MW00443675

THE LAW SCHOOL AT THE UNIVERSITY OF VIRGINIA

HALE   NOTTINGHAM   MINOR

THIS BVILDING
WAS ERECTED BY
WILLIAM ANDREWS CLARK JR.
LL.B CLASS OF 1899
IN LOVING MEMORY
OF HIS WIFE
MABEL FOSTER CLARK
1880-1903
AND IS DEDICATED
TO THE FACVLTY
ALVMNI AND STVDENTS
OF THE LAW SCHOOL
UNIVERSITY
OF VIRGINIA
1 9 3 2

The Law School at the University of Virginia

Architectural Expansion in the Realm of Thomas Jefferson

Philip Mills Herrington

University of Virginia Press

CHARLOTTESVILLE AND LONDON

University of Virginia Press
© 2017 by the Rector and Visitors of the University of Virginia
All rights reserved
Printed in the United States of America on acid-free paper

First published 2017

9 8 7 6 5 4 3 2 1

Library of Congress Cataloging-in-Publication Data
Names: Herrington, Philip Mills, author.
Title: The law school at the University of Virginia : architectural expansion in the realm of Thomas
    Jefferson / Philip Mills Herrington.
Description: Charlottesville : University of Virginia Press, 2017 | Includes bibliographical references and
    index.
Identifiers: LCCN 2016032945| ISBN 9780813939308 (cloth : alk. paper) | ISBN 9780813939469 (e-book)
Subjects: LCSH: University of Virginia. School of Law—Buildings. | University of Virginia. School of
    Law—Design. | Law schools—Virginia—Charlottesville.
Classification: LCC KF292.V573 H47 2017 | DDC 727/.43409755481—dc23
LC record available at https://lccn.loc.gov/2016032945

Cover art: University of Virginia Law School; photograph by Robert Llewellyn

Contents

Color gallery follows p. 128

Foreword

This architectural history of the University of Virginia School of Law is, by and large, a product of the Law Library's Special Collections. Among law libraries, our special collections houses an uncommonly large and diverse array of materials covering the breadth of legal history and scholarship, and its rich repository serves as the Law School's institutional memory. Within our archives we curate thousands of rare books and legal treatises, diverse personal papers, and a vast collection of Law School photographs. Inasmuch as we collect these physical objects of the past, our mission—to acquire, preserve, and provide access to information and knowledge in support of the Law School's goal of excellence in instruction, research, and public service—emboldens us to engage with a broad community of patrons, most especially scholars and alumni. Promoting our collections and providing access to them is as essential to our mission as amassing and preserving them. In the past decade we have digitized hundreds of thousands of objects and made these materials available online in innovative ways. We have written histories, hosted exhibitions, expanded the size and scope of our digital collections, and collaborated with faculty research.

Good scholarship emanating from our collections enables and encourages future research. The creation of the Horatio and Florence Farmer Research Fellowship within Special Collections has proved a successful development in our efforts to discover and promote our materials. Offering a scholar's eye, our fellows have shed new light on the documents in our archives and produced remarkable and powerful tools for exploring and understanding them. In his tenure as a fellow, Philip Herrington began writing a primer on the architectural history of the Law School at the University of Virginia. He quickly uncovered a rich collection of fascinating and underused materials deserving of a much larger project. The result is this book, an important story that recounts the development of the University through the lens of one of its original schools while also relating the history of the Law School through a study of the construction and use of its buildings. Originally housed in Pavilions III and X on the UVa lawn, the Law School left Jefferson's Academical Village in 1911 as it moved through a series of purpose-built, freestanding structures. Often unremarkable as stand-alone buildings, these structures have gone largely unnoticed. But collectively, as Herrington deftly recounts in this book, they tell a compelling and rich story of an institution within an institution. Herrington immerses us in an engaging narrative that recounts these Law School structures as cultural and educational spaces. Their architectural history reflects the changes in and the enduring continuities of the Virginia Law experience, the expanding Grounds and student body, the increasing professionalization of the legal field, and the inescapable pull of Jefferson's architectural influence.

The following chapters reflect the Law School's identity, illuminating the places it has occupied and the people, classes, and ideas that have filled these buildings. Alumni will discover through this book the histories behind familiar Law School spaces such as Mural Hall, student lounges, the library, and Red Square, while those interested in the development of the University of Virginia, American campus architecture, or American legal education will find much of interest as well.

We dedicate this book to our alumni, who with their accomplishments, loyalty, and generosity have helped the University of Virginia School of Law flourish for nearly two hundred years. Their donations built our walls, our character, and our reputation. It is with deepest gratitude to each of them that the Arthur J. Morris Law Library proudly presents this architectural history.

LOREN S. MOULDS
Special Collections
Arthur J. Morris Law Library
The University of Virginia Law School

Acknowledgments

When I came to Charlottesville in 2005 to begin my doctoral work in history at the University of Virginia, I became the latest arrival to fall under the spell of the Academical Village. At the time, the history department occupied a building within sight of the famous Lawn. Experiencing Grounds on a daily basis was something I relished. Little did I know as I strolled along the ranges and among the trees of the University that I would one day study its architectural history from the perspective of a part of the campus I had not yet seen: the Law School, tucked away at North Grounds. What began in 2012 as a temporary research job became a nearly two-year postdoctoral fellowship at the Law School. It is therefore appropriate that I give my first thanks to the University of Virginia School of Law, especially the Arthur J. Morris Law Library, for the opportunity to research and promote its history and to pursue this project.

The Law Library provided me with a wonderful family of colleagues who surrounded me and this project with enthusiasm and encouragement. The vision, leadership, and friendship of Taylor Fitchett, Director of the Law Library, made my postdoctoral fellowship and this project possible. It was Taylor who recognized the dearth of published material on this original school of "Mr. Jefferson's University" and sought to correct it. Taylor's perseverance and passion for the history of the Law School inspired this book, and she provided innumerable means of support to allow it to happen.

There is no way to sufficiently thank my friend and colleague Loren Moulds, Digital Collections Librarian at the Law School, who labored with me throughout this project. Loren and I began our doctoral work together, and through twists of fate we had the opportunity to work together in the Law Library's Special Collections. Not only did Loren shape this book from the beginning through his scholarly input, but he did much of the grunt work of reading drafts, processing images, and providing technical support. In this work I hope he has something of which he is proud, as he played an essential part in producing it. Thanks also to Loren's wife, Kelly, and their children, Ethan and Audrey, for allowing me to stay with them so often during my many visits to Charlottesville working on this project.

Another crucial friend, ally, and co-laborer on this project was Cecilia Brown, Special Collections Archivist at the Law Library. Cecilia pulled countless documents for me and offered invaluable institutional knowledge. Through hundreds of questions and requests, her reserve of patience and kindness never failed.

Many thanks to all the faculty and staff at the Law Library, especially Leslie Ashbrook, Randi Flaherty, Micheal Klepper, Kent Olson, Joseph Wynne, Oleksandra Skulinets, Katherine Bergey, Amber Anglada, Kate Boudouris, and James McKinley.

A number of people connected to the Law School, past and present, from outside the library also played important roles in this project. Thanks especially to Robert Scott, William Bergen, and David Ibbeken for their help in answering questions and reviewing earlier versions of parts of this book. Also thanks to J. Gordon Hylton, Peter Low, Diddy Morris, Mary Wood, and the late Daniel Meador for their kind assistance.

I also had the help of several people connected with the University of Virginia

Darden School of Business; thank you to Mark Reisler, C. Ray Smith, Karen King, and Susan Wormington.

At University of Virginia Facilities, thanks to Benjamin Hays and Garth Anderson, who were always so generous with their knowledge of the University's history and architecture.

Elsewhere at the University of Virginia and throughout Charlottesville, I want to thank the staff of the Albert and Shirley Small Special Collections Library, Richard Guy Wilson, Ed Roseberry, Kristin Jensen, Brian Hogg, Sarita Herman, Matthew Riley, Keri Matthews, and the late Werner Sensbach. Thanks especially to my friend Erin O'Hare for providing access to the image archive of the *University of Virginia Magazine,* Coy Barefoot for his help in finding photographs of North Grounds, and Audrey Golden for her careful reading of much of this work. And many thanks to Christopher Young for his wonderful floor and site plans for this book and his enthusiasm for this project.

At Clark Hall, thanks to "that chap climbing the tree"—you've inspired me and so many others!

Thank you to the staff of the University of Virginia Press, particularly Mark Saunders, Boyd Zenner, Mark Mones, Angie Hogan, and Morgan Myers, for their belief in this project and their work to produce a beautiful publication. Also at the Press, thanks to my friend Stephanie Lovegrove for her kindness and encouragement.

Outside of Charlottesville, my thanks go to Luanne Greene of Ayers Saint Gross, Alan Dynerman, Murray Whisnant, David J. Neuman, Melba Levick, and my dear friend Laura Kolar. Also thank you to William Richards at the American Institute of Architects; Christian Anderson at the University of South Carolina; Charles Holland at the University of Florida; James Stimpert at Johns Hopkins University; Sabrina Sondhi, Jocelyn Wilk, and Janet Parks at Columbia University; Rebecca Fenning at the William Andrews Clark Memorial Library, UCLA; Lisa McCown at Washington and Lee University; and Keith Longiotti at the University of North Carolina.

No words can express my gratitude to Lydia Mattice Brandt for her boundless support, editorial and otherwise, on this project. You are truly the best, both as a friend and as a scholar. Eternal thanks to you for the many hours you spent reading chapters and discussing ideas and the countless words of wisdom you provided that helped push this project further than I'd imagined it could ever go. I look forward to a career of collaboration with you. I know you join me in thanking Sharon, Nikki, Ashley, and everyone else in GC for the sustenance they provided us during the writing and revision phases of our respective projects.

And finally my thanks and love go to my sister, Mary Herrington, and my mother, Jenny Herrington, for their never-ending enthusiasm for anything I do. You can now add the history of the law buildings at the University of Virginia to the list of subjects about which you never imagined you'd know so much.

THE LAW SCHOOL AT THE UNIVERSITY OF VIRGINIA

Introduction

At the University of Virginia, change has often been accompanied by regret. In 1916, the University's *Alumni News* reported with dissatisfaction on the response of visiting alumni to various alterations made to Grounds, as students and faculty call the revered campus. One alumnus bemoaned the construction of Cabell Hall, which in 1898 closed the southwestern vista of the mountains. Another lamented the paving of the University's roads. A third resisted an invitation to examine Minor Hall, the new home of the Law School, completed in 1911. The first purpose-built Law School building at the University, its red brick walls, white columns, and arched doorways spoke to an effort by the architect to harmonize with the historic campus, but the alumnus never got close enough for an inspection. Rather, he "lost himself in a fog of memory and spoke tremulously of the austerities of the two rooms under the Rotunda that once housed the School of Law; and he never did look at the new building, but hurried away to look at the old."[1]

The writer for the *Alumni News* recognized that the changes to the University, including modifications to its built environment, sparked strong emotion. Physical alterations were especially worrisome because some observers perceived them as emblematic of less tangible, more threatening systemic changes. The writer thought the feelings of the nostalgic alumnus misguided. "He does not want anything changed," he concluded, "because he fears that if details are altered, fundamentals will be altered as well. He does not want new buildings, new courses, new requirements for degrees, because somehow he fears that if they are introduced, something essential in the old scheme will have to be absolutely destroyed to make way for them." Such melancholic alumni were "prone to confuse . . . principles with their outward symbols." The writer ended with a recommendation: "Turn your faces away from the past and look toward the future. And if you can not do that, at least do as Janus did—look both ways at once."

The architectural history of the University of Virginia is the story of an institution doing just that: trying to look both to the past and to the future at once. This book follows the architectural career of one of the eight original schools of the University—the Law School—to tell the story of how one branch of this historic and history-conscious institution negotiated the past and future through its buildings over the course of nearly two hundred years. This is, then, an architectural history of the University, though one that primarily looks beyond the famous core of buildings designed by the University's founder, Thomas Jefferson.

As the masterwork of Jefferson and a UNESCO World Heritage Site, the original "Academical Village" at the heart of the University has rightly attracted the attention of scholars intrigued by the inspiration and intention behind this distinctive, artistically rich historic complex. Constructed between 1817 and 1826, the Rotunda, pavilions, ranges, and Lawn arguably make up the most recognizable collection of college buildings in the world, and images of the Academical Village continue to dominate popular conceptions of the University. Yet today the original Jefferson ensemble comprises only a small fraction of a campus of over 1600 acres. Scores of non-Jefferson buildings dating from the 1850s onward spread out in all directions, especially to the west and northwest. Although the story of Jefferson's creation of the Academical Village has long dominated scholarship on the architectural history of the University, the buildings that followed and soon outnumbered the Jefferson complex also tell their own compelling narrative. As the University of Virginia has expanded and changed to achieve its educational mission, it has remained preoccupied with the past, always mindful of its connection to a celebrated American statesman and his architectural masterpiece.[2]

As one of the eight schools originally chosen by Jefferson to form the University's curriculum, the Law School has played a central role in the development of the University since its establishment in 1819. Jefferson considered the study of law an essential purpose of the institution. His Academical Village would "form the statesmen, legislators & judges" so essential to the success of the new American nation, the well-informed citizenry "on whom public prosperity, & individual happiness are so much to depend." Jefferson did not conceive any of the subjects at the new University as stand-alone disciplines, including law. Rather than the professional degree it has become, law in the earliest days of the University was part of a liberal arts curriculum. Jefferson thought it necessary that all students at the new institution learn "the principles & structure of government, the laws which regulate the intercourse of nations, those formed municipally for our own government, and a sound spirit of legislation, which banishing all arbitrary & unnecessary restraint on individual action shall leave us free to do whatever does not violate the equal rights of another."[3] The Law School held its first classes in Pavilion III of the Academical Village. For almost one hundred years it stayed within the original village (or in the adjacent Rotunda Annex, constructed in the 1850s), occupying an important position within the University, as Jefferson had envisioned. While the Law School's current location at North Grounds, a complex one and a half miles north of the Rotunda, suggests a peripheral relationship with the University, the Law School in fact originated in the educational designs of the Sage of Monticello.

The Law School is well positioned to serve as a case study in the evolution of the University's historic Grounds. Despite Jefferson's expectations, the Law School almost immediately reorganized itself around the primary goal of professional legal training, and the buildings that followed reflected that purpose. But while the Law School moved away from the Academical Village and Jefferson's plans for its role in a liberal-arts curriculum, its buildings tell an essential story of the University. Perhaps alone of the original schools of the University, the Law School moved or built anew with each new phase in the University's development. As the school participated in the University's gradual expansion to the west and north, each of its new buildings emerged as a different response to the push-pull between old and new, helping reshape the campus into a landscape dominated not by the Academical Village but by architectural responses to it. In 1911, the Law School moved into its first freestanding law building, Minor Hall. The school's enormous growth led to three subsequent construction projects: Clark Hall (1932), Withers-Brown Hall (1974, 1979), and a dramatic expansion of Withers-Brown, Law Grounds (1997, 2002). Each of these buildings emerged at a turning point in the history of the University, and each represents an effort by the Law School and the University to work out in red brick the difficulties of reconciling the veneration for the past with the needs of the present and future. Change and nostalgia have always been in tension at the University, and a focus on the Law School buildings allows for a closer examination of these competing forces.

While this book is primarily concerned with the architecture and history of the University of Virginia and its Law School, its study of the transformations of the University campus between 1820 and 2000 speaks to broad themes in campus planning and the evolution of higher education in the United States.[4] The progression of the Law School as seen through its buildings provides insight into how the University reconciled the desire for modernization in the late nineteenth and twentieth centuries with the draw of the past. The push by the American Association of Law Schools and the American Bar Association around 1900 to standardize and professionalize the practice of law helps to explain the Law School's ambition for its first purpose-built structure, the "modern" Minor Hall. This Progressive-Era emphasis on specialization acted on other departments as well, helping to fragment a university purposefully designed by Jefferson to be interconnected and interdisciplinary. By the mid-twentieth century, the specialization of disciplines

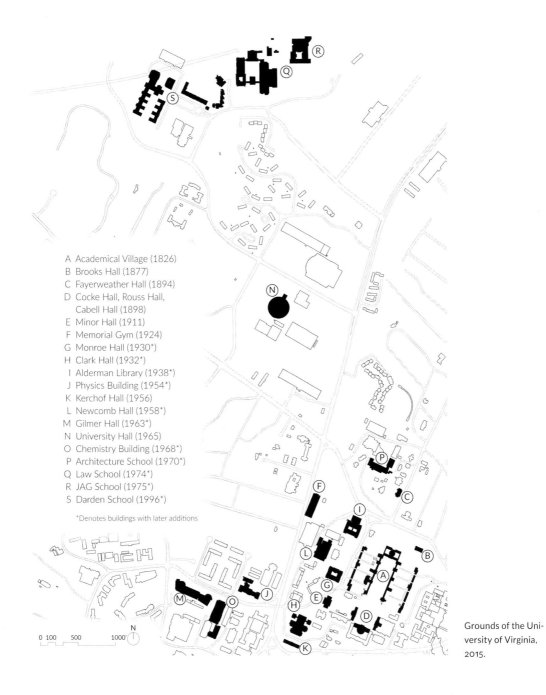

A Academical Village (1826)
B Brooks Hall (1877)
C Fayerweather Hall (1894)
D Cocke Hall, Rouss Hall,
   Cabell Hall (1898)
E Minor Hall (1911)
F Memorial Gym (1924)
G Monroe Hall (1930*)
H Clark Hall (1932*)
I Alderman Library (1938*)
J Physics Building (1954*)
K Kerchof Hall (1956)
L Newcomb Hall (1958*)
M Gilmer Hall (1963*)
N University Hall (1965)
O Chemistry Building (1968*)
P Architecture School (1970*)
Q Law School (1974*)
R JAG School (1975*)
S Darden School (1996*)

*Denotes buildings with later additions

Grounds of the University of Virginia, 2015.

at universities across the county resulted in the development of the "multiuniversity" in the United States, a term denoting the massive expansion of post–World War II institutions of higher learning into complex, multifaceted campuses with large student bodies and administrative bureaucracies. The University of Virginia and the Law School both experienced unprecedented growth at this time, leading to the creation of the North Grounds satellite campus. Here midcentury modernism expressed itself both architecturally and more broadly as students and faculty at the Law School experienced the opportunities—and isolation—of the University's push in the 1960s and 1970s to keep step with sweeping technological, demographic, and cultural changes.

Using the Law School as a case study for the University of Virginia's development demonstrates that people, rather than abstract forces, were responsible for shaping the historic campus. In fact, usually a very small number of people controlled the design of the University's buildings and Grounds. Central to this story are the ways in which key historical actors worked to create buildings that satisfied both their reverence for the past and their personal ambitions and aspirations for the University. For example, the second chapter, which examines Clark Hall, focuses on the interactions of several main players: William Andrews Clark Jr., the fabulously wealthy law alumnus whose cosmopolitan background influenced the building's design; Allyn Cox, the New York muralist whose desire for an epic central hall created one of the University's most imaginative and unexpected interiors; the University's Architectural Commission, whose series of rejected plans for Clark Hall reveal the challenges of balancing old and new, small and large at the University; and President Edwin A. Alderman and Law Dean William Minor Lile, close friends who communicated extensively about the new building and played a major role in choosing its site, appearance, and interior treatment. Although the number of players was small, the variety of characters and agendas illuminates the muddied, complex process of expanding the University of Virginia, particularly when the University contemplated changes within sight of the Academical Village.

While the Law School's buildings illustrate broader themes in the architectural, spatial, and cultural development of the University, they also tell the specific story of a department using physical space to define its growing institutional autonomy. The relocation of the Law School to the North Grounds campus was only the most conspicuous episode in a long process through which the Law School grew increasingly distinct and at times distant from other disciplines within the University. Ironically, the Law School's central role in the success of the University made its movement away from the center possible. In its first twenty years, the Law School saw high faculty turnover and much shuffling of its curriculum and organization, but it quickly became one of the University's most popular and profitable programs. By the early 1900s, law students made up nearly one-third of the total attendance of the University; the Law School was also the only department at the time that made a profit. In the twentieth century, capable leadership and loyal alumni enriched the Law School's coffers and assured its place among the nation's top law schools. Yet the Law School's size, financial capabilities, and national prominence (it remains the second oldest continuously operating law school in the United States) allowed it to develop an institutional identity apart from the University, a reality borne out in its architecture.[5]

Considering its connection to Thomas Jefferson, its long history, its national reputation, and its considerable influence in American politics and law through its alumni, the Law School warrants further study and documentation.[6] In addition to its purpose as an architectural case study for UVa's development, this book also serves as an institutional history of the Law School. Further, it works to expand the historiography of American legal education, making connections between architecture and changes in admission standards, curriculum, and the legal profession. Although American law school buildings have received little scholarly attention (even in the institutional histories of various law schools), these structures have much to say about the evolution of legal education in the United States and the relationship of the study of law to higher education.[7]

This book consists of four chapters, which follow the Law School through its four principal architectural programs. Chapter 1 tells the story of the Law School's transition through various spaces within the Academical Village to the construction of its first official home, Minor Hall, completed in 1911. After cycling through two of Jefferson's pavilions, the Law School became one of a number of departments to occupy the University's first major post-Jefferson building, the Rotunda Annex (1854), designed by Robert Mills, architect of the Washington Monument. The Rotunda Annex fire of 1895 set the Law School on a course toward its first freestanding building. Minor Hall was an effort to keep pace with the law schools at Yale, Harvard, and the University of Pennsylvania, each of which had recently constructed its first law building. Minor Hall continued the campus expansion initiated by Stanford White in the 1890s with his Cabell, Rouss, and Cocke buildings at the southern end of the Lawn. But while the White buildings maintained the Lawn as a dynamic and essential element of University life, Minor Hall stood apart, aloof and autonomous. Its construction began the westward movement of the campus and the University's transition to detached, specialized buildings.

Chapter 2 follows the Law School in the 1930s from Minor Hall to its most iconic home, Clark Memorial Hall. With its marble-walled, mural-decorated central hall and massive size, Clark Hall signaled the Law School and the University's desire for grandness, but its carefully considered exterior spoke to the appeal of continuity with a more intimate, bucolic past. Paid for by a large donation from William Andrews Clark Jr., a wealthy alumnus, Clark Hall allowed the Law School to indulge in a building far more opulent and internally complex than Minor Hall and reassert itself as a national rather than state law school. Nevertheless, Clark Hall's materials, classicism, and massing reinforced its ties to the local and familiar.

Chapter 3 focuses on the 1960s and 1970s, when the Law School moved to North Grounds, part of the most dramatic geographic expansion in the University's history. Situated between a highway bypass and a shopping center, North Grounds typified the suburban, automobile-centered campus of the era. A relocation prompted by the explosive midcentury growth of the University and the Law School, the development of North Grounds offered the Law School room to expand and diversify its student body and curriculum. It also fanned anxieties about the anonymity and isolation of twentieth-century mass education. Despite the use of red brick and thin, column-like piers, the appearance, layout, and utilitarianism of the new building contributed to feelings of dislocation among students and faculty.

Finally, chapter 4 moves to the 1990s, when the Law School engaged in a dramatic remodeling and expansion of its North Grounds building. With the construction of a central pavilion reminiscent of the Rotunda and Clark Hall, the new "Law Grounds" complex announced a postmodern return to classicism and a departmental interest in reasserting the Law School's connection to the historic University. Nevertheless, the fact that the Law School funded this massive redevelopment of its building and landscape through a sophisticated private fundraising apparatus reinforced its self-sufficiency.

Studied separately, the Law School buildings offer historical and architectural significance at the local level. Studied together, they tell a compelling story of continuity and change at an American university, one known worldwide for its physical beauty and ties to Thomas Jefferson — a place peculiarly conscious of its history and hesitant to venture too far from the confines of the past, yet always striving forward.

I

The Academical Village, the Rotunda Annex, and Minor Hall

In the winter of 1909–10, a concrete basement and steel framing heralded the arrival of "that many years myth, the law building," situated at the base of Monroe Hill in what was then the southwest corner of the University of Virginia.[1] The rising building stood just a short distance from the University's historic Academical Village, designed by Thomas Jefferson and completed over eighty years before. Soon christened in honor of famed University law professor John Barbee Minor, the new law building featured the familiar red brick and white columns of the earliest University buildings. Yet its Colonial Revival exterior disguised a modern addition to the campus. With its concrete foundation walls, steel girders, electric lights, and lavatories, this was indeed a building of the new century. Its most essentially modern features, however, were less tangible. Minor Hall represented a fundamental departure from the fluidity and external orientation of Jefferson's nineteenth-century campus. Like the seven other original schools of the University, the Law School first existed in ephemeral form; there was no designated law building. Its substance came from being part of a whole, a University embodied

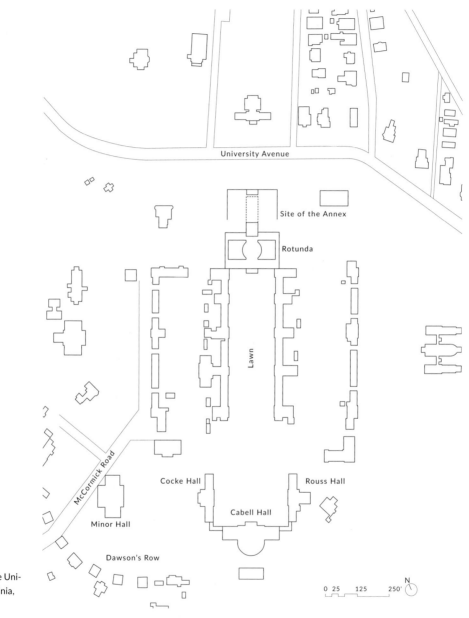

University Avenue

Site of the Annex

Rotunda

Lawn

McCormick Road

Cocke Hall

Rouss Hall

Cabell Hall

Minor Hall

Dawson's Row

Grounds of the University of Virginia, c. 1911.

0 25   125   250'

N

in a tight orbit of red brick and white columns. To complement an interdisciplinary curriculum, Jefferson made the Lawn the center of the campus, an outdoor classroom inviting to all disciplines. But through the next eight decades, the Law School slowly revolved out and away from the Academical Village, growing in size and developing its own institutional identity. The Rotunda Annex, an ungainly 1850s classroom building, contained the Law School and several other departments throughout much of the late 1800s, but the fire of 1895 fully unleashed the centrifugal forces of change. When, in 1911, the Law School finally moved to its freestanding building, it achieved an unprecedented physical autonomy that announced its distinctiveness and self-reliance. While stylistically (if superficially) deferential to the Academical Village, Minor Hall embodied a modern emphasis on professionalization, specialization, and a segregation of disciplines that set it apart from Jefferson's original design.

When John Tayloe Lomax, the University's first law professor, arrived in Charlottesville in the summer of 1826, he must have been wide-eyed at the sight of the nearly completed Academical Village, sited on a ridge just west of Charlottesville. Thomas Jefferson, whose long work had finally brought ideas of a "Central College" to fruition, had monitored its progress from nearby Monticello. He designed a distinctive, interconnected complex rather than a single large college building, finding the latter "ugly, inconvenient, exposed to the accident of fire, and bad in cases of infection." Jefferson likely had in mind the main edifice at the College of William and Mary, his alma mater, where professors and students studied, slept, ate, and worshipped almost entirely under one roof. The University, he believed, "should not be an house but a village."[2] While Jefferson initially conceived of a very broad plan with a central lawn 750 feet wide, the topography of the site required a narrower lawn of 200 feet, which enhanced the village-like intimacy of the complex. This "village," unlike most towns and campuses at the time, was dominated not by a church but by a library: the Rotunda, which, when Lomax moved to the University, was nearly ready for the arrangement of its hundreds of newly purchased books.

View of the University of Virginia from the south, 1831, published by J. & F. Tallis.

Built between 1817 and 1826, the Academical Village was a U-shaped complex consisting of ten pavilions, 108 dormitory rooms, the Rotunda, and the central Lawn. It was a plan of clearly legible hierarchies of space. The head of the complex was the Rotunda, the library and symbolic repository of knowledge, which looked down the cascading terraces of the Lawn to an unobstructed view of the Blue Ridge Mountains. The two-story pavilions, laid out along the east and west sides of the Lawn and linked by long one-story rows of dormitory rooms, served as both professors' residences and classroom space. In back of each pavilion was a garden, protected from marauding animals by brick serpentine walls. Behind the

Jefferson attended
the College of
William and Mary
from 1760 to 1762
and remembered
the second version
of its main building,
now called the Wren
Building, constructed
between 1709 and
1716. Seen here
c. 1858, it burned
in 1859 and again in
1862. Between 1928
and 1931 the College
restored the build-
ing to its colonial
appearance.

gardens were the ranges, additional rows of brick, one-story student dormitory rooms. This open yet interconnected design well expressed Jefferson's intention that the University be a seat of interdisciplinary learning. The pavilions, distinct but unified, symbolized the interdependence of the University's eight original schools. Chosen by Jefferson, these were Ancient Languages, Modern Languages, Mathematics, Natural Philosophy, Moral Philosophy, Chemistry, Medicine, and Law. As the center of the complex, the Lawn served as both a grand concourse and a forum, a means of traveling between buildings but also a meeting place in which all disciplines mingled.[3]

In his Academical Village, Jefferson combined many elements common in

American architecture of the day, including fanlights and double- or triple-sash windows, with Roman and Renaissance forms and decorative elements. While the Rotunda was famously inspired by the Pantheon in Rome, the designs of the ten pavilions made use of a variety of ancient Roman precedents and the classically inspired works of sixteenth-century Italian architect Andrea Palladio. Jefferson employed various facade configurations and classical orders to make each one unique but utilized scale, materials, and color to visually unify the complex. For the Rotunda, pavilions, and covered walkways lining the Lawn, Jefferson used only unfluted columns but played with an assortment of Doric, Ionic, and Corinthian capitals and bases, his models again all Roman or Roman-inspired. For the walls, Jefferson employed red brick laid in a decorative Flemish bond pattern. Later generations have often reduced "Jeffersonian" architecture to its most basic elements, combining red brick, unfluted white columns, and round arches with Georgian, Colonial Revival, Beaux-Arts, and other styles to produce buildings that in scale, massing, and detail had little in common with the works of Jefferson. For most observers, these loose connections were sufficient. When writers for the school newspaper saw the design for Minor Hall in 1909, an essentially Colonial Revival building with red brick laid in Flemish bond and unfluted white columns, they wrote that it would be "metamorphosed into a harmony of Roman architecture" to match the Academical Village. Just as many later colleges and universities would draw inspiration from Jefferson's campus plan, the University of Virginia itself would seek in varying degrees to emulate Jefferson's style, filling the expanding Grounds with red brick and white columns.[4]

The University of Virginia was one of the largest American building projects of its time, and its rural setting likely made the scale of the complex all the more impressive. Rural campuses were common in the United States—in fact, their abundance was a distinguishing characteristic of American higher education—but the University of Virginia stood apart in a number of ways. First, it was remarkable because of its ambitious and fully executed design—most colleges could only build as meager funds became available, which made constructing large, unified complexes impossible. The University was further distinguished by its unusual three-sided plan. This layout was not unprecedented in the United States; the plan of Union College in Schenectady, New York, designed by the Frenchman Joseph-Jacques Ramée in 1813, was similar to Jefferson's scheme but was never fully executed. American campuses at the time usually consisted of one large building, often with a pair of auxiliary structures (as at William and Mary), or, as was increasingly common, a cluster of buildings arranged around greenswards or courts. The University of North Carolina and the University of South Carolina, both of which predated UVa, featured collections of fairly large buildings facing center greens. What was revolutionary about Jefferson's plan was his balance of unity and detachment. By radically distending the arms of the complex to connect classrooms and living spaces and crowning the head of the campus with the Rotunda, he achieved a singularly impressive, monumental, and cohesive result.

The plan of the Academical Village reinforced Jefferson's idealistic vision that the University's eight schools would be co-contributors to a liberal education, providing future leaders of the republic with a broad interdisciplinary knowledge rather than a choice of specialized fields of study. Thus Jefferson conceived of law as a liberal art rather than a professional degree. In this regard he was not unique; several American colleges since the American Revolution had created law professorships, and nearly all of these institutions provided scholarly rather than practical legal instruction. For this reason, law courses at most colleges struggled to attract students, and many institutions abandoned legal education entirely after a few years of poorly attended lectures. When the state of Virginia established the University in 1819, only two collegiate law schools in the United States had had much success in graduating students directly into the practice of law: the College of William and Mary and Transylvania University in Lexington, Kentucky. These schools attracted students because they offered vocational legal training. Others tried this approach but failed for various reasons; David Hoffman, professor of law at the University of Maryland, supported practical legal instruction but lacked support from his home institution. Regardless, most aspiring lawyers did not need a college degree to pursue their chosen profession. They received their legal training at private, for-profit law schools, such as the well-known Litchfield Law School in Connecticut, or learned their trade through apprenticeships or self-directed study. Therefore Jefferson's concept of legal education was at odds with the main objective of most young Americans studying law, which was joining the bar. This tension between an academic and a professional legal education was not lost on Professor Lomax, who soon conceded that students' "demand for the law is as for a trade." From its beginning the Law School existed uneasily in the Academical Village, as law students resisted the liberal arts model of legal education that Jefferson's architectural scheme supported.[5]

By the time Lomax began his professorship, the rhythms of living, teaching, and studying in the Academical Village were well established. The University first held classes in 1825, but its failure to secure a law professor forced the postponement of law classes until the following year.[6] Even though the Rotunda was not yet complete, the pavilions and dormitories were finished and in use, their expert design and craftsmanship a contrast to the lingering roughness of the site. Lomax moved into Pavilion III, the second pavilion constructed in the Village. Built in 1818–19, Pavilion III was perhaps the finest of the group, being one of only two pavilions whose porticoes featured the elaborate Corinthian order. Jefferson called the pavilion "Corinthian Palladian," a nod to his use of the works of Palladio in its design.[7] Unable to find adequate stone masons in the United States, Jefferson had the pavilion's Carrara marble capitals carved in Italy, from whence they were shipped to New York, then to Richmond and finally Charlottesville. In addition to giving Pavilion III a fine portico, Jefferson surrounded the building with an entablature ornamented with scrolled modillions, egg-and-dart molding, and dentils. On top he constructed a parapet, a low decorative wall that disguised the roof of the building and made the pavilion appear taller and more stately. Jefferson directed that expensive oil-struck brick be used for the facade of this and other pavilions, which provided a precise, smooth wall surface. Reaching out from the second story under the roof of the portico was a deck with a chinoiserie railing. This shaded outdoor living space, raised above the ruckus and dust of ever-present students, provided fine views of the Lawn.[8]

Like his fellow professors, Lomax lived and worked in his assigned pavilion. Pavilion III was a busy, crowded place. Not only was it a classroom, with students coming and going, it was also home to Lomax's very large family, which in 1826 included his wife, six daughters, and two sons. Like Pavilion VII, its neighbor two doors down, Pavilion III had two entryways from the Lawn, a reflection of its mixed use. The central entry, a double door, opened into a large lecture room that did not communicate with any other room in house. This separation of teaching and living spaces allowed the professor-in-residence and his family some privacy. The other entry, a single door located to the right, opened into a stair hall that provided access to the rest of the building. At the back of Pavilion III's main floor, directly to the rear of the lecture room, was a dining room

Pavilion III, c. 1890, showing the building before the removal of its parapet.

that overlooked the back garden. In the basement were the kitchen, with its large hearth, and other rooms used for storage, food preparation, and sleeping quarters for enslaved workers. On the second floor were a large drawing room, two bedchambers, and a small spare room. Jefferson had not expected the University professors to have families, and his design anticipated a collegial intimacy between professors and nearby students. Put into practice, the Academical Village was far less serene than Jefferson had imagined it would be. Despite there being no door between the lecture room and the other parts of the house, Lomax likely taught amid the smell of cooking and the sounds of children and animals emanating from

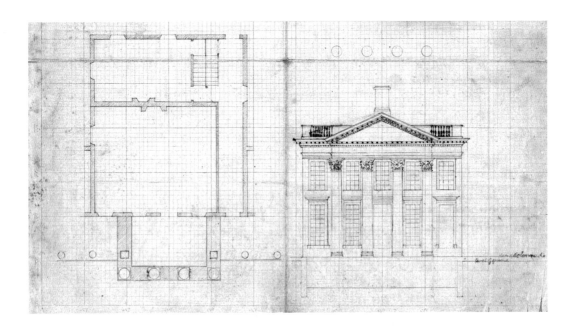

Thomas Jefferson's
elevation and
first floor plan for
Pavilion III.

all sides. Students, enslaved workers, colleagues, toddlers, and livestock all made their presence known continually to Professor Lomax at Pavilion III.[9]

Whatever travails he faced as the father of eight children—a ninth arrived in 1828—and overseer of dozens of students, Lomax enjoyed easy access to the Rotunda, one of the most impressive libraries in the United States. By 1828 it held over 8,000 volumes. Its catalogue that year listed 375 law titles, many selected for purchase by Jefferson prior to his death in 1826. Novelist and biographer Margaret Bayard Smith, of Washington, D.C., who visited the University in 1828, spent two hours with the "charming" Lomax at the Rotunda, "looking over books and conversing on literary subjects." Thanks to Jefferson's careful selection of an expansive yet practical list of law titles, Lomax could step out of his front door and within moments peruse books on chancery, merchant law, maritime law, and ecclesiastical law in the circular reading room.[10]

Lomax resigned in 1830 to become a judge on the Fifth Circuit of Virginia; his replacement was John Anthony Gardner Davis.[11] Like his predecessor, Davis experienced little separation between his personal and professional life while at the University. Although Davis, an alumnus of William and Mary, owned a fine brick home at "The Farm," just east of Charlottesville, he nevertheless moved into Pavilion III with his wife and four young sons when he began his professorship. He subsequently moved to Pavilion X, across the Lawn at the southeastern corner of the Academical Village. Pavilion X remained the home of University law professors for approximately the next hundred years. Like Pavilion III, Pavilion X had a four-columned portico, although here Jefferson used Roman Doric columns accompanied by a Doric entablature with triglyphs and metopes. Pavilion X also combined a classroom with living space, but whereas Jefferson separated the lecture room from the living quarters at Pavilion III, he used a conventional single entry into a central hall at Pavilion X. In 1837, the Board of Visitors, the governing body of the University, approved Davis's request to use the student dormitory rooms adjoining the pavilion, which provided him much-needed work space away from the constant activity of Pavilion X. In his ten years at the University, Davis's family grew by three daughters, making for seven children in all.[12]

However much Davis's children created a sense of mayhem about him, they were more easily controlled than the students, whom Davis, like Lomax before him, had to superintend. The Lawn may have encouraged camaraderie and intellectual exchange, but it also became contested territory as boisterous students challenged the authority of faculty. Often rowdiness manifested itself in the form of pranks. In 1832, Davis, along with John Patton Emmet, professor of natural history, and Robert Patterson, professor of natural philosophy, awoke to find their pavilions smeared with "filth & ordure"—likely animal feces. The same night students attempted to smoke a dormitory they believed inhabited by the Board of

Pavilion X, seen here in the right foreground, was the home of law professors for nearly a century. This view of the Academical Village from the south, c. 1891, shows Pavilion X prior to the removal of its parapet and the Rotunda before the fire of 1895.

Visitors.[13] Unfortunately, not all student behavior was so harmless. On November 12, 1840, Davis heard gunshots coming from the upper portion of the Lawn and stepped out from Pavilion X to investigate. Two students had decided to celebrate November 12 — an annual night of disorderliness — by wearing disguises and shooting their guns in the Academical Village. Spying Davis, other students warned the two to stay away from Pavilion X, but the pair proceeded toward him. When they reached Davis, the professor attempted to forcibly remove one of the students' masks. After a "slight scuffle," the student retreated several feet from Davis and then shot him in the stomach. The two students fled the Lawn while others carried Davis inside. He died two days later. His killer fled the state of Virginia, escaping prosecution.[14]

After five years under the next law professor, Henry St. George Tucker, the University hired in 1845 the man who would be synonymous with the Law School for the next fifty years: John Barbee Minor. Minor arrived at the University as it was beginning to lose its rough edges. Although a student riot that year got so out of hand that the University summoned the local militia, overall the institution was mellowing as well as expanding. The attrition rate, as high as two-thirds of the student body in the early years, had greatly declined, and student behavior improved to such a degree that, in the 1848–49 academic year, the University issued no expulsions or suspensions. The University of Virginia was becoming an established and respected institution. Minor, an alumnus of the University, had witnessed much of this evolution himself, having enrolled in Davis's junior law class in 1831. Minor and Davis became friends, and the professor eventually hired Minor as a tutor for his young sons. Minor's connection to Davis proved doubly felicitous: not only did Davis inspire him to pursue a career in law, but Minor fell in love with Davis's sister, Martha, whom he likely met within the walls of Pavilion X. They married in 1834. In 1845, when he accepted the seat recently vacated by Tucker, Minor established a dynasty of sorts at the Law School; his son, Raleigh Colston Minor, taught law at the University from 1895 to 1923, while his great-nephew, William Minor Lile, taught from 1893 to 1932.[15]

By the time Minor began his professorship, the Law School curriculum had undergone a number of changes in response to the demand for practical legal education. The most substantive change was the division of the two-year program into discrete junior and senior classes. Initially, the junior class focused on the more practical aspects of law, including common and statute law, equity, and procedure. The senior class was more theoretical, covering the law of nature and nations, the science of government, and principles of jurisprudence. This way students entering the Law School solely for practical training could leave after the first year. Although the Law School later reversed the content of the junior and senior years, students could bypass the junior course or take the two courses in one year. Only students who completed both courses received a "certificate of law." To enhance the opportunities for practical training in the Law School, Professor Davis had organized the Law Society in 1833, which functioned as an early moot court. In 1840, the University established the degree of bachelor of law, which officially ended Jefferson's plan for law to be part of the arts and sciences curriculum.[16]

Jefferson's design for integrated living and teaching spaces was also breaking down, albeit slowly. Jefferson himself made the first accommodation: in 1826, he designed the freestanding Anatomical Theater west of the campus so that the professor of medicine did not have to conduct dissections in his pavilion. Soon after Minor began his professorship, serious discussion began about the need for a more significant alteration to the Academical Village. In 1850, the Board of Visitors, determining that "the existing buildings are totally insufficient for the accommodation of the increasing number of Students," asked two of its members, Andrew Stevenson and Thomas Jefferson Randolph (a grandson of Thomas Jefferson), to serve on a classroom building committee.[17] Aside from the growing student population, the desire for a classroom building also reflected professors' frustration with the constant use of their pavilions for teaching purposes. Jefferson's holistic architectural ensemble was a noble experiment, but sustained use required its modification.

The classroom structure, built into the sloping ground north of the Rotunda, was the University's first definitive architectural step away from the Academical Village model. Although the architect, Robert Mills, joined the new structure to the back of the Rotunda in an effort to simply extend the Village, its construction nevertheless pulled apart some of the living and teaching spaces purposefully unified by Jefferson. Constructed between 1851 and 1854, the Rotunda Annex was a massive four-story, solid-brick structure, topped with a gabled roof. Measuring fifty-five feet wide and one hundred feet long excluding its porticoes, it was a hefty commission even for Mills, who designed the Washington Monument, the National Treasury Building, and over a dozen courthouses in South Carolina.[18] Mills' plans devoted most of the first and second stories to lecture rooms, the largest measuring fifty by forty-five feet.[19] In 1852, the Board of Visitors reserved rooms on the lower floors for Chemistry and Materia Medica; Natural Philosophy had

rooms on the second floor by the time of the 1895 fire.[20] On the third floor, which corresponded to the main floor of the Rotunda, was a one-and-a-half story public hall that seated twelve hundred people. It took up almost the entire floor, with entry halls and staircases in the area closest to the Rotunda.[21] At the north end of the public hall was a replica of Raphael's famous *School of Athens,* painted by French art copyist Paul Balze. The painting hung in an arched niche, framed by pilasters. At the mezzanine level in the public hall was a balcony with additional seating; overhead was a large plastered ceiling embellished with medallions. On the fourth floor were additional rooms: a large room to the south and at least one room to the north, separated from the larger by a lath and plaster wall. Here by 1895 the Engineering Department had a mechanical drawing room and an instrument room.[22]

Invisible from most points on the Lawn, from the side and back the Annex, seen here from Carr's Hill c. 1890, was a conspicuous tail on the back of the Rotunda.

Although professors on the Lawn still found themselves surrounded by students, smells, and sounds, the Annex made it possible for some of them to close the doors of their pavilions and retreat into exclusively domestic space. Eventually, John B. Minor succeeded in joining their ranks, moving law classes out of Pavilion X and into the ground floor of the Annex. By the time of the 1895 fire, the school had two rooms there: one for a lecture hall, the other for a library. James P. C. Southall, who attended the University in the early 1890s, recalled that "just before the hour for Mr. Minor's lecture, the long flight of stone steps leading down to the basement was usually crowded from top to bottom by eager disciples of law in anticipation of the arrival of their master."[23] These exterior steps stretched down on either side of the Annex and provided an excellent location for class photographs.

While the Annex pulled instruction out of many of the pavilions, beginning the University's evolution into a more segmented campus, the new building likewise foreshadowed other developments in the appearance and layout of Grounds. The Annex was the first of many large buildings at the University whose apparent size the administration sought to diminish in one way or another. As was true with the Annex, the goal was to maintain the scale of the University and preserve the primacy of the Rotunda. After seeing the plans for the Annex, Andrew Stevenson of the Board of Visitors assured the University rector, Joseph C. Cabell, that "the whole Building is made subservient to that of the Rotunda & calculated to aid its appearance & add to its beauty."[24] As the University grew throughout the late nineteenth and twentieth centuries, the Academical Village remained intact and free from the shadows of larger buildings, even as these buildings took on nearly all the educational and administrative activities of the institution. In the case of the Annex, Mills's placement of the building directly behind the Rotunda made it largely invisible from the Lawn. He thus satisfied the concerns of the visitors that the new structure might overwhelm other buildings on Grounds.

Also in keeping with later developments at the University, Mills mimicked Jeffersonian architectural elements in order to integrate the Annex with existing University buildings. The Annex's red brick, column capitals, and window

moldings matched those of the Rotunda, though the Corinthian capitals were made of cast iron, a new technology less costly than carved marble. But whereas the porticos and piazzas of the Academical Village reinforced the connectivity and indoor-outdoor nature of Jefferson's University, and the diversity of pavilion designs invited the attention and study of passersby, the Annex exterior was little more than a veneer covering a functional interior. As a work of art, the Annex had

University of Virginia School of Law faculty and students on Annex steps, 1890s. John B. Minor sits center front.

few admirers; one detractor in the 1890s called it "a monstrous tail . . . only ending apparently when the bricks gave out."[25] Yet it succeeded in providing usable, specialized space. Indeed, the Annex's functionality likely soothed any immediate misgivings about its appearance. In 1853, when the Annex was still under construction, Stevenson praised the "whole building capacity of lecture room, Laboratory &c" as "not surpassed by any institution of the kind, and equalled probably by very few." Emphasizing its utility, he believed there was "nothing . . . to prevent its development for the most perfect instruction in agricultural, manufactural & pharmacopoeial Chemistry."[26] Like its closest descendants, New Cabell Hall (classroom building, 1952) and Newcomb Hall (student activities building, 1958), the Annex was a behemoth pushed to the background, its hulking mass trimmed and fitted as needed to cover its utilitarian purposes.

For over forty years, the Annex succeeded in keeping a number of departments housed together and physically tied to the Academical Village; but a fateful spark destroyed it along with the celebrated Rotunda, initiating the most substantial material changes seen at Jefferson's University to that time. One result of the destruction was ultimately to free the Law School to attain its own building. At 10:15 on the morning of October 27, 1895, senior law student Walter Scott Hancock was preparing for Sunday church services when his landlady called out to him that the University's public hall, housed in the Rotunda Annex, was on fire. Hancock "thought nothing of it," but he got ready and arrived at the University Grounds fifteen minutes later. He found the blaze much worse than he expected. An electrical burst, possibly caused by a passing trolley, had sparked the fire in the upper portion of the Annex, and Hancock found that "the rear end of the Annex near the roof was smoking & the flames had just burst out." By that time, law professor Raleigh Colston Minor had directed an effort to douse the fire using the University's engine and hose, but this failed due to an insufficient amount of water and water pressure on Grounds. Hancock came upon a "great crowd of students & others," some of whom "were running here & there helpless as to what should be done on account of the small supply of water." At first helping with the hose, Hancock soon realized the Annex was doomed and began to assist in salvage efforts.[27]

The fact that the fire began on the top floor of the Annex allowed time for heroic professors, students, and community members to rescue what portable treasures they could hoist into their arms and skirts from the lower floors and the Rotunda. Not everything could be saved. Despite frantic efforts to remove it from the public hall, the *School of Athens* was lost. Twelve-year-old Margaret Bell Dunnington, daughter of chemistry professor Francis Perry Dunnington, reported that students and faculty "tried very hard to get out The School of Athens and had it all undone but one corner when they were obliged to go and leave it." Hancock meanwhile "hastened to aid in removing the physical apparatus" of natural philosophy professor Francis Smith, which poorly withstood its hasty exit. John T. Thornton, a nephew of Smith's who witnessed the fire, wrote that "Uncle Frank's valuable physical apparatus was carried out but the greater part so broken as to be practically useless." Despite the location of the Engineering Department on the top floor, some of its equipment also made it out of the building, though perhaps in similar condition to that of Francis Smith.[28]

A more successful, even miraculous survival was the law library, which, but for its removal from the Rotunda to the Annex in 1894, would likely have perished with most of the University's books. Located on the ground floor of the Annex, the area was easily accessible and far from the initial blaze. By the time Hancock arrived in the Law School's rooms after dumping a load of Smith's equipment, he "found all the important books removed." He "took up an armfull of such as remained & hastened out," likely depositing them in the grass near the Annex. In the catalogue of 1895–96, the University reported that "nearly all those [books] belonging to the department of law" survived the fire; these books likely included at least some of the law volumes first purchased at Jefferson's request for the University. At this time the law library numbered "several thousand" books.[29]

Another survival dear to the Law School was a marble bust of Professor John B.

Saved from the Rotunda fire, the bust of John Barbee Minor followed the Law School through its changing spaces. For much of the twentieth century it stood in Clark Memorial Hall's Mural Hall.

Minor, commissioned by law alumni and only recently unveiled to the public at a ceremony the previous June. Carved in white marble by Richmond sculptor Edward Virginius Valentine, the life-size bust commemorated Minor's fiftieth anniversary at the University. The bust's polished granite pedestal bore the inscription: "HE TAUGHT THE LAW AND THE REASON THEREOF." At the unveiling ceremony, which took place in the Annex's public hall, James B. Green, law instructor and chairman of the bust committee, likened the white marble to Minor's "purity of character" and the granite pedestal to "those basic principles governing man's intercourse with his fellow-man, embodied in his teachings and enduring as rock."[30] Minor died scarcely a month after the ceremony, his funeral also taking place in the public hall; the committee placed the bust in the Rotunda, where it stood at the time of the fire. When it became clear that the Rotunda would burn along with the Annex, students and professors focused their salvage efforts on the older building, removing portraits, important papers, books, and a life-size marble statue of Jefferson by sculptor Alexander Galt. In his 1905 history of the fire, Morgan Poitiaux Robinson reported that "while this work [of salvaging] was at its height, a student (whose name the writer much regrets that he was never able to ascertain) rushed into the Library and, by reason of the intense excitement under which he was laboring, gathered sufficient strength to pick up the marble bust of Mr. Minor," and carried it to safety. "Elated by his success," he returned and saved the pedestal as well. The Rotunda's dome, bright with flame, crashed down into the shell of the building at 1 p.m., about three hours after the fire started; the fire was under control by 2:30. The University held classes the next day.[31]

After the fire, law classes resumed in Washington Hall, also called Hotel B, at the north end of the East Range, one of the two long rows of buildings Jefferson designed for student housing at the periphery of the Academical Village.[32] Almost immediately thoughts turned to a new, freestanding law building. This

The Rotunda in flames, October 27, 1895.

determination to have a separate building was part of a broader shift taking place at the University, pushed to the fore by the recent destruction. The University had completely outgrown Jefferson's plan. In the forty years since the construction of the Annex, a number of new buildings had sprung up on the edges of Grounds. Unlike the Annex, these structures stood independent of the Academical Village and reflected little interest in replicating its architecture. Most of these buildings were auxiliary in nature: the stone, Gothic Revival Gatekeeper's Lodge (1850s; nicknamed "Chateau Front and Back") and Chapel (1890), the functional brick Infirmary (1858; now known as Varsity Hall) and Chemical Laboratory (1868), the Second Empire–style Brooks Museum (1877), and the columned, eclectic Fayerweather Gymnasium (1893; Fayerweather's architect, John Kevan Peebles, who later designed Minor Hall, did believe his plan for Fayerweather referenced Jefferson). Instruction remained almost wholly within the original Jefferson footprint or, until the fire, in the Annex. Whatever the beauty or symbolic significance of Jefferson's cohesive academic ensemble, the ungainly Annex confirmed that what the Academical Village enjoyed in charm it lacked in elasticity. The hodgepodge architecture of the newer buildings, however, seemed to foreshadow a less harmonious, less architecturally and spatially homogeneous campus. Anxious to enhance the prestige of the University through this unprecedented expansion, the administration and faculty now sought to develop the University in a more organized and visually unified way.

Only four days after the fire, the faculty outlined in a report to the rector and the Board of Visitors their recommendations for the restoration of the University, including suggestions for new construction. The faculty proposed that the Annex, "an architectural blunder," not be rebuilt but that the Rotunda itself be restored with such interior changes as to make it more usable in its role as the University's library. Next, the faculty recommended new buildings for the departments left homeless by the fire: Academics, Natural Philosophy (Physics), Engineering, and Law. The report urged that the Rotunda and Academics Building be the top priorities, followed by Physics, Engineering, and Law, with the faculty advising the

Brooks Hall, located northeast of the Rotunda, 1914. Constructed in the Second Empire style in the 1870s, it was an object of ridicule at the University through most of the twentieth century. Nearly demolished in the 1970s, it ultimately survived decades of scorn little changed.

Board "to observe this order in their erection, if but one can be erected at a time." Law likely held last place because of the equipment needs of Physics and Engineering. Whatever the order of construction, the faculty sought a cohesive architectural scheme, hoping that the additions would "create an harmonious combination with the original Jeffersonian group." Signifying the importance of the project, the faculty recommended that the architect be "a man not of local repute only, but of broad and national consideration." The rector and visitors ultimately approved these proposals, agreeing that new, freestanding buildings were in order.[33]

Soon the law faculty began to consider what it wanted in a new building. Freestanding law school buildings were a relatively recent phenomenon in higher education. Like the University of Virginia, most colleges and universities held law classes in structures designed for other purposes. The law school at Yale moved into its new building in 1895 after spending twenty years housed in the New Haven County Courthouse. Likewise, prior to the completion of its opulent new building in 1900, the University of Pennsylvania Department of Law met in historic Congress Hall, over two miles from the West Philadelphia campus.[34] Collecting information, the Law School looked at Austin Hall, designed by architect Henry H. Richardson in his signature Romanesque style for Harvard Law School in the 1880s. This building, with its spacious reading room, fireproof bookroom, airy lecture halls, and student locker rooms, cost $135,000. Such a price was out of UVa's budget, but Austin Hall provided some idea of how to configure a modern law school building, and even a smaller structure would seem spacious compared to cramped Washington Hall. The Law School submitted a detailed building report to the Board of Visitors, but the plan was ignored due to the priority of repairing the Rotunda and creating new classroom space for other schools.[35]

As the Law School admired the fashionable architecture of East Coast law schools, it also considered how it compared to these schools in other ways. Despite its impressive pedigree, the University of Virginia School of Law was not at the forefront of American legal education; in fact it was in some danger of becoming an educational backwater. During his fifty-year tenure, John B. Minor succeeded in attracting students, but he resisted reform. Although he changed the organization of law classes from time to time, the standard curriculum under Minor in 1895 was little different from what it was in 1845. Minor faced little in the way of challenges to his method of doing things. While the University expanded the law faculty by hiring a second professor, James Holcombe, in 1851 (succeeded by Stephen Southall in 1866 and James Houston Gilmore in 1884), Minor remained in charge of the school. Unlike Jefferson, Minor believed that the Law School's purpose was to train students to step directly into legal practice. Yet by the 1890s, Minor's unwillingness to substantively alter the program's curriculum made it unclear if law students were indeed receiving adequate preparation for their pro-

fession. Minor required students to memorize and recite law, and he adhered to the lecture method of instruction, while many law schools were following the lead of the dean of Harvard's law school, Christopher C. Langdell, who popularized the case method. Whereas the lecture method relied on professors' delivering their interpretations of legal decisions to students, the case method required students to read and analyze judicial opinions rather than memorize and recite law. Professors who adhered to the case method typically used the Socratic method to encourage students to discuss law in the classroom. After Minor's death in 1895, his great-nephew, William Minor Lile, who had joined the law faculty in 1893, took charge of modernizing the school. Although Lile resisted the case method (the Law

Austin Hall at Harvard University, shown prior to 1895. The University of Virginia School of Law could only dream of such a building from the basement of the Rotunda. H. H. Richardson, architect, constructed 1882–84.

School finally adopted it in the 1920s), he updated and expanded the curriculum, increased the standards for admission (at the time, students could enter without a high school diploma), enlarged the faculty and library, and lobbied tirelessly for a purpose-built law structure.[36]

While the Law School reorganized itself following Minor's death and the Rotunda fire, the University made decisions about how to expand its campus in a way that respected the symmetry, aesthetics, and impressiveness of the original Jefferson complex. Newly popular Beaux-Arts planning, with its emphasis on monumentality, regularity, and stylistic cohesion, was an obvious source of inspiration. Beaux-Arts design drew from the architecture, decoration, and urban planning of imperial Rome and the Renaissance; the gleaming white porticoes, stately domes, and broad avenues of the grandiose Chicago Columbian Exposition of 1893 introduced the style to the American public and led to the rapid adoption of Beaux-Arts buildings and plans across the country. Beaux-Arts plans were particularly well suited to universities, which were growing both in number and size and needed campuses that accommodated large new buildings yet evoked timelessness and grandeur. The balance and classical ornamentation of the Beaux-Arts made it attractive to the University of Virginia, which wanted its new buildings to be sympathetic with Jefferson's design. After the University fired Kentucky architect Harry McDonald, who had been hired to restore the Rotunda, it commissioned the firm McKim, Mead & White of New York—one of the most prominent purveyors of the Beaux-Arts—not only to rebuild the Rotunda but also to create a new complex at the foot of the Lawn to replace the facilities lost with the destruction of the Annex.[37]

McKim, Mead & White, by the mid-1890s renowned architects of domestic, commercial, and institutional buildings, had recently designed two Beaux-Arts campuses that drew inspiration from Jefferson's designs: the new uptown campus of Columbia College (now Columbia University) by Charles McKim, and the new Bronx satellite campus of New York University by Stanford White. Both featured monumental, domed central libraries reminiscent of the Rotunda.[38] White, who planned the Rotunda restoration and new trio of buildings at the south end of the Lawn, was reportedly "scared to death" of the commission due to his admiration for Jefferson's buildings.[39] Nevertheless, White aimed to improve upon the Rotunda design by making changes he believed were consistent with what Jefferson himself would have wanted had the necessary funds and technology been available in the 1820s. He converted the central block of the building into one large dome room, making a more explicit connection to the Pantheon in Rome, Jefferson's inspiration for the Rotunda. At the other end of the Lawn, the new academics, physics, and engineering buildings, named Cabell, Rouss, and Cocke Halls respectively, formed a U-shaped court and featured the red brick and white columns of their predecessors, though White differentiated the new complex from the Academical Village by using Greek rather than Roman details. White purposefully used the sloping terrain to diminish the apparent mass of the buildings and make them subordinate to the Rotunda. This new and grand Beaux-Arts composition at the foot of the Lawn provided a template for University planning, informing the style and massing of subsequent expansions.[40]

In 1898, the Cabell-Rouss-Cocke complex was complete, and academics, physics, and engineering moved into their new quarters. The Law School made do with "two small rooms" in the new northwestern terrace wing of the Rotunda (a Stanford White addition), which it used as classrooms, and "two still smaller rooms" in the Rotunda basement, which became "crowded with books and furniture." There was no new building in sight. In a 1905 report to President Edwin A. Alderman, law professors William Minor Lile and Charles Graves, the latter hired in 1899, laid out the school's needs, which included a new building. They couched their argument in economic terms. The Law School provided, and thus the Law School should receive: "Financially, the Law School is the only fowl in the poultry yard of the University that lays golden eggs. It has always been characteristically modest. It has asked for little, and received less." Lile and Graves maintained that Law was "the only department that has proved a good financial investment," making $25,000 and spending "less than one half of that amount." Therefore, the Law

Cabell Hall, 1914. Designed by Stanford White and opened in 1898, this structure formed a court with Cocke and Rouss Halls that closed the southern end of the Lawn.

School had earned "a home of its own—a well equipped LAW BUILDING, housing a complete Law Library."[41] Alderman apparently agreed, but he needed to cajole the state legislature into providing the money. In the meantime, the University commissioned McKim, Mead & White to construct two additional buildings, the President's House at Carr's Hill and the Refectory (now Garrett Hall) south of the West Range.

A new law building was indeed on the horizon. Alderman made his case for funding in the winter of 1907–8. That February, while on vacation in Florence, Italy, Lile wrote to the president: "I see you have been pouring honeyed words into the ears of the legislature, touching, among other things of lesser importance, a Law Building. I pray that your eloquence fell upon willing ears and that you gathered them in like unto ripe corn." In fact Alderman had already emerged victorious. Writing to Lile in March, Alderman happily shared the good news in his first sentences: "My first impulse is to tell you that the Legislature, which adjourned yesterday, has provided $65,000 for a Law building." In the 1905 report, Lile and Graves had asked for at least $100,000, so $65,000 was a somewhat disappointing amount, although Alderman expected to obtain an additional $10,000 in the next legislative session, providing a total of $75,000 with which "to build a worthy and noble home for the Law School." From Naples, Lile responded, "Your letter containing the gratifying intelligence of the handsome results of your labors with the tribunes of the people—and especially the news of the prospect of a home for the Law School—has just reached me, and has made the delights of Naples doubly delightful."[42]

President Alderman expected McKim, Mead & White to design the new law building; he thought the firm responsible for bringing about a classical renaissance on grounds the obvious choice to take on this new commission. Writing to Lile, Alderman confided that "McKim, Meade [sic] & White will doubtless draw the plans," and he likewise informed the firm itself that, while he had "not yet been empowered, by the Board of Visitors, to select architects," he favored them because of their "utter sympathy with our architectural scheme." McKim, Mead & White responded the following day, agreeing that they were "in entire sympathy with the architectural scheme of the University of Virginia," but two months later the firm declined the commission after receiving further details from Alderman. Why? A number of factors explain this decision. For one, Stanford White, architect of the restored Rotunda and the Cabell-Rouss-Cocke complex, was now gone, murdered in 1906 by millionaire Harry Thaw in response to White's relationship with Thaw's wife, Evelyn Nesbit. And while the firm assured the president that their "connection with the University ha[d] always been most gratifying," the University of Virginia commissions had been trying ones, in part because of the University's limited budget. The Law School commission was likely too meager to be worth the trouble. In fact the firm told the University that the proposed budget of $65,000–$70,000 was unrealistic given the Law School's specifications, informing Alderman that they could not see "how such a building could be erected for less than $105,000 or $110,000." Perhaps even more objectionable than the budget was the fact that the commission was not assured; the University had decided to invite other architects—John Kevan Peebles of Norfolk, Taylor & Hepburn of Norfolk, and Carpenter & Blair of New York—to submit drawings. Overall, the firm declared, "The plan is not one that commends itself to us for many reasons, and would, we are sure, bring upon us the criticism of members of our profession if we gave it support." McKim, Mead & White did, however, provide the University with some preliminary sketches they had prepared for the building, and offered advice should it be solicited.[43]

Alderman was "greatly distressed" that McKim, Mead & White chose not to pursue the commission and blamed the Law School for what now seemed an overly ambitious plan. He felt that "the specifications as outlined by the Law Faculty call[ed] for an entirely too large a building [sic]," one that would "probably have to be cut down in a great many respects." Meanwhile happier news appeared in the form of replies from the three remaining firms, who all expressed interest in submitting proposals for the new building.[44]

As Alderman corresponded with architects, he also thought about the site of the new law building and its relationship to the future development of Grounds. The McKim, Mead & White classroom buildings and dining hall had closed the south end of the Academical Village, but the new law building would be the first step toward a cohesive, grander campus plan that rippled out and away from the buildings on the Lawn. To develop this new plan, Alderman hired Warren Henry Manning, a well-known landscape architect based in Massachusetts who had previously worked in the office of American landscaping pioneer Frederick Law Olmsted. Manning was recommended by Charles Duncan McIver, president of the North Carolina State Normal and Industrial College (now the University of North Carolina at Greensboro), who had hired Manning to oversee the layout of the Greensboro campus. Writing to Manning for advice regarding the site of the new law building, Alderman explained that "the University of Virginia has on a beautiful site a singularly impressive and harmonious group of buildings, due to the genius of Thomas Jefferson and Stanford White. There are a few blots on it, due to the lack of genius of other folks." Alderman hoped to avoid more "blots" — likely the Brooks Museum, the Chapel, the Chemistry Lab, and other outliers that through their architecture or location appeared to be haphazard additions to the University rather than the result of careful long-range planning. Manning agreed to visit the University, arriving in Charlottesville in June 1908. He delivered a proposed campus expansion plan to Alderman that October.[45]

Although Manning's initial plan does not survive, evidence suggests that he imagined a vast expansion of the Beaux-Arts plan initiated by Stanford White. A surviving revision from 1913 features scores of regularly placed buildings surrounding enclosed courts, each small complex working to replicate the intimacy and scale of the original Lawn. In October 1908, the placement of the new law building within this Beaux-Arts plan was a matter of great importance to President Alderman, who imagined the new home of the Law School as the launching point for an expanded and beautified campus. In his first scheme, Manning put the law building near the hospital, adjacent to the East Range, but this idea met with "universal disapproval." The hospital was among the most vocal objectors; it wanted the site for its own "symmetrical expansion of the hospital plant" and otherwise thought the "large numbers of students, with professors lecturing, &c, would of necessity be detrimental to the quiet and privacy of patients in the hospital." The law professors, meanwhile, were "somewhat panic stricken at the thought of the building being put at that place," and for Alderman the site was "a surprise and a disappointment." He wanted the Law School building to be "a logical part of some logical scheme." Nevertheless, Alderman generally approved of Manning's overall plan, which he praised as "intelligent and farseeing." He told Manning that such a plan "would have been worth an incalculable sum if Mr. Jefferson could have had such a thing placed in his hands seventy five years ago. It is a big noble comprehensive scheme that greatly appeals to my imagination."[46]

As President Alderman envisioned the new law building as an essential step toward a grander University of Virginia, he wanted it fully integrated into the planned arrangement of new structures lining lawns and courts, evenly expanding outward from the Academical Village. Wanting the new structure to clearly relate to the Thomas Jefferson and Stanford White buildings on the Lawn, Alderman proposed a site just west of the southwest end of the Academical Village, where the law building would form a "quadrangle" with Cocke Hall and the Refectory. The president's suggestion prevailed. Yet while Alderman was a visionary, he underestimated the rate of growth about to take place, telling Manning that his plan was "of such a nature as to make realization in anybody's lifetime now living quite impossible." Manning recognized that the University would grow quickly, as had institutions of higher learning across the country. He asked the president, "Do you realize that the Universities of Wisconsin, Minnesota, California, Chicago, and Stanford University, have all grown up within the memory of men now living who are not old men[?] . . . I have had numerous dreams that have come to be realities in my professional life, and I believe that I will live to see the time when the greater part of the plan that I have outlined to you will be executed provided you have the same faith in the future growth of the south that I have, and believe the University of Virginia ought to take the leadership in this growth."[47]

While the campus planning that accompanied the construction of the law building revealed the University's desire to expand in a way that replicated the symmetry and order of the Academical Village, the design of the law building demonstrated an attempt to complement the building vocabulary of the original structures. In their proposals for the new building, submitted in the late spring or summer of 1908, the competing firms certainly recognized the University's commitment to new buildings that at least superficially matched Jefferson's work. Hepburn & Taylor acknowledged the necessity of building "along Jeffersonian lines," declaring that "the building should harmonize with all these which have done their part in placing the University at the head of our American universities in point of beauty and harmony in the architecture. . . . Nothing should be permitted to enter into the design which would clash with pre-existent structures." Likewise Carpenter & Blair remarked that "the University of Virginia is noted for its many classical examples of buildings," and therefore they "chose . . . for [their] chief architectural motif a colonade [*sic*] of coupled columns." The University selected Peebles, who made a successful bid with his own design in red brick and classical columns.[48]

John Kevan Peebles, a native of Petersburg and graduate of the University of Virginia, was experienced in merging the old and new, incorporating modern amenities and interior layouts into designs for buildings that were stylishly venerable. After completing his engineering degree in 1890, Peebles served as an architecture apprentice in Nashville, then in 1892 moved to Norfolk, where he established a partnership with James E. R. Carpenter. That year, the University hired Peebles to design Fayerweather Hall, its new gymnasium. With its red brick and Corinthian portico, Fayerweather suggested a return to Jeffersonian classicism, but in reality the building had little in common with the Academical Village. Peebles claimed that Fayerweather "follow[ed] the lines laid down by Jefferson, being classic in feeling and in detail," but as Richard Guy Wilson, David J. Neuman, and Sara Butler have argued, Peebles used "fragments of the familiar" to repurpose

Jeffersonian motifs for contemporary needs and preferences.[49] In the 1890s and early 1900s, Peebles primarily worked in the Colonial Revival style, which borrowed widely from early American architecture; these buildings succeeded in appearing historic though they often combined elements in ways that had no colonial precedent. In this phase of his career Peebles designed a number of elegant Colonial Revival houses in Norfolk; he was also responsible for several Colonial Revival hotels, including the Monticello Hotel (1898) in Norfolk and the Hotel Zimmerman (1902) and Hotel Richmond (1906) in Richmond. His reputation for excellence in traditional design helped him win his bid for an expansion of the Jefferson-designed Virginia State Capitol in 1902. The commission confirmed Peebles' reputation as an authority on Jefferson buildings. Nevertheless, Peebles designed buildings that suggested his lack of interest in conforming too closely to historical precedents, and indeed for most of his clients a light veneer of history would do. As the chair of the Board of Architecture for the Jamestown Exposition, which opened in Norfolk in 1907 to celebrate the tercentenary of the founding of Jamestown, Peebles helped design the architectural centerpiece of the fair, a large Colonial Revival auditorium. A brick, domed building with a hipped roof and Corinthian portico, flanked by arcades leading to wings, the auditorium more closely resembled a contemporary school or courthouse than anything related to Jamestown. Its dome, balustrades, quoins, stringcourses, festoons, white keystones, and brick walls were all standard Colonial Revival features. Observers, seeing its roof, red brick, white columns, and symmetry, likened the building to Monticello, and indeed the impression that the building recalled colonial Virginia mattered more than its true pedigree.[50]

As he began the design for the law building at the University of Virginia, Peebles considered the plan of at least one other law school structure: the red-brick, classically styled home of the University of Pennsylvania's Department of Law. Like his own designs, this building displayed a freehanded engagement with the past. Dedicated in 1900, the structure was part of a wave of construction at UPenn taking place under the supervision of the Philadelphia firm of Walter Cope and

John Stewardson. For the Philadelphia campus Cope and Stewardson drew inspiration from Oxford and Cambridge as well as the American Gothic Revival and Colonial Revival styles. This versatile combination allowed Cope and Stewardson to build red brick and stone buildings that recalled both the great universities of England and the late-eighteenth-century golden age of Philadelphia. The University of Pennsylvania law building, which Peebles personally examined in January 1909, recalled the Eng-

The University of Pennsylvania Department of Law Building was another impressive law building in the Ivy League. Cope & Stewardson, architects, photographed in 1900 at the time of its dedication.

glish Baroque, specifically the garden facade of Hampton Court Palace. With its vaulted ceilings, grand staircase, and mosaic tile floors, the building was far more splendid than anything the University of Virginia School of Law could dream of constructing.[51]

Although Peebles lacked the budget of the University of Pennsylvania, he designed a building that achieved adequate stateliness through its massing and ornamentation. And rather than attempting a simplified version of the English Baroque in imitation of UPenn, Peebles created a straightforward Colonial Revival building that matched the scale, palette, and classical vocabulary of the University of Virginia without specifically referencing anything built by Jefferson. Begun in fall 1909, Minor Hall was named for John B. Minor, an obvious but nevertheless ironic choice since the building symbolized many of the reforms in legal education that Minor so vehemently resisted. It was a nearly square two-story central block over a basement, with a hipped roof, a recessed portico with unfluted Ionic columns, and one-story side wings. Peebles based the building's scale and central-block-with-side-wings configuration on Stanford White's nearby Cocke Hall; Minor Hall further resembled Cocke in that both buildings achieved greater unity through the use of a heavy entablature. The one-story wings, a common feature of many University of Virginia buildings of the time, made Minor Hall more imposing while also reducing the ponderousness of the central block. Minor Hall enjoyed an enviable site at the edge of Monroe Hill, overlooking a small depression that the University transformed into McIntire Amphitheater in 1921. Set apart from other University buildings on its overlook, the columned Minor Hall made an imposing temple of law.

Despite the University's determination to spatially and architecturally venerate the Academical Village in its new construction, Peebles' design for the law building reveals that this desire was largely superficial. Minor Hall offered the illusion of pedigree: like Colonial Revival buildings generally, it relied on the suggestion of the historic past. Minor Hall's series of five front entries, each with French doors and fanlights, trimmed in limestone and capped with corbels, loosely referenced the series of arches on the Lawn and ranges, but these were also standard features of Colonial Revival institutional buildings nationwide. Peebles and the Jamestown Exposition Board of Architects had used three such entrances on the fairground auditorium. Minor Hall, in fact, introduced the French-door-and-fanlight entrance to the University canon; in the following decades, architects repeated this element on many University buildings, including Thornton Hall, Newcomb Hall, and New Cabell Hall. At Minor, Peebles used a few Jeffersonian trademarks—such as red brick, white keystones, and unfluted columns—as visual cues denoting that the building belonged at the University. Overall, the design of Minor Hall succeeded in fitting in. When *College Topics,* the student newspaper, learned of plans for the building's "Doric style of architecture," it declared approvingly that Minor Hall would have "nothing of the beautiful Brooks Museum appearance," disparaging the 1870s Second Empire structure northeast of the Rotunda that the newspaper found "in discord with classic designs seen in the other buildings" of

the University.[52] Yet Minor Hall was just as much a product of the fashion of the day as the Brooks Museum was in its time. The new law building would in fact have been at home at any number of campuses across the country then embracing the brick-and-columns version of Colonial Revival.

While the placement and the exterior design of the law building spoke to the University's desire to preserve the visual primacy of Jefferson's campus, in truth Minor Hall heralded a transition away from the Academical Village. The Cabell-Rouss-Cocke complex had dramatically expanded the University's square footage, but its U-shape formation at the foot of Lawn extended the Academical Village and maintained the Lawn as a dynamic and essential part of University life. In con-

Minor Hall in the 1910s, prior to the construction of McIntire Amphitheater.

trast, Minor Hall was freestanding and autonomous. Further, unlike outliers like the Chemistry Lab and the recently constructed hospital, which stood removed from the Academical Village for reasons of health and safety, and the Chapel and Brooks Museum, which served auxiliary purposes, Minor Hall housed one of the University's largest schools. This was the beginning of a reorientation of the University, one in which instruction and campus life expanded away from the Academical Village. Minor Hall stood apart because the Academical Village could no longer accommodate the Law School's twentieth-century requirements. The building's traditional exterior made this newness more acceptable to its consumers. Peebles' design was not an academic response to Jefferson's Grounds but rather a mollifying Colonial Revival skin—one with enough shades of the familiar to cloak Minor Hall's modernity in nostalgia for the previous century.

Minor Hall's "colonial" architecture was a bridge of sorts—a means of safe passage from old to new. In the two years that Minor Hall took to complete—roughly October 1909 to September 1911—*College Topics* frequently reported on the progress of the building in terms connecting it with both the past and the future. The newspaper continued to praise the appearance of the structure, reporting that "the architecture is Colonial, conforming in that respect to other buildings of the University," and again that "it is in the prevailing style of colonial architecture." *College Topics,* however, devoted more space to the building's "modern" features—its materials, use of new technologies, conveniences, and furnishings. When completed, the new law building would be "one of the most modern in the United States." Sounds peculiar to twentieth-century construction heralded the undeniably modern aspects of Minor Hall's construction: "The familiar chug, chug of the little steam engine, that was used to grind rock [for the concrete basement], has ceased, but the ring of the hammer and the clamping of bolts are heard in its stead. The steel framework arrived recently from Baltimore, and already the derrick is creaking merrily as it swings it into place." Unlike the buildings of Jefferson's time, Minor Hall had "adequate toilet facilities, janitors' closets, and other conveniences. . . .The entire

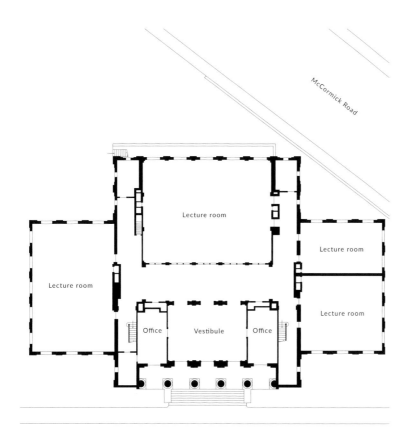

0 5   25   50'   N

First floor of Minor
Hall, transcribed
from original plans.

building is heated by steam and lighted by electricity. All rooms are ventilated after the most approved methods." The furniture, "in mission style," was "of the most modern type"; in short, Minor Hall had "every convenience of a thoroughly up-to-date nature." *College Topics* was likely correct that the building was "the largest and best equipped of the kind in the South," as most southern law schools did not yet have buildings constructed specifically to house them. Visitors to the building entered a spacious vestibule with the dean's office on the left; from there, wide halls led to four large lecture rooms and three restrooms. Upstairs was a large library with a skylight and space for eighty thousand books, two study halls, several small work-spaces, and an additional restroom. The materials and technologies used, as well as the specialized spaces offered, indeed made much of this building's interior "thoroughly modern," even as its exterior was more mindful of the past.[53]

Unlike the Academical Village, where Jefferson dynamically linked the indoors with the outdoors to draw various disciplines together, Minor Hall's exterior was respectful of but less engaged with its surroundings. The passivity of Minor Hall's facade well reflected the new reality of the modern campus building. The Law School's size, its desire for a variety of spaces, and the availability of up-to-date amenities, like plumbing and electricity, led it to construct a new building that symbolized its efforts at modernization, departmental distinctiveness, and increasing self-sufficiency. Its four walls housed a vital core of law professors, students, and staff, working in a specialized space, devoted to specialized tasks. Efficiency, segmentation, and focus had replaced the Academical Village's interchangeability. Whereas the Academical Village cultivated a philosophy of higher education grounded in the ideals of the Enlightenment, Minor Hall championed a Progressive-Era prioritization of expertise. But if Minor Hall's interior told a twentieth-century story of the University of Virginia, its exterior did so as well: it announced that the Law School and the University had not rejected the aesthetics and tradition of the Academical Village, even as these institutions outgrew its confines. Rather, Minor Hall's serene exterior quietly set the precedent for future expansion. As other schools likewise spiraled out from the Academical Village in the quest for larger and more varied types of space, the University continued to use architecture to temper the stresses of change.

By 1930, the Law School outgrew its new building and once again headed west, this time with grander ambitions to be worked out with red brick and white columns. Minor Hall's twentieth-century modernity was a double-edged sword: its newness was soon out of date.

2

Clark Memorial Hall and the Allyn Cox Murals

While Minor Hall represented the Law School's tentative transition into a twentieth-century law program, Clark Memorial Hall affirmed the institution's place among the nation's top law schools. Subsequent generations considered the Clark Hall era the school's golden age, with "a 'coincidence of quality' among the academic curriculum, the faculty, and the physical facilities."[1] In fact, when compared to the University law buildings that came immediately before and after it, Clark Hall was opulent, its grandness a symbol of the Law School's success. Situated in a prominent location just southwest of the Academical Village, Clark Hall was a large, three-story, red-brick building with Corinthian columns, a marble attic, and a prominent pyramidal roof. Inside was a surprising interior space: Mural Hall, a glass-ceilinged, marble-walled atrium, decorated with paintings by Allyn Cox. Clark Hall was especially impressive given its construction in the early years of the Depression. Started in 1930 and open for classes in 1932, it predated the Public Works Administration, which funded many grand American college buildings, including the University's Alderman Library. Clark Hall was the imposing product of friendship and good fortune. William Andrews Clark Jr., a Law School alumnus and heir to riches made in the copper mines of Montana, gave $350,000 for its construction, a gift prompted by his fondness for Law School dean William Minor Lile. Clark's generosity, which also included funds for the elaborate interior decorative scheme, spoke to the fact that he wanted a first-rate building for the School of Law. He got what he paid for. Whereas the limits of state funding clipped the high hopes attached to Minor Hall and the North Grounds campus of the 1970s, Clark's money created a building that fully conveyed the Law School's aspirations in brick and marble. Clark Hall was and remains a major landmark of the University, its scale and decoration linking it to Jefferson's Rotunda and Stanford White's Cabell-Rouss-Cocke complex.

Yet, despite felicitous beginnings and impressive results, the construction of Clark Memorial Hall was hardly straightforward. The familiar brick-and-columns facade of Clark Hall belies the complex history of its design. The new home of the Law School was borne out of overlapping interests and input from various stakeholders. Designed by the University's four-member Architectural Commission, the building had to satisfy President Alderman, the Board of Visitors, and the Law School faculty, all of whom weighed in on this important new University building. Cox and Clark made no attempts to control the design process, but Clark's gift of elaborate murals commissioned especially for the new building shaped the entire project. Although diverging at times in the particulars, all stakeholders agreed that the new building should be monumental. The problem with this desire for grandness was familiar to the University. As had been true with the Cabell-Rouss-Cocke complex in the 1890s, the University was cautiously ambitious regarding the design of Clark Hall, wanting bigness but nothing too big, newness but nothing too new. Ultimately the commission managed to produce a building that harmonized with the pastoral campus while also standing out as something remarkable and urbane. The commission created in Clark Hall a building that was local yet not provincial, modest yet stately, intimate yet ample. Cox's murals, with their bare bodies and

Clark Memorial Hall.

epic scale, and Clark's desire for a suitable monument to his wealth and his late wife, proved to be essential components in a formula that allowed Clark Memorial Hall to be both forward and backward facing, seemingly progressive yet comfortably nostalgic.

Clark Hall may never have been built had not William Andrews Clark Jr., a resident of Los Angeles, decided to visit his friend William Minor Lile in Charlottesville in the fall of 1929. Clark, the son of self-made millionaire Senator William Andrews Clark, had received a bachelor of law from the University of Virginia in 1899. Given his lifelong attachment to Lile, it is easy to imagine that Clark was no stranger to Pavilion X, the home of the Liles, during his years at the University.

Portrait of William Andrews Clark Jr., painted in 1932 by H. Medina, Paris. Clark commissioned the painting to hang in Clark Hall.

Clearly a bond formed between the Alabama-born law professor and the more worldly law student. In later years, Lile joined Clark on fishing trips on the Flathead River in Montana. With access to the fortune made by his robber baron father, Clark enjoyed a life of travel and leisure and the pursuit of expensive hobbies. As he got older Clark became an avid bibliophile, and he enjoyed sending Lile handsome and expensive volumes.[2]

As was true with his gifts of books, Clark provided the funding for the new law building with a casual generosity. When Clark visited in 1929, Lile entertained him much as he did other out-of-town guests: lunch with friends, then tea at the Farmington Country Club, followed by a drive to Ash Lawn and Monticello. A tour through Grounds included a stop at Minor Hall. Clark, as an 1899 graduate, had not attended classes in the building, and he no doubt perceived the boxy brick structure as a considerable improvement over the cramped rooms in the Rotunda. Yet Clark recognized, with a nudge from Lile, that the Law School had outgrown its new location: "I confess that I brought this to his attention in a very casual way," Lile wrote in his journal. In passing, Clark made an amazing offer: a donation of $100,000 toward a new building. Although a staggering sum, Lile knew it would not be enough for an entirely new structure. Speculating that Clark was worth $50 million, Lile scribbled that $300,000 would be "a mere bagatelle" to the amiable, enormously rich Clark. As such, he hoped for more: "Perhaps, who knows?—when we exhibit the plans for the new building to him, he may open up his heart & his purse, & offer to finance the erection entire!"[3]

Although Minor Hall was not yet twenty years old, the Law School and legal education had experienced a number of changes in the previous two decades that prompted Lile to want a new building. The changes are best understood in terms not only of the growth of the student body but also of an expanding curriculum and evolving standards in legal education. Minor Hall was built to house a maximum of 250 students, but by 1929–30 there were over 300 law students at the University.[4] The increase in numbers was not simply the result of the Law School admitting more students; the extension of the law curriculum from a two-year to a three-year program in 1908 meant that students had to stay an additional year to earn the law degree. When Dean Lile subsequently reorganized law classes for the 1909–10 academic year, he raised the number of required courses from twelve to twenty-five. Although these changes occurred while the

William Minor Lile, c. 1920s.

Law School was planning Minor Hall, limited funding prevented the construction of a building better suited to accommodate growth. Dean Lile embraced the opportunities that an enlarged curriculum offered, but Minor Hall had only four classrooms. It also had almost no faculty office space, a serious problem given the demands of the expanding curriculum on the small number of professors. By 1925, the law faculty consisted of six full-time professors; only Dean Lile had an office in Minor Hall. The establishment of the student-published *Virginia Law Review* in 1913 created an additional need for room that Minor Hall could not provide. All of these developments were part of the ongoing modernization of the Law School, which corresponded to sweeping changes in American legal education. The fact that the Law School began requiring at least one year of college prior to enrollment in 1918 exemplifies its gradual transformation into a professional, graduate-level degree program during the first half of the twentieth century. In 1922, the

Law School increased its admission requirements from at least one year of college to two.[5]

Hoping for a larger donation that would pay for a more accommodating building, Lile and a small group of University administrators, including President Alderman, cleverly chose to submit two sets of drawings to Clark: one for an addition to Minor Hall, the other for an entirely new building. Alderman asked the Architectural Commission, the University's board of architects, to prepare the drawings. Although the plans are lost, written descriptions provide some idea of what the commission had in mind. For the more modest scheme, the Architectural Commission proposed constructing a freestanding law library beside Minor Hall and connecting the two with an arcade. The location of Minor Hall at the base of Monroe Hill, together with its close proximity to McCormick Road, made expansion to the rear impractical. By moving the library into an adjacent building, the second floor of Minor Hall could be converted into classroom and office space. The commission explained that "a balanced composition would be changed to a balanced central motive with unbalanced wings." This asymmetry was allowable because Minor Hall was at the side rather than the central axis of the McIntire Amphitheater, which the University had constructed in front of Minor Hall in 1921. Regardless, this plan was largely subterfuge. In a letter, Alderman told Clark that while expanding Minor Hall would alleviate the overcrowding problem for the next few years, "of course, the proposed *new* building of the type indicated in the drawing would care handsomely for the needs of the Law School for an indefinite period." The design for this new building was "almost identical" to the Doremus Memorial Gymnasium at Washington and Lee, completed in 1915. The gymnasium itself looked something like an aggrandized Minor Hall. The president graciously concluded his letter to Clark with "I want to do what you want to do," but his words hardly masked unwritten hopes that the millionaire's generosity—or vanity—would prompt the grander plan.[6]

The fact that both proposals reserved space for decorative murals suggests that this ostensibly superfluous feature was indeed a critical part of Clark's vision for the

Law School's expansion. Although there is no record of Clark specifically including murals in his initial gift of $100,000, they were certainly part of the package by the time the University presented him with the proposed building plans a few months later. The commission clearly noted that three interior walls of the proposed Minor Hall library addition "would provide ample spaces for murals." Alderman, in turn, emphasized how the large walls of a new building would "quite gloriously set forth" the murals when he encouraged Clark to make a larger donation.[7] Clark readily agreed to provide $350,000 for a new structure even though he confessed to Alderman that he had not really taken the time to inspect either set of drawings. A delighted Lile wrote in his journal: "My faith was not in vain! . . . Alderman is as happy at the fulfillment of this long cherished dream of both of us

Doremus Memorial Gymnasium at Washington and Lee University. Flournoy & Flournoy, architects, completed 1915. Undated photograph.

as was I." Alderman meanwhile shared with Clark that Lile had been to see him, "full of pride and happiness and profound rejoicing." Both the president and the dean recognized that the attainment of a magnificent new building for the Law School and University was one of the crowning achievements of their careers.[8]

The Clark gift was one of the largest financial donations the University received between World War I and the Depression, a time when limited state support threatened the University's ability to keep up with its peer institutions. Such philanthropy proved essential to the University's ability to expand its curriculum, physical plant, and endowment. Although the University did not receive the enormous windfalls during this period that a few other schools enjoyed (for example, Princeton received $15 million from the estate of Henry Clay Frick in 1919), a bequest of $6 million from alumnus Philip du Pont in 1928 did much to revive its finances. Paul G. McIntire, a Charlottesville native who attended the University for one session before embarking on a career as a stockbroker, provided a number of substantial gifts during these years, including $120,000 for the McIntire Amphitheater, $155,000 for the School of Fine Arts, and $200,000 to establish the School of Commerce. Frederic W. Scott, a member of the Board of Visitors, gave $300,000 in 1929 for the University's new football stadium. Clark's donation was one of these exceptional gifts, made all the more exceptional by the fact that it would build and equip a single building.[9]

Clark attached only a few strings to his donation, but these stipulations had a considerable impact on the building program. First, Clark wanted the new building to be a memorial to his first wife, Mabel Duffield Foster Clark, who had died in 1903 shortly after the birth of their son. Second, Clark would commission the murals himself, paying for them apart from the $350,000 building gift and hiring well-known decorative painter Allyn Cox for the project. He imagined that the murals would depict scenes of law, running from "the time of Moses . . . to the time of our Revolution." In other respects, Clark was content to exert little influence over the project. Writing to Alderman in May 1930, Clark explained, "The site for the new building, the exterior and interior plans & general scheme of affairs I am perfectly satisfied to leave in your hands or those of your advisors." Clark's letters to the University about the project, of which at least twenty-eight survive, convey enthusiasm for the new law building, but he used his demanding schedule of business meetings and international travel to deflect questions about almost any aspect of the project besides the murals. For Clark, the murals were the centerpiece of the design. John K. Peebles remarked to his fellow Architectural Commission members, "It is our idea that Mr. Clark is largely building the structure around this [mural] hall."[10]

Clark's preoccupation with the law-themed murals may be attributable to the eccentricity of a wealthy man, but his personal history helps explain his desire to include a dramatic art feature in the new law building. Clark was born in 1877 in Deer Lodge, Montana, where his father was a banker and mine operator. Clark Sr., a native of Pennsylvania, had a knack for business and the necessary ruthlessness to compete in the hardscrabble world of mining in the wild west of the Montana Territory. The elder Clark's success in mining earned him the nickname the "Copper King of Montana," and by the time of his namesake's birth, he was already quite rich.[11] Despite being born in a log house in the American Northwest, William Andrews Clark Jr. enjoyed a cosmopolitan upbringing in line with his father's ambitions, which could hardly be contained by the state of Montana. Clark Sr.'s commercial empire made foreign travel possible and often necessary, and he and his family spent much of their time in Europe. Mrs. Clark, born Katherine Louise Stauffer, preferred France to Montana, and she lived there year-round with her three sons and two daughters until 1883. On his many trips to Europe for business and to see his family, Clark Sr. developed a passion for art, and his financial resources soon allowed him to create one of the most impressive art collections in the United States.[12]

Clark Sr. also enjoyed building fine homes, through which he displayed his success and indulged his love of the fine arts. In 1884, he began construction on an ornate mansion on Granite Street in Butte, with hand-painted ceilings that may have sparked the younger Clark's fondness for the decorative arts. Despite the

The ornate mansion of William Andrews Clark Sr. at Fifth Avenue and Seventy-Seventh Street, Manhattan. Completed around 1907, it was demolished in 1927 and replaced with an apartment building. Undated photograph.

mammoth size of the new home, Clark's family resided primarily on the East Coast. Clark Sr. wanted his children educated in New York, and he established a residence for them in Garden City, Long Island. The elder Clark eventually took up residence himself in New York, where his unbridled ambition took on staggering proportions in his new mansion at the corner of Fifth Avenue and Seventy-Seventh Street in Manhattan. This showcase of new money was one of the largest residences constructed on Fifth Avenue during the Gilded Age, rivaling the homes of the Astors and the Vanderbilts in size and surpassing them in ostentation. Designed by the New York firm Lord, Hewlett & Hull with flourishes by Henri Deglane of the École des Beaux-Arts in Paris, the French Renaissance structure of over a hundred rooms took more than a decade to build. When the mansion was finally completed around 1907, critics dismissed it as outmoded and garish. Its exceptional collection of 225 paintings included works by Gainsborough, Rembrandt, Van Dyck, and Titian. Two picture halls, a sculpture hall, and two other art galleries took up half of the main level; the ground floor housed an additional gallery for porcelain, tapestries, and other art objects. After Clark Sr.'s death, many of these works went to the Corcoran Gallery of Art in Washington, D.C.[13]

Unlike his father, who became notorious for his Gilded Age excess and the bribery scandals that sullied his bids for public office, William Andrews Clark Jr. garnered public recognition primarily for his charitable contributions. His philanthropy included founding the Los Angeles Philharmonic in 1919, funding the construction of the Alice McManus Clark Library at the University of Nevada (a memorial to his second wife), and bequeathing his valuable personal library to the University of California, Los Angeles. Unfortunately the only published biography of Clark is a largely unsympathetic treatment in William D. Mangam's *The Clarks: An American Phenomenon,* a 1941 tell-all written by the former secretary of Clark's brother, Charles Walker Clark. Mangam attributed Clark's "sudden and unprecedented interest in undertakings which were of a public nature" to a desire to mask his romantic relationships with several younger men. A more balanced examination of Clark's life suggests he was a man with a great love of art, music, literature, and education, who sought to promote these interests as he grew older. Clark may have wanted to keep his personal life private, but Mangam's classification of all of Clark's good works as a "smoke-screen" was unmerited and malicious.[14]

Clark perhaps loved nothing more than books, and his generosity reflected his desire to share his passion with others. Not only did he fund the construction of library buildings for two universities, but he also made gifts of smaller numbers of rare or fine press works to friends and public repositories. Lile received a number of books from Clark, including a limited edition four-volume set of Dante, bound in vellum. In 1930, Clark sent to the University of Virginia a remarkable first edition of Jefferson's *Notes on the State of Virginia* that contained an inscription from Jefferson to the Marquis de Lafayette. University librarian Harry Clemons wrote to Clark, "It is not easy to express to you how delighted we are by this acquisition. . . . As a result of your gift, the Virginia Collection at the University is in the way of containing the most notable set of editions [of *Notes on the State of Virginia*] in existence." Clark's gift reveals a bibliophile's delight in discovering and passing on treasures of unique value to the public.[15]

In 1923–24 Clark constructed a building for his personal library adjacent to his home in Los Angeles; here he first commissioned Allyn Cox. Designed by Robert D. Farquhar, a Los Angeles architect trained at the Massachusetts Institute of Technology and the École des Beaux-Arts, the building was a red-brick Italian

Renaissance–style structure, an example of the Mediterranean-inspired architecture especially popular at the time in southern California. Outside, Farquhar used a light touch, limiting ornamentation primarily to decorative door and window surrounds. Meanwhile the interior treatments were heavier, reminiscent of the lavish rooms of the Clark family's Fifth Avenue mansion. Clark wanted paintings on the barrel vault of the library's vestibule, and Farquhar recommended Cox, whom he had met in Italy. Farquhar recalled that Cox's "years in Italy from early youth, the guidance of his artist father Kenyon Cox, his studies at the American Academy in Rome, his excellent work in New York, all seemed to me to justify my recommending him to Mr. Clark."[16] Cox transformed the vault into a polychrome wonderland of painted clouds, niches, broken pediments, pastorals, and muscular male nudes, reminiscent of the sixteenth-century interiors of Palladian country houses. Clark was so happy with Cox's work that he asked him to paint ceiling panels and two large wall scenes in the library's drawing room. Clark then commissioned the painter for two philanthropic projects: murals for both the University of Virginia Memorial Room at the American Legion Building in Paris and Clark Memorial Hall.[17]

Clark's enthusiasm for Allyn Cox's work therefore merged with his devotion to the University of Virginia, his friendship with Dean Lile, and his philanthropic spirit to prompt his gift of a grand new Law School building with an impressive, decorative interior. The choice of murals reflected Clark's personal taste; simply, he liked them. He clearly inherited at least some of his father's inclination toward dramatic effect in the arts and architecture. It seems Clark found in Cox a satisfactory means of stamping a building with his own penchant for florid, often larger-than-life decoration, a way of infusing structures with his own personality. And like his father, he thought of buildings as incomplete without art.

While Clark stipulated that the building should house murals and serve as a memorial, it was up to the Law School and the University to work those elements into a design that met their own needs and desires. The site for the new building was the first consideration. Dean Lile first thought of the location of the Brooks

Museum, itself the gift of a wealthy donor, Lewis Brooks of Rochester, New York, who in 1876 gave the University funds for a "suitable building for a Cabinet of Natural Science." Though built in the familiar brick, the Second Empire ornamentation and verticality of the Brooks Museum had made it unpopular by 1900, when Beaux-Arts classicism and the Colonial Revival prevailed in American architecture. On a visit to the University in 1915, President William Howard Taft referred to the building's "majestic ugliness," urging it be kept unchanged as a reminder of architectural folly. *College Topics,* the University newspaper, described the Brooks Museum in 1909 as a "horrible example of 'bastard renaissance' thrust upon the

Vestibule of William Andrews Clark Jr.'s personal library in Los Angeles, painted by Allyn Cox. The building and collection are now the William Andrews Clark Memorial Library, UCLA.

reluctant vision of every visitor to the University . . . a production of the Archi-tectural 'Reign of Terror.'" The building was on a conspicuous site just east of the Rotunda, facing the "Corner" district and Charlottesville. Lile wrote in his diary that "if we could hire some incendiary to set fire to the Brooks Museum, that site would be ideal," but he quickly moved on to consider a rise just southwest of Minor Hall along the largely undeveloped McCormick Road, the most likely direction for University expansion. The University approved this selection. Dawson's Row, an arc of antebellum brick dwellings used as student housing, stood on a portion of the site; at least one of these houses would have to be demolished. Houses D and E of Dawson's Row would block the view of the structure, and siting the law build-ing further back was undesirable "from the standpoint of first impressions," since the University and law faculty meant for the new structure to impress. Crowning a prominent point, and visible from the sacred Lawn, the selected site spoke to the importance of the Law School to the University.[18]

In March 1930, President Alderman asked Dean Lile to call a meeting of law faculty to prepare a list of what was wanted in the new building "in the way of class rooms, offices and library, etc." Although their recommendations were mod-est, they reflected changes in legal and higher education that had occurred over the past two decades as well as the desire for the Law School to reclaim a position of national prominence in the legal academy. Alderman asked that Clark's gift be kept confidential, as he wanted to reveal the news on Founder's Day, April 13 (Thomas Jefferson's birthday). Lile wrote that the surprised faculty "had a sort of love feast" about the news, delighted by the prospect of a new building. Over the next two weeks, the law faculty, working in secret, prepared a set of recommendations that aimed to expand and improve upon the facilities offered in Minor Hall. The most noteworthy feature of this list was the number of specialized spaces, reflective of a more contemporary, expansive understanding of the uses of college buildings. See-ing the new law building as a place where students and faculty should fraternize as well as study or teach law, the professors asked for smoking, lounging, and locker rooms. Although the report did not specify a division of social space between students and faculty, ultimately the new building would have separate student and faculty lounges. Anticipating twelve law professors in the future (as opposed to the current seven), the law school requested a dozen offices, located near the library to facilitate teaching preparation and research. The library itself also needed to be bigger. Whereas the current library had approximately twenty-three thousand books, the report requested that the new library hold seventy-five thousand. The faculty also wanted a moot court room, "a luxury, but quite desirable," with a bench, bar, and seating for at least fifty people. Smaller spaces included offices for the *Virginia Law Review,* a grading assistants' office, a filing room for administrative records, and a storage room for catalogs, back copies of the *Law Review,* and so on. The recommendations did not suggest that the faculty expected the sex ratio of students to equalize anytime soon. In 1920, the University began admitting women to the Law School and other graduate and professional programs, but the number of women remained quite low until the 1960s. The faculty report asked for toilet rooms to accommodate an enrollment of five hundred men and only twenty-five women. For more ideas, Lile sent a questionnaire to deans of law schools with new buildings, wanting Clark Hall to keep pace with its contemporaries.[19]

Although the law faculty got to weigh in on the numbers, types, and sizes of spaces in the new law building, its design automatically fell to the University's Architectural Commission, an architectural planning group established by President Alderman in 1921. This group controlled the design and expansion of the University through the interwar period and ensured the dominance of red-brick classicism on Grounds. The four original members of the commission—head of the architecture school Fiske Kimball and architects R. E. Lee Taylor, Walter Dabney Blair, and John Kevan Peebles—had all previously worked for the University. Kimball, a trained architect, designed the McIntire Amphitheater; Peebles won the commission for Fayerweather Gymnasium (1893) with his partner, James E. R. Carpenter, before designing Minor Hall in 1909. Peabody Hall (1914) with its Doric portico was the work of Taylor and his firm, while the Ionic-columned Cobb Hall (1917) was the work of Blair. The commission's first building on Grounds was Memorial Gymnasium (1924), modeled loosely on the Baths of Diocletian. When Kimball left the University in 1923, professor and architectural historian Edmund Campbell replaced him on the commission. The Monroe Hill Dormitories and Monroe Hall followed in 1929–30. While all of these buildings made use of red brick and classical columns, cornices, and pediments, the commission freely blended Georgian, Colonial Revival, and Beaux-Arts elements with motifs taken from Jefferson, producing a variety of architectural and decorative configurations. Frequently, building materials and scale made these diverse buildings appear "Jeffersonian," even if they had little in common with the Academical Village or each other in terms of style. As they would with Clark Hall, the members of the commission showed deference to the Rotunda, paying close attention to massing and site placement to diminish the apparent size of larger buildings.[20]

The Architectural Commission called the law faculty report "the most satisfactory preliminary memoranda they had ever had from faculty committees" at the University and resumed the design work initiated by President Alderman's request for two sets of plans to be sent to Clark. There was much to be done. Although the commission's proposal for a new building had succeeded in prompting a larger donation from Clark (even if he had hardly glanced at the drawings), the design disappointed Alderman and the Board of Visitors. As expected, this initial proposal appropriately fell within the parameters of the red brick and classical columns tradition: "The architectural motifs used are either Jeffersonian or such as would harmonize with them." Yet the considerable flexibility within this tradition meant that there were nearly endless ways to configure various elements. The scheme submitted to Clark (the one resembling the Washington and Lee gymnasium) consisted of a large central block with a long recessed colonnade, three central doorways, and side wings; inside was a two-story library with "high arched windows" and wall space for the murals. Taylor believed it "really most successful," but Alderman and the visitors disagreed, even judging the design less attractive than the one prepared for the addition to Minor Hall. Taylor wrote to Campbell of his dismay: "To say that I feel discouraged at the way architectural designs are passed on by the powers-that-be would be putting it mildly." Alderman thought that the large windows behind the front columns were "factory-like" and that the structure looked too much like a public building, perhaps a post office. This critique brought to the foreground a problem that would plague the design for the next few months: how to design a building that was large and imposing but not institutional—and certainly not industrial. Over the course of 1930, the Architectural Commission struggled to produce a design that would satisfy themselves, Alderman, the Law School, and the Board of Visitors. Clark, at least, had simplified the process by declining to participate. By October, however, little progress had been made. John Lloyd Newcomb, Alderman's assistant, wrote to Dean Lile that "the Board of Architects has literally made up a dozen different plans for the exterior of this building. None of these plans has been satisfactory."[21]

There were two primary obstacles to a successful design: the commission had to create a sufficiently grand scheme within the limits of the University canon, and they had to incorporate the murals within an appropriately dramatic interior space. Regarding the first problem, the commission encountered various notions of what constituted a "monumental" design. R. E. Lee Taylor reported that Frederic W. Scott, a member of the Board of Visitors, "said no monumental building should have wings," a criticism of the initial building proposal. Yet monumentality could only be expressed using the amalgamation of Jeffersonian classicism, Colonial Revival, and other styles that the University administration found palatable— styles that, rather than inspiring a feeling of grandness, often made buildings appear smaller and more domestic. Wings, in fact, had been a primary way that the commission kept large new buildings from overpowering the campus; Memorial Gymnasium, with its Roman Bath design, had two conventional Colonial Revival wings that reduced the apparent mass of the building. President Alderman, meanwhile, nervous that the design might be too austere, made it clear that the building should not have a flat roof but rather the traditional sloping slate roof found elsewhere on Grounds. The president liked Manning Hall, the law building at the University of North Carolina, which achieved a modest stateliness through its mass,

hexastyle portico, and location at the end of a court. Blair therefore proposed a design for the new law building that strongly resembled Manning Hall: a simple two-story hipped-roof structure with a classical pediment and cornice, Corinthian columns, and two one-story wings with arched windows and balustrades. Other members of the Architectural Commission, however, worried about the use of a pediment as a major feature of yet another University building. In any case, the Blair plan was likely too modest to satisfy the visitors or the law faculty.[22]

President Edwin A. Alderman admired Manning Hall, completed in 1923 for the University of North Carolina School of Law. He suggested it as a model for the new law building at the University of Virginia. William Kendall, architect, undated photograph.

The problem of showcasing the murals overlapped with the complexities of achieving monumentality, as the murals were a primary way in which the building's interior could achieve the desired stateliness. Certainly by July 1930 the commission had decided to display the murals in an imposing central hall rather than in the library. The floor plan for Blair's Manning Hall–inspired design reveals one problem with the inclusion of a grand mural hall; if too large, the hall could compromise the building's educational purpose. In Blair's scheme, the hall consumed almost the entire central block of the building, taking space away from the library and classrooms. Another issue was how to handle the roof of the building if the hall was exceptionally tall. A surviving design by Taylor illustrates the problem. Unsure how to incorporate the lofty hall into the exterior design, Taylor awkwardly inserted a towering projection with no relationship to the rest of the building. The commission likewise struggled with interior treatments for the mural hall. At one meeting "a great many sketches were shown — some of these treated the side

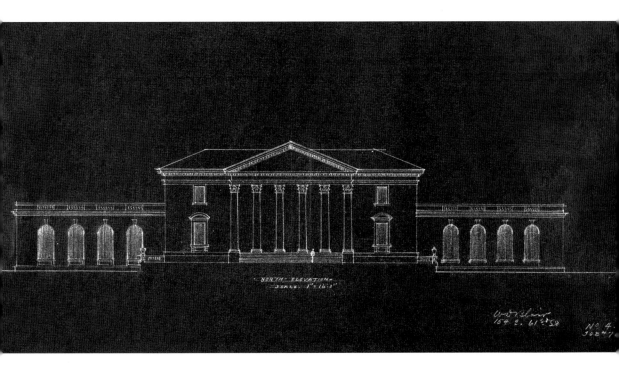

walls with arches, some with piers, some with pilasters, all in various proportions and with different feeling." One model put forward was McKim, Mead & White's Franklin National Bank in Philadelphia (1916), which had a large central hall with a skylight set in a coffered barrel vault. Arches and pilasters decorated the walls. Eventually practicality superseded the most elaborate schemes and simplified the design process. In midsummer, Taylor visited the law libraries at Harvard and Columbia, and he reported to the commission, "Nothing that I saw at Harvard or Columbia approached in magnificence the room which we have been drawing (except the Main Library of Columbia) and when we consider the comparative resources of those two places with Virginia, I am afraid we were shooting at the stars." Taylor suggested that the commission "make the Great Hall much less mon-

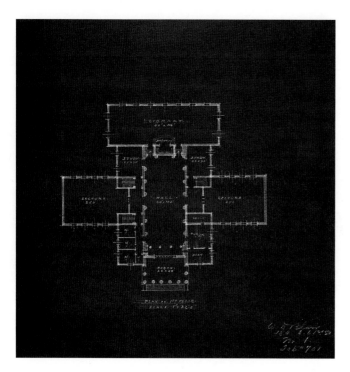

Proposal for Clark Memorial Hall, plan of first floor, Walter Dabney Blair, 1930.

umental, but still keep it architectural and with a certain bigness of scale," despite the "disappointment to give up such a fine monumental room as we have been contemplating." Dreams of vaults and arches would go unrealized, but Mural Hall survived as the central and most impressive feature of the new building.[23]

Although the Architectural Commission decided to reduce the size of Mural Hall, the group still had to come up with a grand overall design "in view of the openly expressed disappointment of the Visitors that the former sketches did not have a more monumental character." In a new plan, Taylor sought to render monumentality through a more explicitly Jeffersonian scheme. Starting with the idea of an octagonal mural hall, he topped the building with a likewise eight-sided dome; in front he placed a hexastyle portico. The roof of the building, Taylor explained, was "not unlike the treatment of the mass over the octagonal hall at Monticello." Although the design clearly drew from both Monticello and the Rotunda, Taylor likely also found inspiration in John Russell Pope's Union Station in Richmond, which he admired. He probably paid even greater attention to the eight-sided dome of the Shedd Aquarium in Chicago, which Taylor mentioned in his description of the plan. As Blair did in his plan, Taylor placed two large lecture halls on either side of the central mural hall. He kept the library at the rear but placed it perpendicular

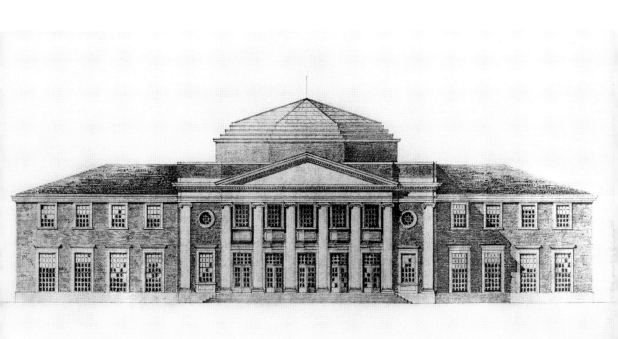

to the main building in a long projecting four-story wing. The ponderous exterior garnered the immediate censure of Campbell, who found it lacked "any merit whatsoever." Especially damning was Campbell's comparison of the building's long projecting rear wing to the "old burnt Academic Bldg addition to the Rotunda." The design likely also failed because its dome and portico made it appear too much like the Rotunda.[24]

While the Architectural Commission struggled with a design, Dean Lile became increasingly anxious about the project. By late spring 1930, Lile had met with the commission and seen preliminary sketches, which he found, "in general, attractive and satisfactory." He was "especially glad when they declared that this would be the handsomest building that has ever been erected on the grounds." Several

Proposal for Clark Memorial Hall, elevation, R. E. Lee Taylor, 1930.

months later he was less content. In October, he wrote to Newcomb, Alderman's assistant, of a visit from Charles Walker Clark, brother of William Andrews Clark Jr. As Lile explained, "[Clark's visit] has reminded me that our architects seem to be taking a tremendously long time to lick the plans of the new Law Building into shape. I have heard nothing from them for several months. I have never seen any of the elevations at all." Lile feared that, without plans to show Clark, their benefactor might interpret the University's sluggishness as "apparent indifference," and he hoped Newcomb would "put a small coal of fire on the backs of these slow-moving gentlemen."[25]

Fortunately for everyone, the commission was on the verge of a finding a solution that balanced grandness with approachability and newness with veneration for the older portions of Grounds. In mid-October, Taylor told Peebles that the main problem was one of scale and massing: "As I got them [the Board of Visitors], they felt that this particular building should be a compact monumental mass. I think they meant that it should have more kinship to such buildings as the Lincoln Memorial, the Temple of the Scottish Rite, University Rotunda, or our own War Memorial here in Baltimore, than to such open compositions as Homewood, Brandon, the New Academic Building [Monroe Hall], or the [Monroe Hill] Dormitories which we did some years back." The commission hit upon a compromise, one that included elements of both compact monuments and sprawling, more domestic plans. In several ways this new plan was an expanded version of Minor Hall. Both buildings featured a large central two-story block of seven bays with a recessed portico with no pediment, and both had one-story wings at either side. Clark Hall, however, was far grander. Whereas Minor Hall featured four columns with Ionic capitals set between two engaged half-columns, Clark Hall had six freestanding columns with more ornate Corinthian capitals set between pilasters. And while Peebles had capped Minor Hall with a simple hipped roof, the Architectural Commission chose for Clark Hall a marble attic topped by a pyramid, making the roof the most outstanding feature of the building's exterior. Monuments mentioned in Taylor's letter likely inspired the Clark Hall roof design. The attic resembled the one used at the Lincoln Memorial, which had been completed in 1922. An even likelier source for both the attic and the pyramid was the Masonic House of the Temple in Washington, D.C., headquarters of the Scottish Rite, designed by John Russell Pope and modeled after the ancient Mausoleum of Halicarnassus.

The Clark Hall roof design achieved multiple aims. The pyramid set upon the square attic had the loftiness, grandeur, and simple geometry of the Rotunda dome without imitating the older structure. Notably, the commission did not eliminate a dome altogether but used the attic to accommodate a domed ceiling in the moot court room. There was likely some symbolism in this placement: the moot court room's location under a dome, under a pyramid, made a sacred space of the room devoted to the ultimate purpose of the study of law — the practice of law. Further, the design's allusions to the Lincoln Memorial and the Mausoleum of Halicarnassus nodded to the building's purpose as a memorial to Mabel Foster Clark. Finally, on a practical level, the pyramid succeeded in disguising the roof and skylights of Mural Hall, which projected upward from the middle portion of the building. Although an unconventional choice and a departure from the standard Jeffersonian paradigms, the pyramid succeeded as the crowning element of a building designed both to stand apart and to blend in. Even though Lile was concerned about "the sharp point given to the roof in the center of the mass," the design won approval from administrators and law faculty alike.[26]

Although the Board of Visitors expressed a desire for a "compact" monumental building, meaning a large structure without wings, the commission recognized that they needed some means of diminishing the apparent size of the structure. They knew that President Alderman and the visitors would not approve any building that appeared to rob the Rotunda of its primacy on Grounds. Yet two-story wings, such as those in Taylor's octagonal dome plan, made the building appear heavy and institutional. The commission therefore chose to distend the body of Clark Hall, pulling the wings outward, lowering them to one story, and connecting them to the central block with arcades. In this regard the building did in fact

The Carroll family mansion, "Home-wood," with its Palladian five-part plan consisting of a central block, hyphens, and flanking dependencies. Constructed Baltimore vicinity, c. 1801; now part of the Johns Hopkins University Homewood campus.

take on the Palladian massing of such historic homes as Homewood at Baltimore and Brandon on the James River, each consisting of a central structure and two flankers, connected by hyphens. Campbell observed that "such loose connection is the idea of many Va. colonial works" and thus would create a visual link with the past that he believed would help win over the administration. Further, the use of arcades for the connecting hyphens tied the new building to the Lawn and ranges, providing "certain Univ. of Va. sentiment which will surely appeal to [the] Visitors." The rejected Blair and Taylor proposals had placed a large lecture hall on either side of the main block of the building, and the commission kept this general arrangement, putting a lecture hall in each wing (these rooms became known as East Hall and West Hall). Lile was not so sure of the wings: "I feared they would appear to be added as an afterthought, or as subsequent additions for the enlargement of the building." Yet the arrangement did effectively anchor the building to its site and disguised its size, as Clark Hall would in fact be much larger than the Rotunda.[27]

As for the interior of the building, the commission made sure that Mural Hall would be its eye-catching main attraction. Although the commissioners had to abandon any thoughts of an expensive barrel vault, they achieved "bigness of scale" by following Campbell's suggestion for a "pediment scheme," which proposed skylights along either side of a more economical, gently sloping gable roof over the hall.[28] Elaborately decorated pediments, engaged Ionic travertine columns, Ionic travertine pilasters, a travertine floor, and deep-purple, richly veined marble wainscoting created a striking interior that resembled a Roman temple turned outside in. The plan provided ample space for two large triptych murals on either side of the hall, with room for decorative painting above the doorways. The hall also served as a main traffic artery through the building, connecting the office and classroom spaces at the front and sides of the building with the library in the rear.

After such a prolonged design process, the building went up with considerable speed. In his journal, alongside entries about his own failing health, the worldwide economic depression, and the rainstorms that offered relief from the severe drought plaguing Virginia in 1930–31, Lile recorded Clark Hall's progress. In April 1931 he noted the groundbreaking, and by July he observed: "The new Law Building is rapidly going up, the walls complete up to the first floor. House E [of Dawson's Row], that stood immediately in front of the new building, has just been razed, & House D is soon to follow suit." Later that month, the commission asked Lile to provide text for the building's inscription. Due to his "present state of semi-invalidism," Lile "found it no easy task to find or to evolve an inscription sufficiently appropriate in substance & sufficiently dignified & impressive in form, to bear the public scrutiny and criticism which it must undergo for perhaps several centuries." He turned to Leslie Buckler of the law faculty for help, and it was Buckler who wrote the words soon to be carved in marble: "That Those Alone May Be Servants of the Law / Who Labor with Learning Courage and Devotion / To

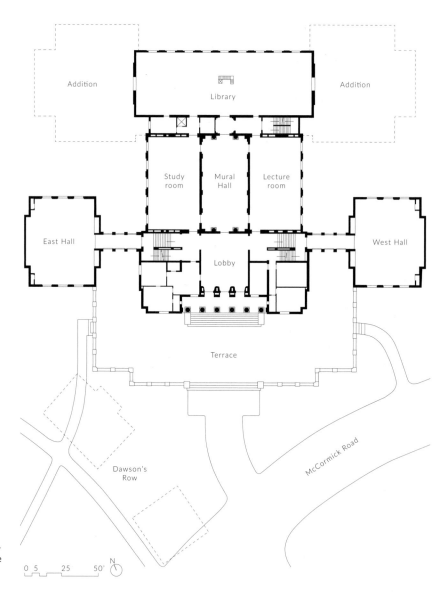

Addition

Library

Addition

Study room

Mural Hall

Lecture room

East Hall

West Hall

Lobby

Terrace

Dawson's Row

McCormick Road

First floor plan,
Clark Memorial Hall,
transcribed from the
original plans.

0 5   25   50'

N

Preserve Liberty and Promote Justice." On July 21, the faculty laid the cornerstone "without ceremony," depositing "copies of the general and special catalogues, the Va. Law Review & a few other insignificant things" in a tin box. In September, the commission asked Lile to come up with the "names of distinguished lawyers & judges" that would appear along the classical frieze of Mural Hall. Clark arrived in Charlottesville that November with "one of his French protégés, Lemire," and "was much pleased with the progress made in erection of the building, & with the building itself, which is now practically under roof." In May 1932, *College Topics* reported that the building was nearly complete, with landscape grading and interior painting left to be done. It opened in September for the 1932–33 academic year.[29]

Clark Memorial Hall, which the *Washington Post* proclaimed "combines beauty and utility to a marked degree," reflected changing expectations in the uses and amenities of college buildings. Whereas Minor Hall housed the basics of legal education—classrooms, a library, study rooms, and the dean's office—Clark Hall had more varied and specialized spaces to suit expanding requirements. The building consisted of a three-story central mass with a two-story rear wing for the library and two one-story side wings for the large lecture halls. An assortment of classroom sizes spoke to an increasingly diverse curriculum; in addition to East Hall and West Hall in the wings, there was a lecture hall on the first floor of the building and three smaller classrooms on the second floor. For professors, there were individual offices and a faculty lounge. Student life dominated almost the entire ground floor of the structure, with office space for the *Virginia Law Review,* a locker room, and a large student lounge. *College Topics* called this last space "one of the most attractive features of the building. It is a large room, 60 by 25 feet in proportion, heavily paneled in wood with its walls plastered in the old Colonial manner. At each end is a big open fireplace, where in winter burning logs may furnish a cheerful touch." The domed moot court room on the second floor provided an elegant, tailored space for practice in oral arguments. Overall the building represented a more expansive view of legal education, with students and professors using the building more frequently, fully, and recreationally. The *Virginia Law Review* found that "the reading rooms, the library and the class rooms are attractively and comfortably furnished with ample accommodations to care for a large increase in enrollment. The Faculty and Student Lounges abound in easy chairs and divans that are extremely conducive to the rest that the tired and over-worked members of these two groups so frequently require." Comfortable leather chairs and crackling fires invited the

building's occupants to tarry, making Clark Hall a more homey structure that stimulated a variety of uses. Law alumni hoped that eventually the University would construct a dormitory and dining hall behind Clark Hall, enhancing the building's all-hours usage and "thus making the Law School a complete unit as is the case at Yale and certain other large Universities."[30]

Although Clark Hall with its ample size, huge columns, and marbled central hall looked something like a courthouse, its domestic characteristics gave this

Library, Clark Memorial Hall, 1936.

ostensibly public building the aura of a private domain. Like Minor Hall, Clark Hall stood in opposition to the interdisciplinary philosophy of the Academical Village, but for the newest home of the Law School this quality was more pronounced. Clark Hall was a self-contained sanctum of legal education, a courthouse reimagined as a members-only club. Its architects may have dressed Clark Hall in materials that recalled the Academical Village, but the similarities ran only skin deep.

What mattered most to the Law School was that the new building served its educational mission while reaffirming its historical significance and national prominence. At the building dedication, held on October 5, 1932, the Law School opened its new doors to a crowd of visitors, invited to gape at the well-appointed if

incomplete new building. The new dean of the Law School, Armistead Dobie, had invited over three thousand University alumni to attend the dedication, including guest of honor William Andrews Clark Jr. Dobie's address portrayed Clark Hall as a successful merger of East Coast sophistication and Jeffersonian sensibility. Its "student lounge would do credit to a metropolitan club" while Mural Hall, when finished, would be "a room unmatched in any Law building on the American continent." In the same breath he proclaimed Clark Hall "a happy blending of the romance of range and rotunda, the lure and lilt of the lawn and the halo of these happy hills." "An eminent New York architect," he assured the audience, "has declared it to be more completely in keeping with the Jeffersonian spirit than any building erected here since the death of the father of this University." In affirming the architectural pedigree of the building, Dobie communicated the comforting

Student lounge, Clark Memorial Hall, 1932.

Mural Hall in 1932, after the installation of the memorial mural but prior to the completion of the side murals and grisailles.

knowledge that the Law School and University could reach "higher and rarer planes of intellectual achievement" without the faculty and students of the Law School becoming "either lazy lotus eaters or enervated esthetes." The old in Clark Hall allowed the new and modish to enthrall rather than disconcert the audience gathered before it.[31]

Some familiar faces were absent at the dedication. President Alderman had died in 1931, replaced by his former assistant, John Lloyd Newcomb. Dean Lile was in poor health and likely away from Charlottesville seeking treatment at the time, but his wife Maud represented him at various functions, including an entertainment she hosted at Pavilion X for William Andrews Clark Jr.[32] Also missing was the complete set of murals by Allyn Cox. Cox had only had time to finish the mural with the memorial plaque to Mabel Clark, which hung in Mural Hall over the entrance to the library.

Two days after the dedication, Clark wrote to President Newcomb expressing his happiness. Not only had he been well pleased with the "general interior arrangement and with the furnishings" of the building, but he declared the dedication ceremony "one of the bright spots in [his] life." As for the murals, he hoped they would "soon be put in place" and would provide "a decided improvement in the entire interior."[33] For now, Clark Hall was a monument with a hollow core, its marble hall the elaborate staging for an attraction yet to come. The Architectural Commission had finished the work of constructing a modern and monumental

THE LAW SCHOOL AT THE UNIVERSITY OF VIRGINIA

law building in appropriately Jeffersonian dress; it was up to Allyn Cox to insert its capstone.

Fully installed by 1934, the Clark Memorial Hall murals were an unexpectedly vibrant feature in a building with otherwise austere finishes. The fact that visitors entered Clark Hall through a vestibule decorated in a muted, functional classicism made the murals, fluted columns, and colored marble of Mural Hall all the more surprising. Mural Hall also contrasted with the building's exterior. While the red brick and white columns reflected the University's commitment to Jeffersonian themes, the murals, with their allegories and classical motifs, were a holdover from the turn-of-the-century Beaux-Arts era. This ambitious if outdated decorative scheme reflected the taste of William Andrews Clark Jr., but it worked well for the purposes of the University and the Law School. With larger-than-life figures set in the temple-like Mural Hall, the murals enhanced the monumentality of the building. They were also the kind of dramatic art program one might find in an urbane public building or the halls of a major American university. Although conspicuous for their abundant nudity, the murals were a conservative decorative art display that looked backward as much as the building that housed them.

The Clark Hall murals therefore were not a precursor to, nor a part of, the well-known rebirth of interest in large public murals that occurred in the United States during the 1930s. The Public Works of Art Project (1933–34), the Section of Painting and Sculpture (later the Section of Fine Arts; 1934–43), and the Federal Art Project (1935–43) were New Deal programs through which the federal government paid artists to create murals for courthouses, schools, libraries, and hospitals. These programs launched a renaissance of large public mural painting in the United States, although the themes explored in these works of art were generally quite different from those of the Beaux-Arts period. While Beaux-Arts muralists often used allegories that relied on the viewer's literacy in classical mythology, New Deal muralists created art that the general population could easily grasp. Understandably, New Deal murals often depicted workers and places of production, such as farms and factories; the artists often used this public forum to call attention to societal inequality. Many New Deal artists were associated with Social Realism, a movement that sought to draw attention to the problems of everyday life and rejected the idealism of the Beaux-Arts. The Clark Hall murals shared no such social or public purpose. Here again, Clark Hall can be best understood as a private rather than a public building: it was a "home" for the Law School. Allyn Cox's work at Clark Hall was essentially a continuation of his commissions for private clients, including William Andrews Clark Jr. Unlike the New Deal murals, with their emphasis on everyday labor and the common man, the Clark Hall murals were impractical and patrician. As imagined by Cox, court was held among muscled Greeks, not suited lawyers. Rather than pulling aspiring lawyers down to earth, the murals drew them toward the heavens, away from the ordinary business of legal practice.[34]

Whatever the trends of American mural painting, the University had almost no history of large wall paintings. The one exception was the reproduction of Raphael's *School of Athens* housed in the theater of Cabell Hall, commissioned by an anonymous alumnus to replace the earlier reproduction that burned with the Rotunda Annex in 1895. Clark attended the University after the fire and before the installation of the new copy of the painting in 1902, so he likely never saw the reproductions and thus was not influenced by either of them. Nonetheless the *School of Athens* had an air of worldliness and grandeur that University leaders found attractive, and they likely enjoyed the thought of creating a similar sensation through the inclusion of large murals in the decoration of Clark Hall.[35]

Allyn Cox, handpicked by Clark for the law school project, had an impressive decorative arts pedigree. His father, Kenyon Cox, was a nationally known painter, illustrator, and art critic in the Beaux-Arts era. Dean Lile wrote in his diary that Kenyon Cox, "during my younger days, was regarded as the most distinguished mural artist in America."[36] The elder Cox trained at the Pennsylvania Academy of Fine Arts and the École des Beaux-Arts in Paris; he launched his career as a muralist when he painted a ceiling for the Manufactures and Liberal Arts Building at the Chicago Columbian Exposition of 1893. He went on to receive a number of large mural commissions, including projects at Bowdoin College, the Library of Congress, and the statehouses of Iowa, Minnesota, and Wisconsin. Allyn Cox's mother, Louise King Cox, was also a painter, best known for her portraits of children. Like his mother, Cox studied at the National Academy of Design and the Art Students League. While attending the American Academy in Rome on a painting fellowship from 1916 to 1920, he left his studies to serve with the American Red Cross in Italy, and it was there that he met the future architect of Clark's private library in Los Angeles, Robert Farquhar.[37]

When Cox returned to the United States, he entered an art world much different from the one his father helped to create. The era of the Beaux-Arts mural was over. While Cox created large murals for the George Washington Masonic National Memorial in Alexandria and the United States Capitol much later in his career, in the 1920s and 1930s he worked almost exclusively on private commissions for decorative painting in fine homes and commercial buildings. Among his works in New York were decorative wall treatments in the homes of Anne Harriman Vanderbilt, Katrina Ely Tiffany, and Helen Huntington Astor; murals of "old New York" in the City Bank-Farmers Trust Company building at 55 Wall Street; and murals depicting scenes from the American Revolution in the Continental Bank building at 30 Broad Street. Through his friend Philip Trammell Shutze, an architect he met at the American Academy in Rome, Cox also executed murals in houses in Atlanta, including an allegorical grisaille and two Italian landscapes for the Andrew Cal-

Allyn Cox with palette and brushes, c. 1940.

houn house and chinoiserie murals in the dining room of the May Patterson Goodrum house.[38]

Cox had to cater to the tastes of his clients, but he was hired for his skill in a number of genres. He was interested in the human form, rendered colorfully or monochromatically, generally nude or partially clothed. Inspired by his father, Cox often painted idealized classical figures, such as in the entry hall of the Calhoun house, where he created an allegory of hospitality showing Jupiter and Mercury visiting Philemon and Baucis. He specialized in faux finishes and trompe l'oeil, such as in the stairway of the Anne Harriman Vanderbilt house, where Cox painted a false niche holding a porcelain statue. He was also interested in painting historical subjects, which later became his life's work at the United States Capitol. Cox employed a wide range of his trademark themes and techniques for Clark Hall, including allegories, grisailles, trompe l'oeil, faux finishes, classical and historical subjects, and human figures.

Allyn Cox painted this stair hall to match Anne Harriman Vanderbilt's pair of chinoiserie pagodas. The statuary niche is trompe l'oeil.

William Andrews Clark Jr. provided the money for the murals as well as ideas for their subject matter. He first imagined a "history of the law" that would illustrate the development of law through various eras, "beginning from the time of Moses, then going on through the Greek, the Roman, the Dark Ages, the Renaissance, Napoleon's [sic] Civil Code, and thereafter to the time of our Revolution, with which our founder, Thomas Jefferson, was so eminent." Ending with history specific to Virginia and the University, his vision of the murals positioned Law School faculty and students as the heirs and torchbearers of legal tradition. Clark did not insist on this idea (and he soon abandoned it), but he wanted the murals integrated into the building design rather than merely applied to the surfaces of the finished structure. As Cox told President Alderman, "Mr.

Clark's idea is, I think, that we can get more interesting results by collaborating on a decorative scheme from [the] beginning rather than by the more usual proceedings." Cox also expressed to the president how thrilled he was to receive the commission, writing that he would put his "greatest effort" into painting "something that is worthy of one of the great monuments of American architecture"—the University of Virginia.[39]

After seeing the classically inspired designs for Clark Hall, Clark and Cox abandoned the historical theme in favor of depictions of an ancient, mythical past. Clark had previously commissioned Cox to create murals of the Rotunda and Monticello for the Virginia Room in the American Legion building in Paris (see color gallery), but both artist and benefactor decided against a similar program at Clark Hall. Cox explained to President Alderman, "For a building as classical as this I feel that an allegorical treatment is more appropriate than one literally historical." Further, Cox believed that the historical subject "never seems to be so architectural as 'the figure.'" Clark shared Cox's appreciation for classical subjects. The vestibule in Clark's Los Angeles library featured a profusion of classical, largely nude figures, and his library drawing room paintings were scenes from Shakespeare's *Antony and Cleopatra* and Dryden's derivative *All for Love*. Most alumni likely continued to expect historical scenes; the president of the University of Virginia Alumni Association of New York, Williamson Fuller, wrote to Alderman that he favored "great historical scenes in the public life of Virginia" for the murals, which the president reported to Cox. Steadfast in his conviction, Cox reiterated to Alderman "that the Anglo-Saxon types and costumes would be difficult to make go with a classical building." Cox also reminded the president that Clark was in agreement with him.[40]

The Architectural Commission, which had settled on a design for Clark Hall in October 1930, planned Mural Hall with a north-south orientation, reserving its long east and west walls for the murals. By December, the interior details of Mural Hall were firmly enough established that Cox was aware that "we have two walls, facing each other, each divided into three panels, but which are closely related between themselves." The divisions consisted of pilasters, which separated the available wall surface on either side into three distinct areas. Despite the pilasters, Cox decided to devote each wall to one subject. In order to justify classical figures, Cox sought out the ancient origins of law: "I take it that there might be said to be two origins of Law. That which comes by Revelation (intuition), the individual[']s relation to Unity, the ten commandments, etc — 2nd, the 'Contract Social,' the relation of the individual to Society, Roman Law, etc." Cox imagined Mural Hall as a visual exposition on the sacred and profane origins of law, with Moses on one side and ancient Romans on the other. Both subjects created possibilities for flowing garments and dramatic compositions.[41]

During a visit to the University in February 1931, Cox presented his sacred-profane concept to President Alderman, his assistant John Newcomb, Dean Lile, and Edmund Campbell, a member of the Architectural Commission. The group approved the general concept with some revisions. Lile and the others "were much impressed by his sketches, and by his enthusiasm for the work." The Romans, however, gave way to the Greeks, as the group preferred using a scene from the eighteenth book of Homer's *Iliad*. Lile wrote, "We tentatively agreed upon two scenes as the motifs of the paintings: one taken from the Iliad, representing a civil trial in Athens, and the other incidents in the life of Moses. I think these murals will be very handsome, & quite appropriate on the walls of the new home of the Law School." Lile estimated the cost at between $30,000 and $50,000, a staggering sum at the time, though of course Clark was paying.[42]

Cox created the murals in four phases: an allegorical memorial painting dedicated to Mabel Foster Clark on the north wall, over the entrance to the library; the three-panel Homeric mural on the west wall; the three-panel Mosaic mural on the east wall; and four allegorical grisailles, representing eight divisions of law, over the doorways on the east and west walls. For each of the murals, Cox began with rough sketches, then developed more detailed cartoons before painting. State law required that the State Art Commission, a state regulatory board, approve Cox's work before the University could accept it, so between 1932 and 1934 Cox sent sketches and cartoons (or photographs of either) to the commission, a bit of bureaucracy that caused tensions and led to some adjustments in the work.[43] During a series of misunderstandings and hurt feelings in early 1932, R. E. Lee Taylor of the University's Architectural Commission wrote to Campbell, who served on both commissions, that Cox was "terribly upset" by the state board's slowness in approving his sketches. Gari Melchers, a nationally prominent muralist and portraitist and a member of the State Art Commission, complained to Campbell of "the same old story: your Art Commission is as usual expected to O.K. anything any donor may offer, and by any author he, the donor, may select." In 1933, Campbell had the unfortunate task of informing Cox of the state board's disapproval of the planned composition of the Mosaic mural, telling Cox, "I also

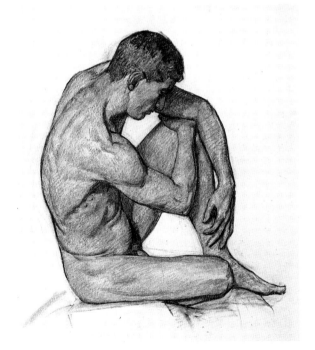

Nude study by Allyn Cox for the Homeric mural, c. 1931.

regret to say that the Art Commission as a whole were not favorably impressed." Cox defended his work to Newcomb, who had succeeded Alderman as president in 1931, assuring him that the donor was happy: "This sketch was seen by Mr. Clark in New York, just before I sent it to Virginia, and he made no criticisms." As the battle between Cox and the State Art Commission escalated, Cox wrote to Newcomb again, saying, "I am putting my whole self into these decorations, and I hate to see a chance missed of doing something really fine and a credit to the University." Campbell finally provided Cox with a detailed critique, explaining that in the board's opinion, "the pictorial ideal seems to lack any original conception. In very simple language, if the Mosaic Law represents 'Love

This surviving cartoon for the Homeric mural illustrates the type of work Cox submitted to the State Art Commission for approval.

God, love your neighbor,' this interpretation seems lost, we have instead Moses actually pointing to the tablet; it seems like a very common-place way to present the idea." Campbell also questioned "what the principal figures are doing in relation to the subject," as many of the characters in the sketches seemed unconcerned about or unaware of Moses's presence in the middle of the scene. Although Cox revised his sketches, he prevailed in his vision for the Mosaic mural as the concept remained largely unchanged.[44]

The first finished portion of the Mural Hall art program, the memorial painting, consisted of a trompe l'oeil bronze plaque bearing the dedication to Mabel Clark, supported on either side by monochromatic female figures. On the left, Eunomia, the goddess of good order, held a torch of enlightenment; on the right her sister, Dike, goddess of fair judgment, rested her hand on a sheathed sword, prepared to defend justice. Painted on canvas at Cox's New York studio, the painting was personally hung by Cox in September 1932, in time for the dedication of the building that October. Until 1934 this was the only mural in Mural Hall.[45] The more colorful Homeric and Mosaic murals, painted from 1932 to 1934, featured brightly painted, larger-than-life figures set against detailed backgrounds (see color gallery). Cox first worked on the Homeric mural, telling President Newcomb that "the three large panels for one side wall are progressing well, and I hope to have them done, and put in place, before so very long."[46] He ultimately installed both sets of murals at the same time, in 1934.

In an era when the classics still figured prominently in education, most law faculty and students likely had some familiarity with the inspiration for the Homeric mural, the *Iliad*. In the eighteenth book, Homer describes a remarkable shield used by Achilles in his battle with Hector. Crafted by the god Hephaestus, the shield depicts an unfolding legal trial in the heart of a beautiful city. As described in a then-current translation by A. T. Murray:

> But the folk were gathered in the place of assembly; for there a strife had arisen, and two men were striving about the blood-price of a man slain; the one avowed that he had paid all, declaring his cause to the people, but the other refused to accept aught; and each was fain to win the issue on the word of a daysman. Moreover, the folk were cheering both, shewing favour to this side and to that. And heralds held back the folk, and the elders were sitting upon polished stones in the sacred circle, holding in their hands the staves of the loud-voiced heralds. Therewith then would they spring up and give judgment, each in turn. And in the midst lay two talents of gold, to be given to him whoso among them should utter the most righteous judgment.[47]

Although the legal question raised by the scene is somewhat ambiguous, in essence the scene demonstrates the importance of law as a means of settling disputes.

In the Homeric mural, Cox depicted men as actors. At the center stood a youth, likely the party claiming to have paid the blood-price in full. He argued before

West wall of Mural Hall showing the Homeric mural and over-door grisailles.

a group of men who talked amongst themselves, debating the merits of his case. Many of them sat on marble blocks, the "polished stones in a sacred circle." On the far right side of the mural, a herald held back an emotional man and woman, probably the family of the murdered man. This was the only woman in the scene who appeared invested in the trial; the other women—a single figure in the background of the central panel, holding a pail, and a group of three figures in the left panel, one carrying sticks, another bearing a basket of eggs—were, unlike the men,

THE LAW SCHOOL AT THE UNIVERSITY OF VIRGINIA

involved in work. Although the three women may have been discussing the trial, their position outside the circle, their visual focus on each other, their symbols of labor, and their proximity to the only child in the scene emphasized their exclusion from the proceedings. While the composition may have reflected Cox's desire to correctly portray the low status of women in ancient Greece, the predominance of men in the mural signified Clark Hall as a male space despite the presence of female law students.

The abundant male nudity in the Homeric mural further conveyed a locker-room-like, same-sex intimacy to Mural Hall that matched the private men's club atmosphere of Clark Hall. Although most well-educated Americans at the time would likely not have been shocked by nudity in public art, Cox's decision to paint a number of figures with exposed genitals in an academic building was unexpected. Cox had studied under his father, whose use of the nude form in his own artwork heavily influenced the son. Kenyon Cox, however, struggled with the censure of those less receptive to nudity in art. Wishing to help his son avoid the same struggles, he wrote to Allyn at the American Academy in Rome in 1918 with the suggestion that he cover up the male genitals in his work: "As art you are right, but you are likely to get into trouble with the prudish, and I know by experience how difficult it is to get it out of people's heads that you are indecent if you once get it in." Although little of Allyn Cox's work for private clients in the 1920s included human figures, Clark allowed Cox to freely indulge in nude forms in his private library. When Cox began sketching out the Clark Hall murals, he believed that the inhabitants of Mr. Jefferson's University would also be receptive to bare bodies.[48]

In the more chaste Mosaic mural, Moses stood on the side of a mountain, pointing to the Ten Commandments. Below him various men, women, and children, many colorfully clothed, struck dramatic postures. Cox intended for this scene to illustrate the bestowing of sacred law rather than simply retelling the biblical story in which Moses angrily breaks the sacred tablets in response to his people's apostasy. In Cox's treatment there was no telltale golden calf, and some figures,

East wall of Mural Hall showing the Mosaic mural and over-door grisailles.

rather than trembling in fear, appeared curiously detached from what Moses was doing. Cox described the subject of the mural as "Moses exhibiting the tablets of the law—the law of the relation of the individual to the race; defining the limits beyond which personal freedom of action can not go without hurting others. I am emphasizing the spiritual side of the subject in contrast to the Homeric panels, which deal with the aspect of the law as a settler of disputes between two parties."[49]

Although the murals were retardataire in subject matter and execution, Cox nevertheless received an invitation from the Architectural League of New York

THE LAW SCHOOL AT THE UNIVERSITY OF VIRGINIA

to hang one set of panels in its 1934 exhibition. The Architectural League, a group founded in 1881 to promote artistic collaboration, included decorative painting in its annual shows. The 1934 exhibition catalog, mindful of the hard times in the country, called the exhibition "a flag of courage and hope in these days of adversity. It is a combination of traditions; some of the old and a little of new." At the exhibition, Cox's Mosaic mural hung alongside the equally large murals of artist George Biddle, which laid bare the hard labor of agricultural workers. Another set of murals by John Holmer, created for the new Ohio State Office Building in Columbus, placed workers at the center of industrial and agricultural progress. Although the works of Biddle and Holmer were not radical, they were of their time in a way the Cox murals were not. Regardless, the league thought enough of Cox to reserve him an entire wall at the American Fine Arts Building, "the only gallery in New York large enough to hold the panels." While Cox had planned to hang the Homeric and Mosaic murals in Clark Hall in May, he wrote Newcomb asking for a delay due to this "very flattering unsolicited offer" to show his work, which Newcomb granted. The University and Law School were no doubt pleased that artwork commissioned for their new building warranted inclusion in a New York show. The Mosaic mural succeeded in attracting attention. The *New York Times* published large photographs of the panels in its Sunday edition. Clark wrote to President Newcomb to thank him for allowing Cox to exhibit the panels, informing him that "they have been much praised by the critics in New York." One prominent admirer of the mural was art critic Royal Cortissoz, a well-known traditionalist and writer for the *New York Herald Tribune.* After seeing the panels at Cox's studio, Cortissoz called the work "a true monumental decoration, so beautifully painted that it does my heart good to think of it." Cortissoz was ill and on leave from the newspaper, but he directed his assistant, Carlyle Burrows, to devote space to the mural in the *Herald Tribune.*[50]

The Mosaic mural finally arrived in Charlottesville in June, where it joined the Homeric mural, which previously had been rolled, boxed, and shipped to Clark Hall. Here all six panels were stored, unopened, until Cox arrived that summer to install them and paint the four over-door grisailles that remained as the last unexecuted portion of the Mural Hall design.[51]

The over-door grisailles, located in the corners of the room over the doors on the east and west sides of the hall, were perhaps the most technically sophisticated of the Mural Hall decorative group. Here, Cox depicted the study and practice of law through the veil of classical allegory. Cox wrote to Newcomb that he designed the panels "as an enrichment to the architecture, and frame for the big paintings," but he nevertheless "tried to make them interesting in themselves at the same time."[52] Whereas Cox painted the other murals at his studio in New York, he painted these directly on the walls, perfectly matching the surrounding stone. Again showcasing his skill in trompe l'oeil, Cox executed the murals as sculptural relief panels, all in a gray monochrome. He divided each grisaille into two, creating eight scenes, all painted as sculpted allegories of the divisions of law. On the west wall at the left was a depiction of crime and punishment: two thieves robbed a traveler, while above, Justice, depicted as a goddess seated on a throne, wielded her sword. On the west wall at the top right was civil law, represented as a Roman official, with contract law below, where a central figure literally "cut a contract" between two parties. On the east wall at left on the top was canon law, or laws governing the Church, with a Catholic bishop wearing a mitre. At the bottom was admiralty law, showing classical figures working at a busy dock. Finally, on the east wall at the right was civil law. The upper portion with two female figures represented equity staying the hand of common law; the lower portion demonstrated a tort or civil wrong, as shown by a chariot driver who had caused an accident that brought about bodily harm and property damage. The grisailles contributed to Mural Hall's sanctuary-like quality, a respite from rather than a conduit to the world and its problems.

Unfortunately there is little record of what must have been an abundance of conversation about the murals when Cox finished installing the colorful panels and painting the remaining grisailles. It is clear that the murals did not enjoy universal admiration. The *Washington Post* reported that "the murals have aroused a great deal of discussion from both a legal and an artistic point of view. Some critics of art have called the panoramas plethoric, the figures blatant in coloring and pose and have cited distracting elements in the scenes depicted." Some disliked the allegorical rather than historical subject matter, finding the connection between the murals and the subject of law unclear. As the *Post* noted, "Being the most conspicuous thing in the building, [the murals] are naturally supposed to be vitally significant in the development of law. Some authorities contend that in this they fail." Some viewers "had expected possibly an impressive representation of Roger Brooks Taney in trial on the Dred Scott case or John Marshall handing down a celebrated decision," and these persons "were surprised—some pleasantly and some not so pleasantly." The *Post* did not report any opinions on the nudity in the Homeric mural, only mentioning that "according to Mr. Cox's conception of Homeric customs, the figures are conspicuously undressed."[53]

Yet the Homeric nudes did raise a few eyebrows. When Cox wrote to President Newcomb about varnishing the murals, which would prevent any modifications, he asked: "Has it been decided that man is the noblest work of God, or is a little more drapery wanted?" Considering that members of the law faculty, President Newcomb, and the State Art Commission all signed off on the design, perhaps pride prevented the addition of fig leaves. The University had begun to get used to the life-size nudes now adorning the walls of one of its grandest buildings. "We hear less complaint about the nudes as time goes on," Newcomb responded to Cox. The artist varnished the murals in November 1935, sealing the story of the Law School's foray into decorative art.[54]

With the completion of the murals, the monument was finished. While the Law School enjoyed a few years of quiet growth in its stylish new setting before the disruption of World War II, the University turned to other projects. Clark Hall ushered in a new era of development. With Clark Hall, the University began investing again in more substantial buildings, and these new buildings did more than simply blend in with the edges of the Academical Village. As Richard Guy Wilson, David J. Neuman, and Sara A. Butler have observed, Clark Hall was part of a new collection of "foreground" buildings at the University. Whereas Monroe Hall,

Clark Memorial Hall grisailles by Allyn Cox. *Left to right:* west wall, left, "Punishment" and "Crime"; west wall, right, "Civil Law" and "Contract Law"; east wall, left, "Canon Law" and "Admiralty Law"; east wall, right, "Equity staying the hand of Common Law" and "Torts."

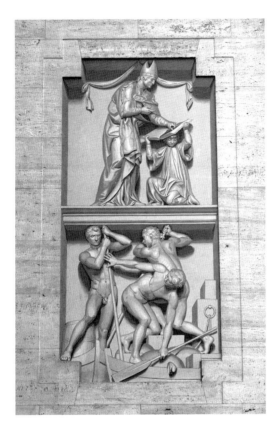

designed by the Architectural Commission and completed in 1930, was a fairly simple, modestly scaled classroom building that called little attention to itself, Clark Hall and two of its Depression-era successors, the Bayly Museum (1935) and Alderman Library (1938), boasted a size and richness of detail that made them major landmarks of the University. After World War II, the University would fall back into "background" (though large) buildings with New Cabell Hall (1952) and Newcomb Hall (1958) before Gilmer Hall, constructed 1961–63 just down

McCormick Road from Clark Hall, commenced a new period of landmark construction. Like the law building, these new structures raised a variety of questions about how to build forward-looking structures that were recognizably part of the University of Virginia.[55]

Critically for the Law School, Clark Hall provided the facilities the school needed to establish itself as a truly national law school of the twentieth century. As legal education became more standardized and more competitive, Clark Hall allowed the Law School to keep ahead of a new contingent of quickly expanding rivals. In its description of Clark Hall in 1934, the *Washington Post* affirmed that Clark's money had not been spent in vain: "One of the foremost law schools of the country is contained in Clark Memorial Hall. With its attractive setting, its first-rate lecture and class rooms, its complete library facilities and its model moot court room, it is a worthy home for the venerable institution."[56] Brick and columned, but also streamlined and up-to-date, Clark Hall allowed the Law School to commemorate its history without succumbing to mothballs. It was a "venerable institution" newly invigorated, at least for the foreseeable future.

Like most monuments, Clark Hall survived to see its builders pass away. Initiated through the friendship of William Andrews Clark Jr. and William Minor Lile, it rose from its site on McCormick Road as the final years and days of these two men waned. Clark died of a heart attack on June 14, 1934, at his summer retreat at Salmon Lake in Montana. The *Los Angeles Times* reported that "news of his death, received here late in the afternoon, came as a shock to literally thousands of men and women who either enjoyed his personal friendship or felt grateful to him for the cultural and educational opportunities which had been opened to them by his princely munificence." The Los Angeles Philharmonic Orchestra performed three selections at Clark's funeral in tribute to its principal benefactor. He was laid to rest in a mausoleum in Hollywood Cemetery with his two wives and son. Lile soon followed, dying on December 13, 1935. He was interred at the University of Virginia Cemetery. In a tribute, Dean Armistead Dobie wrote: "On him, fortunately for the University of Virginia Law School, fell the task of developing and modernizing this law school at the close of the career of his kinsman, the great John B. Minor. With missionary ardor he brought to this task his extraordinary gifts of personality and scholarship. . . . Probably his was the greatest influence that prompted the late William A. Clark Jr. (his friend and former pupil) to give to this University, Clark Hall, the magnificent new home of the law school."[57]

3

The Move to
North Grounds

Like Minor Hall before it, Clark Hall had a freshness that quickly dulled into obsolescence. By the mid-1960s, when Clark Hall turned thirty years old, its occupants complained of noise, filth, and congestion, despite the addition of two library wings and a third floor. Aged by time and cigarette smoke, the dinginess of the Allyn Cox murals reinforced the general shabbiness of the building itself. The faded Greeks and Hebrews presided over a space that was now more like a train station than a temple: the student body had more than doubled, and their voices filled Mural Hall with an enormous roar as they hustled through it. These additional bodies put a great deal of pressure on the fabric of the building, overwhelming classrooms, library, and lounge alike. Clark Hall was not just old and overcrowded; it was also out of fashion. On the University Grounds, new buildings eclipsed Clark Hall's outmoded Roman magnificence. Gilmer Hall, a flat-roofed, concrete-framed science building, and University Hall, an indoor stadium with a clamshell dome, announced the infusion of modern design into Jefferson's campus. Across the country, other law schools were abandoning Gothic and Colonial

Revival structures for the luster of newness. Despite growing dissatisfaction with Clark Hall, few would have suspected that the Law School would soon inhabit its own modern building a mile and a half away. Soon it would abandon its columns, murals, and proximity to the Rotunda for clean lines and elbow room. This latest law building would be part of a new satellite campus called North Grounds, its site cut from a tract of fields and forests nestled behind a suburban shopping center. Here would be a new and very different Academical Village.

Whereas Clark Hall had been a classical temple of law, its lavishness underwritten by an eccentric alumnus, the latest law building emphasized functionality and accessibility. Long, large, and bereft of ornamentation, the structure was distinguished by its heavy cantilevered third floor and two bulbous south-facing projections that gave it a sphinxlike presence on Massie Road. Its utilitarianism was in part the result of economy: a dependence on limited state funding allowed for none of the frills of its predecessor. There would be no murals and no marble halls. But its generally ahistorical design was also deliberate. Concerned by the ascendance of expanding law schools throughout the country, the Law School used modern architecture to affirm its relevance and academic prestige. In order to attract and house its growing faculty and student body, the new law building's design favored square footage over finishes and prioritized convenience and access. The North Grounds complex, which also included the Graduate School of Business Administration and the Judge Advocate General's School, was easily reachable by car, but more critically its massive scale allowed for greater curricular flexibility and a much larger, presumably more heterogeneous student body. Both its functionality and ahistoricism oriented the Law School away from the Jefferson grounds and toward the nation's other top law schools, many of which were constructing their own modern buildings. As such the design worked to neutralize the Law School's connection to exclusivity or provincialism and affirm its place as a truly national school of law. In sum, the move to North Grounds was both a practical effort to correct the ills of the aging Clark Hall and a philosophical shift that prioritized the future over the past.

Yet while the design of the new law building at first suggests an out-with-the-old approach to campus expansion, in fact this move to the modern was neither a complete throwing off of tradition nor a wholehearted embrace of modern design as art or fashion. In style, the latest law building displayed a conservative modernism, its ribbon windows and exposed courses of concrete subdued by plain brick walls and a nearly symmetrical composition. This was the architecture of compromise and of pragmatism. While prevailing forces pulled the Law School toward a design that trumpeted the new, a smaller but significant counterforce also acted upon North Grounds, lest newness wipe away all tradition. Subtle elements of the North Grounds complex affirmed ties to the University of old. The familiar red brick, the suggestion of columns, and the placement and width of the central grassy mall quietly tied North Grounds to the University's historic and aesthetic orbit. These tempering features, along with a restricted budget, ensured that North Grounds would be no monument to the architectural avant-garde. Rather, the modernism seen here aligned North Grounds with its shopping strip neighbors: practical, con-

The law building, North Grounds, around the time of its completion in 1974. Hugh Stubbins and Associates, architects. The distinctive protrusions on the south elevation of the building housed the ends of the polygonal classrooms inside the building.

ventional, contemporary, and surrounded by parking lots. Here was the Academical Village merged with the automobile campus.

The mid-twentieth century boom time that filled the United States with new homes, stores, factories, and interstate highways likewise transformed American higher education. In the three decades after World War II, rapid population and economic growth prompted an unprecedented expansion of the American university system. Existing colleges and universities doubled, tripled, and quadrupled enrollment, and new institutions of higher learning sprang up across the nation to educate thousands more. Between 1955 and 1970, the number of American college and university students grew from 2.7 million to 7 million.[1] The enrollment of increasing numbers of women and minorities, a thriving American economy, and expanding state and national funding for higher education all contributed to this massive jump in college attendance. Colleges accommodated swelling enrollment with additional degree programs, larger bureaucracies, added acres, and scores of new buildings.

At first it may have seemed that the University of Virginia was largely impervious to the demands of postwar progress. Enrollment, which had risen immediately after World War II as troops returned from overseas, had receded. Between 1950 and 1960, University enrollment only climbed by slightly more than eight hundred students, with three-fourths of this growth occurring in the graduate and professional schools.[2] The most notable change in the student body was that these new faces included the University's first African American students. After an initial rejection, Gregory Swanson successfully sued to become the first black student to be admitted to the University, entering the Law School in 1950. His admission opened the door for others, including John F. Merchant, who became the first African American graduate of the Law School in 1958.[3] Although the racial integration of the University was among the most significant and transformative events in its history, its cultural impact on the University became more apparent with time. Approximately twenty to twenty-five black undergraduates per year attended the University by the mid-1950s. Female undergraduates had yet to be admitted, although pressure for the University to become coeducational was growing. Women already attended at the graduate level. In 1920, seventeen women had entered graduate and professional programs at the University, including Rosemary Davis and Elizabeth Tompkins in the Law School. Nevertheless, in 1960 the University remained a small institution of just over five thousand students, most of them fastidiously dressed young white men in coats and ties, attending classes in red-brick, white-columned buildings clustered in and around the Academical Village. New structures, such as the Georgian Revival, Williamsburg-inspired Physics Building and Newcomb Hall, reinforced a sense of timelessness with their architectural deference to their older neighbors.[4]

The conservative Newcomb Hall, completed 1958, was among the last traditional buildings constructed on Grounds before the modernism of the 1960s. Eggers & Higgins, architects, photograph c. 1963.

Yet beginning in the early 1960s, transformations in the style and scale of its buildings signaled concurrent changes in the size and culture of the University. As the first wave of post–World War II baby boomers approached college age, state and University officials realized that the Charlottesville campus needed to grow quickly. In a 1963 speech, University president Edgar F. Shannon Jr. announced his belief that more students should be enrolled at the University, arguing that "steady growth can be an aspect of great strength to the University, and it fulfills our obligation to qualified applicants."[5] Spurred by the Virginia General Assembly, the University did expand, absorbing the first surge of the baby boom generation. Between 1960 and 1970, the student body doubled from five thousand to ten thousand; by 1975 it would surpass fifteen thousand.[6] Minority enrollment grew, and many new students were women, including the first female undergraduates in 1970. The increase in students and faculty and an expanding curriculum meant the need for many new buildings. Unlike the Physics Building and Newcomb Hall, the new buildings were largely ahistorical, lacking the once requisite fanlights, porticos, and sloping slate roofs of earlier University buildings. First came Gilmer Hall in 1963, then University Hall in 1965, the Alderman Library addition in 1967, and the new Chemistry Building in 1968. These were "modern buildings," both as they were called at the time and as they are loosely classified by architectural historians today.

Modern architecture, which made a somewhat tardy arrival at the University, had its origins in a late-nineteenth-century rejection by some architects of the historical revivalism epitomized in the Beaux-Arts extravagance of the Chicago Columbian Exposition of 1893. These architects saw endless creative possibilities in new materials like structural steel and reinforced concrete, and they dismissed the idea that traditional ornamentation should disguise modern construction. Although the modern buildings that went up at the University of Virginia in the 1960s were hardly radical, they were a departure from the revival styles that had typified the campus. Clark Hall's largely utilitarian interior may have borne subtle testimony to the streamlining influence of modernism, but its neoclassical facade and Beaux-Arts Mural Hall exemplified the preoccupation with historical imitation and ornamentation that modern architects found ill-suited to the needs of the twentieth century.[7]

Modern architecture's emphasis on functionality and economy made it a practical choice for new dormitories and classroom buildings at the fast-growing University, but the modern buildings also spoke to the school's acceptance of a new aesthetic in American public architecture. While modern architecture began as an unconventional approach to building based on theories of architect-intellectuals, its suitability to the needs and technologies of the twentieth century brought it into the mainstream after World War II. During the 1950s, modern became the go-to style for a range of public and commercial buildings, from courthouses and hospitals to high schools and shopping malls. Although most American universities were slow to embrace modernism, by the 1960s it proliferated on campuses as higher education boomed. Challenged by ambitious, expanding state schools across the country, the University could not afford to let its new structures, particularly its science and technology buildings, appear old-fashioned.

Appropriately, the first of the University's large modern structures, Gilmer Hall, was a science building, the new home of the biology and psychology departments. Psychology professor Raymond Bice called the blocky five-story structure "the most modern and complete building of its kind in the country." Its rather basic exterior redirected attention to the interior, with state-of-the-art labs and lecture rooms. Designed by Louis Ballou of Richmond, Gilmer Hall's rectilinear form, lattice masonry screens, and crisply articulated geometry set it apart from other University buildings. With red brick walls laid in Flemish bond and a curving protrusion reminiscent of Jefferson's serpentine garden walls, Gilmer Hall was not completely bereft of University allusions, but its design still raised eyebrows. One undergraduate lamented, "It might be all right at any other type of school but not here at the University." Perhaps even this tepid modernism heralded the University's conversion into a postwar behemoth of higher education.[8]

Observers linked the new buildings to a sea change in the culture of the Univer-

Gilmer Hall, the new life sciences building, heralded the arrival of modernism at the University in 1963. As the University wanted up-to-date buildings but never abandoned its commitment to history and visual conformity, it constructed its modern buildings in red brick. Photograph taken March 1964.

sity, one that favored colossal buildings and anonymous hordes of students over the preservation of an identity grounded in tradition. Students, who were among the most vocal detractors of change at the University, used the term "State U" to describe this monster of mass education. The State U became a way of discussing and frequently disparaging not only modernism as a style but mid-twentieth-century modernity itself. Speaking of Gilmer Hall, a third-year student argued that "the new plan to extend the University into a large 'State U' of 10,000 students will only result in the pattering feet of some 4,000 'freshmen' stamping out the Jeffersonian traditions. The switch to modern architecture, so demanded by this rapid expansion, is one of the first signals of the abandonment of the old ideals."

During the 1960s, the student newspaper, the *Cavalier Daily,* became a staunch opponent of "State-Uism," which it argued threatened to uproot the "Jeffersonian traditions." When pressed to define the term, the paper called State-Uism a "contagious disease" exemplified by "large ugly buildings" and "bevies of coeds in slacks and curlers"—a jab at the prospect of undergraduate coeducation. According to the editors of the *Cavalier Daily,* the rise of the State U had implications beyond the mass production of higher education. It threatened "a 'bigness' which reflects all that is ugly in modern American life and all that smothers the individual caught in a vast, faceless institution." State-Uism signified a broader set of fears: of consumerism; of greater social and sexual freedom; of integration into a global, technology-focused, gender-neutral, heterogeneous society. It was a disconcerting move away from the local and familiar.[9]

The juggernaut of the State U even imperiled the Academical Village. When the University released plans for a large, modern-style addition to Alderman Library within sight of the Rotunda, the *Cavalier Daily* issued an editorial entitled "Eleventh Hour Plea": "No one can say that the University has resisted inroads of functional modern design. . . . Nevertheless, there ought to be a sacrosanctity about the few acres including and just to the west and southwest of Mr. Jefferson's original University, which would preclude ever disrupting its tranquil, charming colonial atmosphere with so ill-fitting a pile of masonry as is the proposed annex." Not everyone agreed with these sentiments. After pointing out that the early buildings were not colonial at all, the fourth-year architecture class endorsed the blending of new and old on the campus. They nevertheless called the Alderman annex an "atrocity."[10]

In constructing modern buildings, even conservative ones, the University had to defend itself against a refrain unique to the institution. Modern buildings were unpopular on many American campuses, but only at UVa did they threaten "Mr. Jefferson's University." The fact that the core of the University was a remarkably intact architectural masterpiece, one designed by a Founding Father, made the ahistoricism of modern buildings especially worrisome. In an effort to diminish the impact of modern architecture on Grounds, University planners avoided constructing new buildings in prominent locations. Some, like Gilmer Hall, they placed far away from the Academical Village; others, like the Alderman Library Annex, they hid partially on the back slopes of hills. Paul Saunier Jr., the assistant to the president for University relations and development, reassured alumni in spring 1962 that "the new buildings needed to serve the expanding enrollment are being located to the north and west of the original Jefferson area, placed where their functional architecture will harmonize with their natural surroundings and will not disturb the classic beauty of the original University grounds." The University was wary of anything too unorthodox. After hiring renowned modernist architect Louis Kahn in the early 1960s to design the new Chemistry Building, the Board of Visitors decided against his boldly geometric plan of a castle-like auditorium with cylindrical towers, encircled by a U-shaped classroom and office structure. For a new design they turned to Anderson, Beckwith & Haible of Boston, who produced a more conventional modern building with brick pylons connected by horizontal concrete expanses and ribbon windows. Printing the architect's rendering in 1965, the *Alumni News* assured readers that "the facade . . . will contain vertical white elements that suggest Mr. Jefferson's architecture for the original academical village. It is thus considered an architectural 'bridge' between the unchanged old University and the new science and engineering complex that is growing up near Scott Stadium." Nevertheless, one graduate responded to the *News* that the building was "more than a disgrace to Mr. Jefferson's architecture. It is gross, massive and in the style of Hitler's offerings to posterity (except maybe a bit worse)." This version of the Chemistry Building was in place by 1968.[11]

Although most of Clark Hall's occupants would never have guessed it, the Law School was about to become the latest University battleground between old and new, small and large, traditional and progressive. In the 1960s, Clark Hall was a relatively young building by University standards, but chronic overcrowding made it prematurely aged. In 1932, Clark Hall opened its doors to 257 law students; by 1960

some 579 students filled its corridors and classrooms.[12] Clark Hall had almost always been cramped. As early as the 1940s, Mural Hall had succumbed to student pressure for more space; study tables, piled with books and papers, covered its travertine floors. When the administration removed the tables, one student complained, "We came here to read the law, not to gaze at naughty murals."[13] The Judge Advocate General's (JAG) School, a military law training facility run by the United States Army, relocated to Clark Hall in 1951 at the invitation of the University. Though welcome, it deprived the Law School of classroom and office space.[14] By the 1960s, as enrollment rose again (it surpassed 700 students by 1965), the situation further deteriorated, particularly in the library. Despite the best efforts of Frances Farmer, Clark Hall's no-nonsense librarian, the law collection was bursting at its seams, quadrupling in size between 1932 and 1953. A new west wing in 1949 and an east wing in

By the 1960s, the library at Clark Hall was overflowing with books, students, and their belongings.

The slovenly condition of Clark Hall in the 1960s and early 1970s attracted pests. In the *Virginia Law Weekly* for March 5, 1971, cartoonist James R. "Jim" Wrenn Jr. depicted law librarian Frances Farmer as the distressed damsel in the clutches of a giant rat atop Clark Hall.

1952, added on either side of the library, proved to be stop-gap measures. In 1960, a law student criticized Farmer for rearranging the library "with amazing indifference to space limitations and lighting facilities . . . resulting in squinting students and congested aisles. . . . As a result of Miss Farmer's artistic touch three tables are no longer available, increasing the discomfort of the already uncomfortable." Student squatters covered chairs and tables with their clothing, books, and loose papers, claiming limited space and exacerbating already unpleasant conditions.[15]

Crowding encouraged slovenliness, and a lack of maintenance robbed Clark Hall of the gloss of its early years. Constant cigarette use, even in areas where it was officially off limits, covered surfaces in soot, leading one student to refer to the building as "fuliginous Clark Hall." The uncleanliness became a particular source of embarrassment in 1959 when the American Bar Association cited the problem in an otherwise positive accreditation report of the Law School. The student lounge, which Dean Armistead Dobie had compared to a "metropolitan club" in 1934, was especially infamous. In 1961, the *Virginia Law Weekly* reported that some cleanup had led to a "modest improvement in the first floor halls," but the lounge, located in the basement, suffered from "continuing squalor." Apparently little changed over the next few years. In 1963, another editorial declared that "the nauseating profusion of spilled beverages, scattered newspapers, paper cups and cigarette butts strewn over tables and floors would be shocking to any visitor to the Law School." In 1965, yet another editorial, "Pigsty," referred to filth littered throughout the building. Once again the lounge emerged as the great shame of Clark Hall, with its "revolting sight of discarded coffee and soda cups; the news-

YOU REELED AT RODAN, YOU GAWKED AT GODZILLA, YOU MOANED AT MOTHRA, YOU GROANED AT GARGANTUA . . . *NOW* YOU WILL VOMIT AT —

VERMIN!

PRODUCED BY: DOYU SEDE LOT IN ASSOCIATION WITH 孔孟子弐

DIRECTED BY: HIRCUM DE LODENT

SEE —
FIERCE FANNIE FIGHTING FURIOUSLY FOR FREEDOM FROM FRIGHTENING FLOCKS OF FURRY FOES FROLICKING, FEEDING AND FORAGING FREQUENTLY ON FRAGILE FILES !

Jim Wrenn

paper pages strewn on the floor, tables and chairs; [and] the spill stains on the furniture." Clark Hall did have janitorial services, but apparently littering students overwhelmed them.[16]

In the early 1960s, the Law School looked to expansion and refurbishment rather than abandonment as the best way to remedy the problems of Clark Hall. A third floor built over the library in 1961 added nine thousand square feet and included three classrooms, a seminar room, five offices, and a faculty lounge and terrace. In 1962, the *Virginia Law Weekly* announced that Frances Farmer had taken the "formerly dark, drab and generally unattractive" women's lounge and "transformed [it] into a cheerful feminine oasis." Three years later, the male-dominated student lounge finally received some much-needed attention, with new furniture "upholstered in fall colors . . . accentuated by occasional pieces covered in scarlet and others in solid black," walnut veneer cocktail tables, matching walnut-grained wastebaskets, an inlaid chess table, and a fire-engine red telephone. The Law School also renovated the moot court room, adding a new counsel table and a judge's bench with witness and clerk boxes, and installed a lunchroom in the basement, where students dined on sandwiches, soup, pastries, and milkshakes.[17]

These largely cosmetic changes were not enough to satisfy Hardy Cross Dillard, the new dean, who feared that the Law School was in danger of losing its reputation as a top law school. Following World War II, legal education had become increasingly competitive. In the twenty-five years after the war, the American Bar Association (ABA) and the Association of American Law Schools (AALS) successfully campaigned for higher standards for both accreditation and the issuing of law licenses. It was in this era that law truly became a graduate-level, professional degree. In 1961 the Law School began requiring an undergraduate degree for admission, following ABA-AALS recommendations. Likewise the ABA and AALS lobbied state legislatures to make law degrees mandatory for persons taking the bar exam. As ABA-AALS standards drove hundreds of unaccredited law schools out of business, they also subjected surviving schools to higher thresholds of accreditation, setting minimums for the number of full-time law faculty and the number of books in law school libraries. These actions concentrated law students in fewer, better schools, and many public schools successfully appealed to state legislatures for larger allocations, allowing these institutions to further improve their law programs. As the line between top and middling law schools became blurred, the legal community scrutinized faculty pay, faculty-student ratios, physical resources, and other factors to reassess the relative quality of law schools across the country. It was under these conditions that Dillard accepted the deanship in 1963. Writing to President Shannon about low faculty salaries, Dillard argued, "Unless and until this situation is corrected our constantly reiterated claim to be in competition with the best law schools in the country is only a self perpetuating myth with only partial validity." According to Dillard, the Law School was not only slipping behind Harvard, Yale, Columbia, and Stanford but also up-and-coming state schools such as Missouri and Florida.[18]

Overcrowding in Clark Hall was especially concerning given state pressure on the University to accept more in-state students as the number of applicants grew in proportion with state population. Anxiety over the lack of space for qualified in-state students became great enough that in 1964, three members of the Virginia General Assembly introduced legislation that would have capped the number of out-of-state students at state-aided colleges and universities at 25 percent. The Board of Visitors publicly restated its policy that the University could not remain a "national" institution without a significant out-of-state population. Likewise President Shannon issued a "blistering" eight-hundred-word response arguing that such restrictions threatened the University's ability to compete with "other institutions of national eminence." Expanding enrollment, therefore, was a strategy that allowed the University to admit more in-state students without substantially altering the in-state/out-of-state ratio. The Law School recognized the need for a similar approach. In a report on the size of the Law School, a committee of law faculty concluded that "there seems to be no room for doubt that—strictly on a Virginia population basis—there will be markedly increased pressure for admission of Virginia students qualified under present standards. It will come abruptly, beginning not later than the fall of 1968." Like the Board of Visitors, the committee feared that enrolling a higher percentage of state students would diminish national prestige, advising that "there must be some balance if this is not to become a provincial law school." Thus the Law School, like the University, chose a path of expansion, nearly doubling its enrollment between 1960 and 1975.[19]

As Dean Dillard charted a course of progress, his eyes fell on Mural Hall with new appreciation, not for its works of art but for its square footage. He was not above dismantling the Law School's most sacred space. Both Dillard and Lindsey Cowen, the associate dean of the Law School, were impatient with the JAG School's presence in Clark Hall, and a proposed JAG building would not be ready for at least two years. Looking for speedier alternatives, Dillard proposed to Cowen that the Law School "might move immediately to reconstruct the mural hall space so as to make it useful while at the same time getting rid of those God awful murals." Dillard asked Cowen about making "some discreet inquiries" regarding pulling the murals down, adding that, "in order to avoid raising a lot of rumors, it would have to be done quietly." Cowen did not object to removing the murals, but he argued against Dillard's plan to bisect the hall into two floors. Cowen had spoken to Frederick D. Nichols, the University's celebrated architectural historian, and Nichols thought such an action "would be a tragic mistake." Mural Hall and its namesake artwork survived. Yet Dillard's willingness to dispose of the murals, even if it took clandestine action to do so, exemplified the ongoing battle over the place of history and sentiment at the University. While many alumni, faculty, and students treasured Mural Hall, Dillard and others saw its preservation as an impediment to more urgent goals. As Dillard summarized in an alumni newsletter, "If we wish to remain vital, the pull of the past and resistance to change must somehow be countered by an awareness of the needs of the present and the demands of the future."[20]

Relief was perhaps in sight. Plans were in motion once again to expand Clark Hall. In 1963, President Shannon responded favorably to Dean Dillard's request that the University construct a new building for the Law School to the rear of

Clark Hall, in the space between the law building and the JAG dormitory (now Kerchof Hall). Substantial additions to Clark Hall subsequently appeared in the new University master plan, produced by Sasaki, Dawson, DeMay Associates of Watertown, Massachusetts, and approved by the Board of Visitors in 1965. The plan called for the construction of three structures to the rear of Clark Hall, connected with Clark to form an interior court. A 28,000-square-foot, four-story west wing, built exclusively for the Law School, would include four new classrooms, ten faculty offices, two student activity rooms, and more library space. South and east wings, totaling 35,000 square feet, would house the JAG School, returning square footage in Clark Hall to the Law School.[21]

The Board of Visitors commissioned the 1965 University of Virginia master plan in an effort to unify the old and new in an era of unprecedented expansion. Specifically, it sought to reconcile the Academical Village and the State U. In January 1963, the Master Plan Committee, a body of six that included President Shannon, voted unanimously to hire the Sasaki firm after meeting with founder Hideo Sasaki and executive director Richard Dober. Sasaki, born in California in 1919 and a graduate of Harvard Design School, was a pioneer in multidisciplinary planning, building a firm in the 1950s and 1960s that brought together architects, civil engineers, civic planners, and landscape architects. In the 1994 book *Invisible Gardens,* Peter Walker, a former student and business partner of Sasaki, and coauthor Melanie Simo credited Sasaki with helping "develop . . . a flexible, pragmatic approach to design that could accommodate both modern and traditional buildings, an approach particularly useful for campus expansion and urban design." According to Walker and Simo, designers at the Sasaki office "were generally aware of the ideological schism between modernism and history, yet they believed that the great historical periods and national traditions of landscape architecture could be integrated with modernism." This ability to reconcile the traditional and the modern made Sasaki especially attractive to the University of Virginia, as did Sasaki's impressive list of academic clients, including Harvard, Brown, and the University of Rhode Island.[22]

Sasaki's multidisciplinary approach responded to the new city-like "multiuniversity," which had a spatial complexity that corresponded to the increasing diversity of campus populations, degrees, and services. The tightly ordered compositions of Beaux-Arts master plans, such as Warren Henry Manning's designs of 1908 and 1913 for UVa, could not accommodate the rapid shape-shifting of both individual buildings and overall campuses in the 1960s. Sasaki associate Richard Dober, who published the landmark *Campus Planning* in 1963, called the state of higher education at the time "desperate and unprecedented," arguing that there was now an unparalleled need for comprehensive campus planning. Dober proposed that universities use "planning modules," such as instructional facilities, research, housing, and utilities, to group similar activities together. The Sasaki firm adhered to this approach with its "clusters" of uses. In an article for *Progressive Architecture* in 1960, Dober pointed to the firm's work at the University of Rhode Island, which had hired Sasaki to correct problems created by rapid growth. Dober credited the firm with effectively reorganizing the university's land-use: "By 1975 the University of Rhode Island campus will no longer be a mosaic of mixed uses. . . . In order of intensity of use, academic, housing, and field spaces will be arranged in bands away from the core." Rather than ignoring the historic stone buildings at the center of campus, the firm worked to integrate them into a coherent, expandable whole.[23]

In their 1965 master plan for the University of Virginia, the Sasaki team likewise sought to keep the Academical Village vital by making it the core of a malleable, pedestrian-friendly set of use-oriented clusters. The plan called for six "teaching centers" bundled around the Academical Village. These included a center of the humanities and social sciences, located in and around Cabell Hall; a science center along McCormick Road, west of Emmet Street, anchored by the new Gilmer Hall; a fine arts center on the north slope of Carr's Hill; a university center, including Alderman Library and Monroe Hall, which housed the Graduate School of Business Administration; a medical center, expanding out from the existing hospital; and a law center. All were located in a ten-minute walking radius. The law center, nearly in the middle of the walking radius, remained firmly tied to Clark Hall. The

Board of Visitors and Governor Albertis Harrison approved the plan in 1966. Paul Saunier, assistant to the president, announced that it would balance the University's "remarkable heritage" with "tremendous pressure for expansion." The plan sought to preserve the architectural legacy of the University through its attention to scale. Sasaki wanted to keep the campus walkable and maintain views of the Rotunda and the mountains, creating a larger, denser, but still recognizably bucolic academic setting.[24]

While the 1965 master plan recommended keeping the Law School at the center of Grounds, the plan was a philosophical road map, not established University policy. Backdoor conversations about relocating the Law School began even before the Sasaki group finished the master plan. In early 1965, Dean Dillard asked law professor Daniel Meador for his thoughts about a new location. Meador expressed reluctance to leave. Believing that the Law School's physical location played a critical role in its cultural and academic relationship to the University, he felt "rather inclined against a building on another site":

> Any other site is almost certain to be remote from the center of the University (Mad Bowl or somewhere around the gym might save us, but these seem unlikely). There is value, both symbolically and actually, in being in our present location. . . . It seems to me altogether appropriate that law as one of the original schools of the University be hard by the Lawn and the core of the institution. Even now, we tend to be thought of by our colleagues in other schools as aloof and apart. I would like to see that attitude on their part softened. But a move way out will only accentuate it and will in fact divorce us still more. I am not rigidly fixed in this view, but in my mind the burden rests on those who would make a case for another site.

As an alternative, Meador suggested that the Law School expand the main library reading room into Mural Hall and one or more classrooms. He believed that the proposed additions could provide enough classroom space for the foreseeable future. Meador's proposal likely received little serious consideration from Dillard because it would not have solved the problem of noise and traffic in the library. Dillard was also coming to the conclusion that remodeling and expanding Clark Hall would carry the Law School through the next few years at most.[25]

Dean Dillard's role in the Law School's move is unclear. In 1995, Meador recalled that "neither Dillard nor the law faculty apparently played any part in that decision [to relocate]."[26] Meador's recollection supports the idea that the University "evicted" the Law School from Central Grounds, a belief that has become part of the school's institutional memory.[27] Dillard's preference for ambitious expansion over cautious, sentimental moderation is apparent in his 1964 inspection report for the University of Florida College of Law, conducted on behalf of the Association of American Law Schools and coauthored with Ralph S. Brown Jr. of Yale. Like UVa's, Florida's law school was working to accommodate sharply inclining enrollment and a growing faculty in an aging building. The College of Law had occupied Bryan Hall, a conventional brick Collegiate Gothic building, since 1914. Dillard and Brown could have written their Florida recommendations to the UVa Law School: "Though we realize that many of you would leave your present conveniently located and generally comfortable building with reluctance, it seems fairly clear that it would be difficult to double its capacity and, especially, to provide an adequate library." Due to space limitations, the new building "would have to be on the perimeter of the campus," but Dillard and Brown reasoned that "a new building and dormitory somewhat removed from the center of things might help [law students] to put away childish things and concentrate on professional training." Thus Dillard did not see a move away from "the center of things" as a regrettable casualty of growth. Separation was part of maturation, both for law students and for the school itself.[28]

Regardless of Dillard's role in the move from Clark Hall, the idea did not gain official sanction until the end of 1966. At that time the University comptroller, Vincent Shea, presented a report to the Buildings and Grounds Committee of the Board of Visitors advising that plans to expand Clark Hall and Monroe Hall, the home of the Graduate School of Business Administration, were insufficient to meet the future enrollment of either school. The committee approved "the general idea of relocating the School of Law and the Graduate School of Business at Copeley Hill with the understanding that further study of the exact locations will be made and the results presented to this Committee at a future meeting."[29] Located north of the new University Hall stadium, Copeley Hill was the site of some of the University's recent land purchases. The proposed relocation gained momentum when the University decided to pursue matching federal funds for graduate school buildings made available through the Higher Education Facilities Act (HEFA) of 1963.[30] President Lyndon B. Johnson signed the act into law just one month after becoming president, making it among the first of his domestic initiatives that came to be known as the Great Society. The funds made available by the federal government through HEFA and the subsequent Higher Education Act of 1965 were a major stimulus for the massive expansion of community colleges and state universities at that time. Relocating the Law School and the Graduate Business School together made sense for a number of reasons, particularly within the context of Sasaki's 1965 master plan. While the plan itself kept both schools in place on McCormick Road, its clustered uses laid the groundwork for a sweeping revision. Pairing the two schools together on a site further away simply required a shuffling of clusters. The Law and Business Schools were the University's only graduate-level "professional schools" apart from the Medical School, so removing them from the ten-minute Central Grounds walking radius proposed by Sasaki would not affect undergraduates. For that reason, the University could relocate the law-business cluster without undermining the sense of intimacy on Grounds that the administration believed essential to the undergraduate experience. There were benefits to such a move for the University and both schools. The University could reclaim prime real estate near the center of Central Grounds, and the Law School and Business School could enjoy unprecedented space for expansion. Further, by moving the schools to a new "professional center," the University hoped to stimulate connections between them. The University had established the Business School in 1954 at the urging of alumni who wanted UVa to play a greater role in producing American business leaders. By fostering closer ties between the two schools, the University expected young law and business students to form social ties that would result in lifelong professional relationships. Meeting to discuss the move, Dean Dillard and Charles C. Abbott, dean of the Business School, concluded that pairing law and business together would promote a "cooperation of faculty and intermingling of student bodies" that would be "virtually without precedent in the educational world."[31] With this experimental partnership in mind, the deans signed off on a move that relocated the Law, Business, and JAG Schools to the wilds of Copeley Hill.

The spot selected for the new law-business complex was one of the last surviving fragments of the rural landscape that once surrounded the University of Virginia. Purchased by the University in 1963 from Mary White Duke and the estate of her late husband, the 117-acre Sunnyside farm well symbolized the confrontations between old and new that shaped its subsequent development. Still standing on the eastern edge of the parcel was the Sunnyside house, constructed around 1800 by Blake Harris as a one-and-a-half-story, hall-and-parlor log cabin. In the 1850s, while owned by Addison Maupin, the house underwent considerable expansion and renovation, receiving a two-story south wing, a front porch, and Gothic Revival embellishments. Now a "picturesque cottage"—an asymmetrical building style popularized by Andrew Jackson Downing—the house and its grounds were named Sunnyside after author Washington Irving's fanciful, much larger home in Tarrytown, New York. An octagonal library outbuilding situated on a high rock foundation enhanced the romantic appeal of the property. When Colonel Richard Thomas Walker Duke Sr. purchased the farm in 1863, the Sunnyside house stood over a mile from the University and two from Charlottesville, but by 1963 the property was no longer rural. In 1945, the University purchased the Massie Dairy Farm to the south of Sunnyside, first using it for housing for returning veterans and then in the 1960s constructing Copeley Hill Apartments, University Hall, and parking lots. In 1959, the sprawling Barracks Road Shopping Center opened just

Sunnyside, the home of the Duke family, probably an early twentieth-century view. The home still stands and is used as faculty housing.

east of Sunnyside; the Charlottesville bypass opened immediately to the west in 1962. Sunnyside at the time of its purchase by the University was already rife with juxtapositions of new and old, as the automobile and the shopping strip collided with the rusticity of an agricultural relic.[32]

Like Sunnyside, Clark Hall was now a relic of sorts. Over the years, the Law School had enlarged its footprint and altered its interiors, but despite the seeming permanence of Clark Hall's marble parapet with its dictum to the servants of law, the Law School prepared to relegate its worn building to the past. In spring 1967, the Board of Visitors publicly announced a $91.8 million capital outlay program that included new buildings at Copeley Hill for the Law School and Graduate Business School. Defending the move, Dean Dillard reassured students and alumni that this was not a sudden decision. Claiming that "space here is so restricted we have been aware for years that we would need more extensive facilities," he pointed out that Clark Hall now housed over four times the number of people it had in 1932. Considering the history of the Law School, with its somewhat nomadic existence in the nineteenth century and its departure from Minor Hall after only twenty-one years, the idea to build anew was not a radical one. Given the inadequacy of the previous additions to Clark Hall, Dillard's assertion that the move was "much more farsighted" than adding square footage seemed logical. When asked about the murals, Dillard gleefully joked that "we will miss that chap climbing the tree," but, as Dillard knew, the physical fabric of Clark Hall made up much of the cultural fabric of the Law School.[33]

Perhaps more importantly, the Law School had always been central to the University. Since the first law classes in 1826, the Law School played a key role in University life, and its occupation of stately Clark Hall underscored its prominence. Severing the Law School's connection with Clark Hall threatened to undermine its relationship to the University. For opponents of the State U, the development of the Duke tract represented the further disintegration of the University community. For these reasons, some members of the Buildings and Grounds Committee hesitated to follow through with the move. Frank Rogers, rector of the University, expressed to President Shannon that he feared the University was becoming "a fragmented institution of magnificent distances." Rogers and two colleagues pulled out maps and "drove over the ground to see if by minor modifications of the existing Master Plan, we could find room for those expansions on land already owned in the 'old' part of the University." While Rogers found two promising alternative sites, on May 31, 1967, the committee resolved the "Law School Graduate School of Business Administration complex be located on the Duke property" at Copeley Hill. Rogers was not convinced; the following year he lamented that "as a result of this fragmentation a law student will be able to complete a three year course *without ever seeing the Lawn.*" This concern over the consequences of the Law School's retreat from the sacred soil of Central Grounds would linger over the project.[34]

For students, the Law School's impending relocation likely seemed too distant or abstract to arouse much immediate concern. Not until the 1969–70 academic year did the student body begin a public dialogue on the merits of removal. Concerns over the move were part of a rising youth culture in the late 1960s that challenged authority and valued community. The student activism of the Vietnam War era had come to Charlottesville. Petitions and antiwar posters routinely littered Mural Hall; law students became legal marshals to aid political protests. Against this backdrop of calls for cooperation and social justice, some law students questioned whether moving the Law School away from the center of the University was a responsible decision. For these students, the issue was not one of architectural style or sentimentality but connectedness. In February, law student R. Vernon Swartsel Jr. wrote a letter to the *Virginia Law Weekly* about the impending reloca-

"I hear there's a mural in there that's worth the price!" This cartoon by law student Lynn S. Kneedler appeared in the *Virginia Law Weekly* on May 2, 1968, the same issue that announced plans for the removal of the Law School and Graduate School of Business to the Duke tract, later renamed North Grounds.

tion, asking, "Is it too late for us as a community—faculty, students and alumni—seriously and civilly to ask whether the Duke tract is really the best location for the Law School?" Swartsel admitted that Clark Hall and its "deteriorating interior" were "entirely inadequate," but he doubted "the wisdom of our moving from the heart of the University, away from the liberal arts, at a time when it seems more important than ever that law students and faculty have some meaningful contact with those disciplines." He was not alone in his concerns about the Law School becoming an "enclave overlooking the shopping center." Within a month, thirteen law students issued a statement of concern about the move, arguing for the "absolute necessity that the Law School be an integral part of the University, both academically and institutionally." Thinking of the embattled world around them, the students maintained that "the complexities of modern society require that the lawyer have a grasp of the economic, political and sociological consequences of specific legal actions." An exasperated President Shannon responded, "The problems of alienation of the Law School from the University will have to be considered secondary, and be worked out later." That May, in the aftermath of the shootings at Kent State University, Shannon faced masses of angry students on the steps of the Rotunda. For now, challenges to the relocation of the Law School receded into the background. Construction began in 1972.[35]

President Shannon's blunt response to the issue of alienation got to the heart of a question central to the earlier State U debates: did the unprecedented pursuit of expansion foster a "build now, fix later" sensibility? As the twentieth century entered its eighth decade, Americans looked out at a country of suburbs and interstate highways and ruminated over the costs and benefits of the nation's spectacular growth. And this conundrum over how growth could help solve problems without creating new ones would continue to visit the University. In 1973, a *Cavalier Daily* reporter visited the site of the new law school construction, encountering masses of metal shooting up from the old acres of Sunnyside. His description included a familiar reticence about the consequences of modernity in the realm of Mr. Jefferson:

Aerial view of Judge Advocate General's School (foreground) and Law School under construction, 1973.

Steel girders thrown against the sky indicate that one more addition to the University community is on its way. This structure is planned for efficient accommodation of graduate students and is located far from the basic academical village. When it opens in 1974, an entire faction will release pressure from the Central Grounds by using the new facility's classrooms; yet, as students attend classes in different areas, a step will be taken away from the old academical village and toward the deterioration of the "community spirit" that once pervaded the Grounds. Perhaps efficiency is the key to successful expansion, but are we losing something in the process?

In a similarly themed article entitled "Sprawling Developments Threaten 'Community,'" two student writers for the *Cavalier Daily* concluded, "In the wake of

View of the University of Virginia, Charlottesville, and Monticello, taken from Lewis Mountain, by
E. Sachse & Co., Baltimore, c. 1856. Although the Rotunda is disproportionately large, this image provides an excellent illustration of the University in the late 1850s, including the Annex, pavilions, ranges,
and Anatomical Theater.

The University of
Virginia, oil on canvas
by Allyn Cox, c. 1930.
William Andrews
Clark Jr. commis-
sioned Allyn Cox to
provide two murals
for a memorial room
in Pershing Hall, the
American Legion
building in Paris,
to commemorate
soldiers of the Great
War who attended
the University of
Virginia. This mural
and one for Monti-
cello both survive
and as of 2015 are
on loan by Pershing
Hall to the Musée
Franco-Américain du
Château de Bléran-
court in France.

Monticello, oil on
canvas by Allyn Cox,
c. 1930.

Homeric mural, Clark Memorial Hall,
oil on canvas by Allyn Cox, c. 1932–34.

Mosaic mural, Clark Memorial Hall, oil
on canvas by Allyn Cox, c. 1932–34.

This artist's rendering of the 1974 law building, later known as Withers Hall, emphasized the new home of the Law School as a contemporary space.

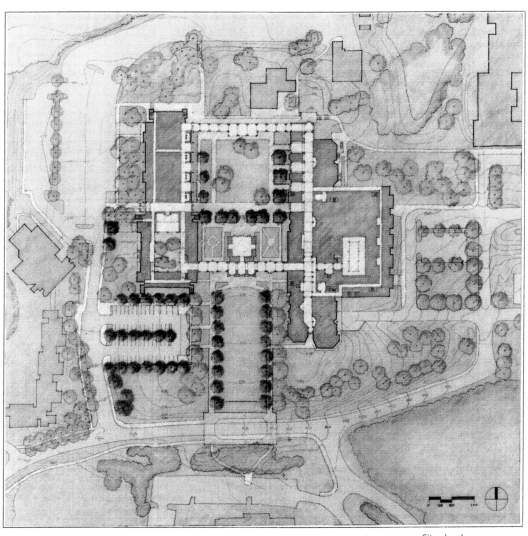

Site plan, Law
Grounds, 1993.

Artist Richard Chenoweth's 1994 watercolor rendering of the Caplin Reading Room, which replaced the
open-air Moyston Court. With paneled walls and
high ceilings, this space epitomized the transformation of the largely utilitarian 1970s law and Darden
buildings into the stately Law Grounds.

unprecedented growth, the fragmentation of Mr. Jefferson's 'academical village' has become a reality, and the struggle now remains to keep the distant branches coordinated and involved both physically and spiritually." It would be up to the architects and building committees overseeing the new law building to either reconcile or ignore the tensions at play between tradition and progress, expansion and anonymity.[36]

In February 1970, the *Virginia Law Weekly* published the first rendering of the new law school building. The three-story structure was long and narrow, its sweeping horizontality broken up only by the thin, two-story piers that supported the immense, overhanging third level. A zigzag of covered skylights broke up the otherwise flat line of the roof. It was a conspicuously modern building. A tree-filled court separated the building from the new home of the Graduate School of Business Administration, represented as only a faint outline to the left. Though only a small black-and-white image, the absence of the classical vocabulary of Clark Hall was obvious. Almost immediately, a law alumnus wrote to the *Virginia Law Weekly,* expressing his disappointment in the design, which he found "a radical departure" and "out of keeping with the general design of the University." "Grecian columns," he explained, had "ever been a hallmark of the University. Why this change?"[37]

A casual glance at the design of the new law building suggests that architects and administrators simply ignored concerns about the separation of the University and the Law School, placing a generic design on an anonymous piece of land sandwiched between a highway and a shopping center. Truthfully, the building and its surrounding complex were the result of a negotiated planning process. While neither University administrators nor the Law School wanted a white-columned, Roman Revival campus at the Duke tract, there was no initial consensus on an appropriate alternative. At least one faction within the Law School hoped for a building of landmark modern design. They reasoned that a conspicuously unconventional building would testify to the Law School's prominence at the University

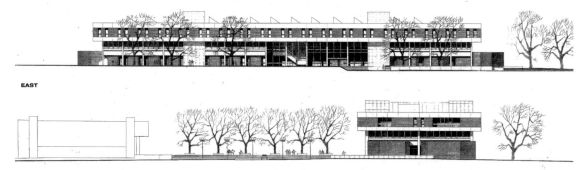

EAST

SOUTH

In February 1970, the Faculty Building Committee of the Law School released Hugh Stubbins and Associates' final conception of the west and south elevations of the proposed law building. The south elevation included the outline of the proposed Graduate Business School building and the cluster of trees left standing in the middle of the site.

despite its peripheral location. Yet for President Shannon, the Board of Visitors, and more conservative law faculty, the institutional and cultural ties between the Law School and the University needed to be affirmed in brick and mortar. The architect and building committee members therefore spatially and visually reinforced the school's connection to the University in key but subtle ways. The use of red brick, white piers, and a Lawn-like common space helped legitimize a building that was essentially an ordinary modern educational structure located on a commuter campus. The results demonstrated that while the University could interpret the Jeffersonian tradition quite liberally, this architectural legacy still mattered. However small, visual and spatial nods to the original campus were an essential means of making modern buildings acceptable at the University of Virginia.

Native Virginians designed Minor Hall and Clark Hall, but for the new law-business complex the University looked outside the state, perhaps hoping that a more urbane, nationally known firm would convey a similar sophistication to the new development. In March 1967, a joint committee of law and business professors met with two architectural firms—Skidmore, Owings & Merrill of New York and Hugh Stubbins and Associates of Boston. The New York firm likely attracted the University's attention because of its strikingly modern Beinecke Rare Book and Manuscript Library at Yale and the campus of the new University of Illinois at

Chicago Circle. The group went on to design some of the tallest buildings in the world, including the John Hancock Center and the Sears Tower. Stubbins's prestigious academic commissions included the Loeb Drama Center and Francis A. Countway Library of Medicine at Harvard, both of which the joint committee toured. Ultimately the group recommended Stubbins to the Board of Visitors' Buildings and Grounds Committee. The professors agreed that Skidmore, Owings & Merrill was "for clients with almost unlimited budgets," which was not true of UVa.[38] Budget constraints in fact plagued the project; in 1969, the Nixon administration cut the federal program that the University expected to provide $3.6 million in matching funds for the project.[39] Working almost exclusively with limited state money, Stubbins designed both the law and business buildings as well as the new home of the JAG School, which followed the Law School to its new location.

Loeb Drama Center, Harvard University. Hugh Stubbins, architect, photographed 1960, shortly after its completion.

Due to the funding shortfall, the University built the complex in stages: first phase one of the law building, then the business and JAG buildings, and finally a second phase of construction on the law building after all three schools had reopened.

Preparation for the law-business complex began with a site plan. It was here that Stubbins and Associates first attempted to reconcile the needs of a modern law school with the desire to transplant some of the character and camaraderie of the Academical Village and Clark Hall to the new site. In order to accomplish this difficult task, the designers worked to create an environment characterized by a sense

The 1968 law-business site plan by Hugh Stubbins and Associates resembled an office park or shopping complex with its asymmetrical arrangement of buildings and abundant parking. While the placement and orientation of the central mall and the law (L), business (B), and JAG (J) buildings remained largely the same throughout the design process, the high-rise dormitory (F) was eliminated and dining and recreational facilities (D/E) only built as the much smaller "Café North" in the late 1970s.

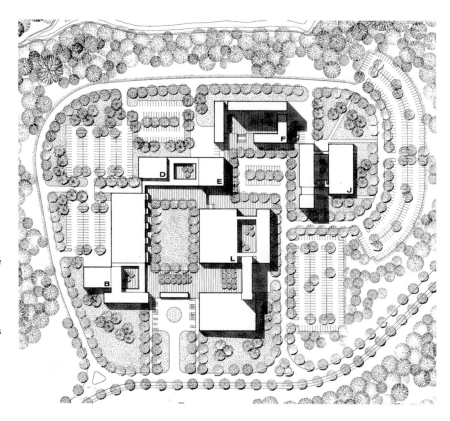

THE LAW SCHOOL AT THE UNIVERSITY OF VIRGINIA

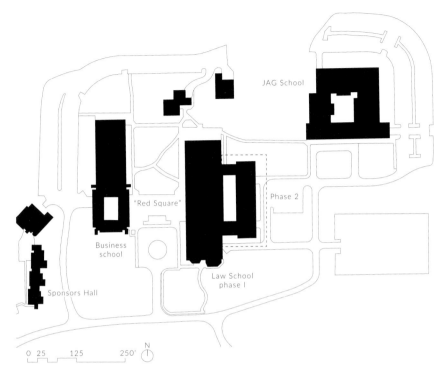

As constructed, the law-business complex was greatly simplified from Stubbins' earliest conceptions. The Graduate Business School (renamed the Colgate Darden Graduate School of Business in 1975) added Sponsors Hall to North Grounds in the late 1970s.

of intimacy and community grounded in tradition. The starting point was not an American but an English model. Dean Dillard hoped that the new law building would "capture the idea of the Inns of Court," referring to the four famous Inns of Court in London—a place where law students could live, eat, study, and congregate.[40] Comprised of lodgings, libraries, and meeting halls, the Inns of Court functioned as nurseries of law, cloistering students together in a de facto legal fraternity. This conception of the new complex embraced a holistic approach to education along the lines of the Academical Village, but it also had a public relations advantage, spinning the Law School's newfound isolation as happy seclusion.

Created in early 1968, the initial site plan showed the influence of both the Academical Village and the Inns of Court. While Stubbins and Associates adjusted the scale and configuration of the buildings over time, the basic layout of this plan survived largely intact. Stubbins' most surprising choice, which had an obvious connection to the Academical Village, was turning the law and business buildings perpendicular to Massie Road, the main thoroughfare fronting the complex. The structures faced each other across a grassy, tree-lined central mall, which Stubbins described as "a space of similar proportions to the original Jeffersonian Lawn." In fact the mall and the Lawn shared a width of two hundred feet. The orientation of the buildings responded to the schools' desire to foster a closer relationship, and in this regard the design mimicked the interdisciplinary purpose of the Academical Village. In contrast to the open central mall, other bits of green space in the site plan were enclosed, turning the buildings in on themselves. Like the cloisters of the Inns of Court, the inward gaze of these interior courtyards reflected the exclusivity and shared vocation of the schools housed within. The JAG building and the proposed dormitory building (never constructed), both sited to the rear of the complex, also featured interior courtyards. Thus through green space Stubbins worked to subtly reference two traditions: one that invoked ties with the University and larger world, and another that fostered separation and privilege.[41]

However much Stubbins drew inspiration from pre-twentieth-century planning models, his layout for the law-business complex also had conspicuous ties to more recent kinds of building projects. With its asymmetric configuration of buildings and ample parking, the site plan more closely resembled an office park or a shopping mall than the Academical Village. Spatially the complex had much in common with its nearest neighbor, the Barracks Road Shopping Center. The automobile-oriented design of the new law-business complex worked against the pedestrian-friendly character of the central mall by establishing this new colony of the University as a commuter school. A driveway and motor court provided the main approach to the complex. The driveway entered the site from the south, terminating in a roundabout with short-term parking adjacent to a brick terrace

that allowed access to the main entrances of the law and business buildings and the mall. A ring road, which survived the planning process with substantial changes, surrounded the entire complex. It provided entry points to six parking lots. Despite the amount of space devoted to parking at the site, the Law School and the Graduate Business School requested more. Stubbins' design provided 844 parking spaces, but the Faculty Building Committee asked for 1,500 spaces. Stubbins

Barracks Road Shopping Center, opened 1959, with the North Grounds complex behind, August 1976.

replied that this "would require an area of approximately 10 acres of relatively flat land . . . cover[ing] most of the buildable land available."[42]

One way that Stubbins attempted to tie his automobile campus back to Central Grounds was by playing up the idea that the site offered views of the Rotunda, which not only promised to tie the new site to Central Grounds and the legacy of Thomas Jefferson but lessened the sense of distance between old campus and new. In one iteration of the site plan, Stubbins identified the "Rotunda View" with an arrow pointing south from the center of the law-business complex. Apparently Stubbins and others believed that the site afforded more sweeping vistas than it actually did. The *Virginia Law Weekly* reported that the complex would occupy "a high knoll with a view of the Rotunda," while Stubbins told President Shannon and the Faculty Building Committee that the Rotunda would be visible from the entrance to the site. Ultimately it became apparent that the site was not high enough for anyone to see the Rotunda from ground level, at least not without an uninterrupted vista. The possibility of Rotunda views from the upper stories of the law and business buildings evaporated when the University insisted that Stubbins reduce the height of the structures. Initially Stubbins planned a more ambitious building program with parts of the law and business buildings reaching five to seven stories high; the never-constructed dormitory was twelve stories. The only Rotunda views available proved to be too expensive for the University to afford.[43]

In 1967–68, as Stubbins and Associates planned the building site, the law professors making up the Faculty Building Committee compiled ideas for their new edifice. They had dozens of new law buildings to consider due to the midcentury construction boom in the legal academy. Neill H. Alford Jr., head of the Faculty Building Committee, hoped to avoid an imitation of any of the University's stock of buildings, historic or modern. Writing to Waller Hunt of the University Planning Department, he explained his desire to move away from the design compromises that characterized Gilmer Hall and the Chemistry Building: "Since we are moving over to a new area, especially when we are not too far from that rather unorthodox field hall [the clamshell-domed University Hall arena], we might use some imagination in building materials. The idea of another building constructed of brick and concrete gives me the horrors." Alford had received Hunt's project criteria for the new building, which specified that the new complex was to use "a type of architecture . . . harmonious with the existing character of buildings at the University of Virginia." He was concerned that the Board of Visitors' penchant for red brick modernism would limit the imagination of Stubbins's design: "Won't his design depend upon the materials he can use? If we come up with structures like the Chemistry and Life Sciences [Gilmer Hall] buildings I expect the law faculty will do more than simply hang me in effigy." He wanted "a different law building," perhaps one in structural aluminum, "something that expressed the uniqueness of the contribution of [the] law school to the legal system." For Alford, a more adventurous design would signify the Law School's high status not only on Grounds but in legal education: "Are we putting one of the nation's leading law schools into a building or buildings of second and third quality? We are not after equality [with the other buildings of the University]. We want something that will be a model for future university design—not simply a hangover from the past."[44]

Alford dispatched law professors on visits to new buildings at a number of law schools, including Wisconsin, Duke, Chicago, Columbia, Rutgers, Northwestern, and Georgia. These were all modern structures, though they fell on a broad spectrum in terms of scale and materials used. Professor Thomas Bergin visited Rutgers and Columbia, which stood at two architectural extremes. Rutgers's law school had recently moved into Ackerson Hall, a forbidding structure of concrete consisting of a massive two-story block supported on piers over a recessed first floor. It was one of a number of matching Brutalist structures (named from the French *béton brut,* "raw concrete") lining University Avenue in Camden. At fifty thousand square feet, it was already too small for its student body. While Bergin considered the Rutgers law building "Spartan," he found the expense lavished on the Columbia law building dazzling, writing to Alford that it was "lush as hell." This building, opened in 1961 and designed by New York firm Harrison & Abramovitz, stood across Amsterdam Avenue in Manhattan from Charles McKim's iconic

Jerome L. Greene
Hall, Columbia Law
School. Harrison &
Abramovitz, archi-
tects, completed
1961.

Columbia campus. While the Rutgers building was squat and economical, Bergin
thought Columbia's was "truly a handsome structure. . . . The general impression
is of an imposing 20th century building." It consisted of a tower standing atop
a heavy podium that abutted the New York City sidewalks. Thin concrete mul-
lions accentuated the verticality of the building. While detractors said the structure looked like a pop-up toaster, it projected a 1960s style of glamour. Bergin
was in awe of the "ferocious amount of money" spent on the building. A wide
pedestrian bridge that spanned Amsterdam Avenue and connected the law school
with the main campus caught the professor's attention. His guide explained that
the bridge, which reportedly cost a million dollars, was necessary because "it's all

inter-disciplinary here." This aside may have made Bergin grimace considering the impending removal of his own school from Central Grounds, where it enjoyed immediate access to other disciplines.[45]

For additional guidance, Alford wrote letters to colleagues at other law schools. One of these was Frank E. Maloney, dean of the College of Law at the University of Florida, who, following the advice of Dean Dillard, was overseeing the construction of the new law building there. Maloney proved an excellent source of advice; he had visited over fifty law schools in the past three years. The new University of Florida law building, designed by the Miami-based firm of Pancoast, Ferendino, Grafton and Skeels, was modern but quite different from the ones at Rutgers and Columbia. A three-story rectangular structure with a slightly cantilevered uppermost story of concrete, its brick facing tied it to Florida's older Collegiate Gothic buildings. Thin concrete piers punctuated the lower two floors. Four rounded concrete stair towers, one on each side of the building, relieved an otherwise boxy design. As UVa planned to do, Florida built its new law school in the remote northwest corner of its campus.[46] Alford also wrote to Charles D. Kelso, associate dean of the University of Miami School of Law, who was something of an expert on new law buildings. He presented "Planning and Design of Law Buildings" at the Association of American Law Schools annual meeting in 1965. By his own count, Kelso had recently toured over a hundred law school buildings. He especially admired the University of Illinois College of Law building, which opened in 1955, calling it "a splendid example of careful planning." Its double-wing construction placed the library and faculty offices in one building and the classrooms, moot court, student lounges, and auditorium in another, with a patio separating the two structures. The University of Utah College of Law "made a similar functional division of its building," and Kelso found the layout here even more appealing. Yet Kelso emphasized that functionality did not mean a new law building could not be attractive; he highlighted buildings at California Western, Arizona, Utah, and Illinois to "illustrate the point that a law building can be beautiful."[47]

Brick and concrete may have given Alford "horrors," but this amalgamation of the traditional and the modern was the compromise of choice in the contentious arena of new design at the University. At a meeting about the law-business complex in February 1968, President Shannon "encouraged the architects to use brick in some manner where possible in view of the Board of Visitors' preference for brick." The Visitors had their wish, and Alford did not get his aluminum building. Stubbins diplomatically assured the president that while "nothing had definitely been established . . . he felt that most likely it would be concrete and brick." He added: "In any case the complex would express the spirit of the University and carry consistency. The mall would be a serene space and the buildings naturally would need some sun control device that would lend shade and shadow to the facades."[48]

As he did with the site plan, Stubbins designed the law and business buildings in an effort to incorporate traditional elements from the historic Grounds into a contemporary formula. He recognized that the law building, the largest and first completed structure at the Duke tract, would set the tone for the complex. To "express the spirit of the University," Stubbins designed a law building that used the requisite brick, made a few other allusions to the Academical Village, and offered "shade and shadow," but all within a clearly modern design. The new law building's consistency with the University relied almost entirely on materials, hues, and the regular, largely symmetrical arrangement of its facade. The limits of the state budget likely made the final product even more conservative than Stubbins intended. While in early 1968 Stubbins proposed a three-part plan consisting of a library, a classroom building, and a faculty office tower, arranged around a U-shaped entrance court, by July the design had changed to a single large, rectangular building of uniform three-story height, with a glass-fronted recessed entry in the place of an open court. Not only could the University not afford such tall buildings, but the design was also too tall for more traditional members of the administration and faculty.[49] After seeing the revised plan, Alford congratulated Stubbins on a design "better suited to our needs than the high rise design," acknowledging the "rock bottom economy requirements" under which the architect labored.[50]

The most conspicuous feature of the building was its broadly cantilevered third level, composed of a thick upper and lower band of concrete faced with brick in between. Along the main or west facade, paired windows broke up the span of brick, but wide stringcourses of concrete ran uninterrupted around the entire building. For the second floor, site of the library reading room, Stubbins wrapped ribbon windows all the way around. This provided views and lighting. Situated just under the cantilevered third story, the ribbon windows benefited from the shadows cast by the broad overhang—the "sun control device" Stubbins mentioned in his description of the building. On the first level, Stubbins angled brick walls at various intervals, creating an undulating facade that provided more of the promised "shade and shadow." Concrete pilotis or thin vertical piers surrounded the building, acting as columns or pilasters and appearing to carry the heavy load of the third floor. Although pilotis were a common feature of modern buildings (Stubbins had used them on the Loeb Drama Center), within the University context they suggested the classicism of Central Grounds. Thus the new law building, while modern in design, had the two key features of University buildings: red brick and white columns.[51]

Seen as three distinct levels—the rhythmic pattern of piers and brick on the first floor, the deep shadow and expansive views of the second floor, and the heavy, overhanging top floor—the law building could be interpreted as a modern expression of the Academical Village, the setback facades, balconies, parapets, and pediments of the older complex merged and abstracted for the new. Yet such a reading would have been lost on almost any observer. Rather, the red brick, the illusion of white columns, and the rhythmic regularity of the building subtly reassured observers that the law building belonged at the University. Since Stubbins chose sympathetic yet standard modern features for the building, his design also succeeded in creating the progressive, forward-facing impression that the Law School desired. Stubbins could not offer a trailblazing design, but he provided the streamlined monumentality that satisfied those who wanted a building evoking preeminence in the legal academy. Although Alford told Dan Meador, now the dean of

Van Hecke-Wettach
Hall, University
of North Carolina
School of Law.
Murray Whisnant,
architect, completed
1968.

the University of Alabama School of Law, that he believed Stubbins did not use any of the plans from other law schools that the committee had gathered, the law building did resemble a number of its contemporaries. It was especially similar to Van Hecke-Wettach Hall, which opened in 1968 as the new home of the University of North Carolina School of Law. Here the architect, Murray Whisnant of Charlotte, also used expanses of brick to soften the appearance of a conspicuously modern design. Both buildings featured elements used at many other modern public buildings, including a flat roof, thick concrete stringcourses, ribbon windows, and tiered levels, although Whisnant avoided the pilotis that gave the UVa building a vaguely classical appearance.

The battles that ensued over the design of the law building were not fought over its general appearance. Rather, differing factions debated whether the law building's modernism necessitated a bare-bones functionality. While functionality was a quality prized by modern architects, the ever-restricting budget at the law-business complex made utilitarianism more a necessity than an aesthetic or philosophical choice. The state of Virginia's demands for greater economy threatened to strip character and interest from the building design. In 1968, Alford wrote to Dan Meador about Stubbins' frustrations: "Although we are happy with Stubbins, I rather doubt the sense of contentment is reciprocated. . . . This is the first contract for a state educational institution that Stubbins has undertaken and he seems to be learning the hard way." The state threatened to gut the building. Letters from Douglas Hamner of the Virginia Division of Engineers and Buildings to the University laid out a number ways to reduce or eliminate nearly all nonessential features of the building. He thought the skylights, which rippled across the roof line and promised to fill the building with natural light, unnecessary: "We cannot justify the skylights presently designed with respect to function. . . . The necessity for having daylight in office areas is not supported by the many recent architectural designs." He requested the east facade be simplified, as "the separate columns and the various angular offsets in the foundation walls will obviously contribute to additional costs." Unsympathetic to the traditional red brick pattern of the University, Hamner rejected the use of Flemish bond and questioned the use of any other "'aesthetic' finish . . . which affects the cost of the structure." Perhaps most alarmingly, he suggested drastically narrowing the wide concourse that bisected the first floor. "Functionally," he declared, "a concourse of approximately half this size would be sufficient." Hamner cut the sizes of offices and reduced the number of elevators. He even challenged the idea of a separate dean's toilet.[52]

Alford complained to Werner Sensbach, the University architect, that the building should not merely be useful but expressive of its eminent purpose as a school of law. He believed that "any touches which will add convenience and grace to the building should not be ignored; the concourse carrying out the spirit and tradition of Westminster Hall, the ancient place of meeting of the English common law courts. The wide concourse thus combines convenience, economy, tradition and grace. A concourse half the width would be no improvement on our present situation [in Clark Hall]—which is intolerable from the point of view of traffic and noise." Alford also took up for the small but symbolic dean's toilet: "A private toilet increases the prestige of the Dean. Thus I think he should have one." Ultimately the dean lost his toilet, but the wide concourse and skylights survived. So did the angled walls, which made both the interior and exterior considerably more complex and expensive to build. Even so, the design of the planned building prompted law student Victor Bernstein, a member of the Student Building Committee, to tell the faculty that "the new building is a disaster at least as far as ambience and aesthetics are concerned." He had little hope for "relief from the general mediocrity of the new law school facilities." The passage of time did not ease concerns about the quality of the structure. Less than six months before the building opened, the faculty reported "considerable disparity between the complex which was originally proposed and . . . the project into which the Law School will move."[53]

In 1972, despite any reservations, workers began clearing the site; soon a huge framework of steel beams forcefully conveyed the reality of the new law building. Construction setbacks delayed the completion of the building, but by spring 1974 it seemed certain that the structure would be ready for classes in the fall. The Law Council, a student-run advisory board, hosted a "Last Tango in Mural Hall" to commemorate the end of the Law School's tenure in Clark Hall. When classes resumed in early September, first-year law students were the first to move in. Until September 23, when the Law School opened the new building to all students and faculty, second- and third-years found themselves disoriented amid "the lame duck atmosphere of Clark Hall that is exemplified by the large empty library, absent administrators and faculty, and the phasing out of Tony's [eatery]." Once noisy and crowded, Clark Hall took on a mausoleum-like aura as it gradually drained of people, furniture, portraits, and the 265,000-volume library. Cleared of its inhabitants and accoutrements, it was no longer the Law School. Ann Graham, the *Virginia Law Weekly*'s managing editor, wrote nostalgically: "Perhaps the most important thing to remember is sitting on the steps of the Law School with friends and watching the hustle and bustle of the whole University passing by. It will be harder now to have a sense of community with Mr. Jefferson's University. Not only will the move isolate us from Cabell's Xerox facilities and from

The new law building under construction, spring 1973.

the bank in Newcomb Hall, but it also takes us away from the history represented by the Grounds and from the broader cross-section of people who make up the University as a whole. Let us not forget."[54]

The new, unnamed law building was entirely different from Clark Hall, just as Hugh Stubbins and the Faculty Building Committee had intended. The most obvious difference was in the relative size of the buildings. Clark Hall was just under 70,000 square feet, of which the JAG School had leased a little over 6,000 square feet; the new building was approximately 136,000 square feet, with the planned phase II adding 60,000 square feet. The new law building also had a much different layout than its predecessor. Whereas users of Clark Hall entered through the front door, where a foyer funneled them into Mural Hall, those arriving at the new building could gain access from multiple entry points, all of which fed into the

The formal "Last Tango in Mural Hall" in May 1974 featured a nine-piece band and included Allyn Cox, painter of the murals, as the Law School's guest of honor.

long central concourse on the first floor. Stretching the entire length of the building, the concourse was 19 feet wide and 350 feet long. From it, faculty and students could enter nine lecture halls, all irregularly shaped octagons, each accommodating a horseshoe-shaped tiered seating arrangement that reflected the latest trends in classroom design. Also on the main floor were three small seminar rooms, the moot court room, and the student lounge. Five staircases and two elevators led up to the library, which took up the entire second floor. Faculty offices, student activities spaces, and additional library stacks made up the third floor. Altogether, the building addressed a number of problems the Law School encountered in Clark Hall. Not only was the new structure much more spacious, but it kept faculty offices away from noisy student spaces, clustered instructional areas together, and prevented traffic bottlenecks by providing numerous entrances on the first floor

and multiple ways of accessing the second and third. While Clark Hall's interior was arranged according to a symmetrical, Palladian model with rooms radiating out from an impressive central hall, the new building prioritized convenience over formality and visual impact.

Understandably, the new building did not immediately feel like home. It was clean, large, and efficient, but these modern improvements, of course, were also the characteristics of the State U. Although many students and faculty members no doubt enjoyed the new facilities, some members of the Law School and University community blamed the new building for fostering anonymity and isolation. Community members most frequently cited the new building's appearance, internal organization, and location as problems, although some struggled to pinpoint exactly what was wrong. As the *Virginia Law Weekly* editorialized, "Perhaps

The "First Boogie at No-Name Hall" in December 1974 in the concourse of the new law building, a far less glamorous location than Mural Hall.

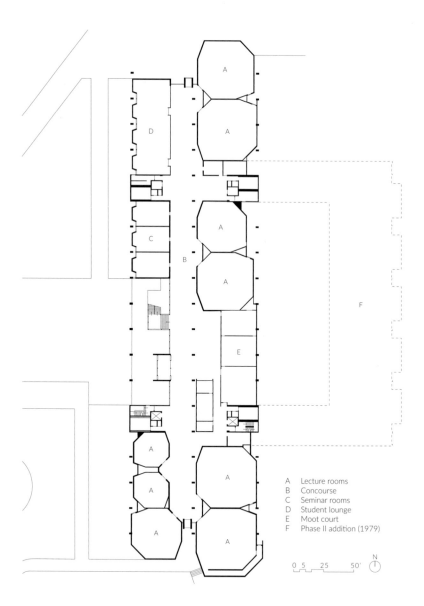

The first floor of the law building included a long central concourse and clusters of octagonal lecture halls.

A   Lecture rooms
B   Concourse
C   Seminar rooms
D   Student lounge
E   Moot court
F   Phase II addition (1979)

0 5   25   50'   N

what the building lacks more than anything else is an intangible—personality."
Certainly its newness meant that it had no softening patina. Meanwhile its name-
lessness made the building itself anonymous and perhaps contributed to an impersonal environment. Students took to calling the structure "No Name Hall." The
Virginia Law Weekly recommended that the Law School name the building as "a
symbolic step toward character," but it remained unnamed until 1983, when it was
christened Withers Hall in honor of alumnus Henry Malcolm Withers.[55] Some
four years after the move, the *Virginia Law Weekly* described the new building as
"a functional but sterile environment in which we spend three years and in which

The library, second
floor of the new
law building.
Renovations in the
1990s removed the
U-shaped stair.

faculty may spend a career." Explaining that the structure had been built "on something of a shoestring budget," the newspaper compared it "to entering the basement of a big city hospital": "The tile floor is a dull grey, the few wall hangings seem deliberately uninspiring, [and] the furnishings are nondescript." While these criticisms had more to do with the building's decoration than its architecture, one University student wrote to the *Cavalier Daily* to explain why he thought the building itself failed: "*Good* modern architecture really does cost a bit—not much, perhaps, but something—more than that which is styled 'modern' only by default. A visit to the new Law School or Medical Education building will be more than sufficient to show that the University simply does not have that little bit more to spend." As some observers had feared during the design process, the economical decor and mundane finishes of the law building had a negative impact on perceptions of the facility, making its functionality seem oppressive rather than refreshingly contemporary.[56]

Other critics of the building blamed its internal organization for a breakdown in the personal exchanges and close relationships between students and faculty that they fondly remembered from Clark Hall. H. Lane Kneedler, the assistant dean of the Law School, told the *Cavalier Daily* that "the new building is not as conducive to faculty-student interaction." The size of the new building alone was an obvious reason why faculty and students encountered each other less frequently; it was simply much larger than Clark Hall. Law librarian Frances Farmer appreciated the new facilities but conceded that she missed "the intimacy of a smaller school." Sharing similar feelings, the Law Council expressed a desire to "return to the Clark Hall intimacy." The council, recognizing "a growing alienation among students and faculty attributable, in part, to the move from Clark Hall to our present building on the North Grounds," believed "that the architectural design of our new building did not allow for enough student-faculty contact other than in the classroom setting." Although Mural Hall had often been ridiculed for being too congested and noisy, now the Law School better appreciated its communal quality. Stubbins had made the concourse wider at the center of the new building, but he and the Faculty

The concourse or main hall of the new law building. Its lockers, tile floor, and institutional appearance invited comparisons to a high school.

"If It Only Had Murals . . ." Cartoon by law student Ann Glover for the *Virginia Law Weekly*, October 25, 1974.

Building Committee decided against a full space comparable to Mural Hall and likewise left the murals themselves behind. Professors Robert Scott and John Jeffries, recent hires to the law faculty, "miss[ed] the openness of Clark Hall and Mural Hall, and especially the opportunities for more casual and informal professor-student contact that existed there." Associate Dean Richard Merrill agreed, citing the loss of Mural Hall for a missing "sense of community" at the Law School. Located in the middle of Clark Hall, Mural Hall had been an inescapable gathering space. One student pointed out that while almost all students and faculty at Clark Hall "came in the front door," channeling them into Mural Hall, faculty at the new building tended to use the door from the parking lot, while students used entrances closer to the street. Thus while the new buildings' designers had worked to remedy the problems of Clark Hall, they unwittingly introduced a new set of issues. Multiple doors, the long concourse, and the separation of faculty offices from students and classrooms made sense in terms of traffic flow, noise, and ease of accessibility, but this layout also decreased opportunities for exchange.[57]

While the size and floor plan of the new law building contributed to feelings of anonymity and isolation, understandably the structure's remote location was largely responsible for a lost sense of community. President Shannon had said prior to the move that the University would have to work out the problems of alienation at the Law School in the future, and now the problems were upon them. Alienation was perhaps the main criticism students and faculty attached to the new site, and it was the most difficult to solve. As Associate Dean Merrill concluded, "The problem of the location of the new Law School is one that cannot be as easily dealt with as its internal layout." In its role as community bellwether, the *Virginia Law Weekly* reported an acute feeling of separation between law students and the University, with executive editor Scot Butler writing that "according to many of its students, when the Law School was located in Clark Hall there was a much closer rapport between it and the rest of the University community than currently exists." While onlookers humorously labeled the new Law School the University's "Culpeper Branch," the relocation had a number of unpleasant consequences despite the comparatively short one-and-a-half mile distance. Writing for the *Virginia Law Weekly* in a piece entitled "Physical Isolation Unsolved Problem for North Grounds," student Pamela Clark reported that law students were "no longer exposed to the campus-wide gossip about courses that flows through the University grapevine." Law students now took very little role in the governance of the University, whereas before they had been regular members of the Honor and Judiciary Committees. Faculty, too, had a difficult time adapting to their new home. While law professors had previously enjoyed easy access to the Colonnade Club, the University faculty meeting spot in Pavilion VII, they now found themselves largely cut off. Clark observed that "while several faculty members are involved in interdisciplinary projects, the social ties are no longer there."[58]

Perhaps the biggest consequence of the move was that the Law School's students soon lost any awareness of or concern about the separation from the larger University community. While faculty may have long remembered and regretted the loss of engagement with Central Grounds, the students who attended classes in Clark Hall quickly graduated. For new students, Central Grounds became irrelevant as it was possible to attend the Law School and never set foot near the Rotunda. North Grounds, as it became officially known in 1974, had an increasingly tentative orientation to Central Grounds, despite its new name. It became an island unto itself. In a 1979 editorial entitled "Secession?," the *Virginia Law Weekly* explored this new reality:

Thomas Jefferson's close university community has grown into a sprawling diversity of individual schools. The Law School, once right in the middle of college activity, even has its own Grounds which it shares, somewhat reluctantly, with the Business and JAG Schools.... The choice becomes one of trying to re-integrate the Law School into the University fold, or letting it continue in its own sphere of interest. While reunification seems the better course, most law students don't care, and most undergrads would rather not. Each group has its own perspective of University life, and each is equally palatable to its members. It is a matter of different Grounds, and as long as they are separate, the students will be, too.

That students cared less and less about the loss of connection to Central Grounds created an interesting epilogue to the State U narrative. Opponents of the State U had feared a world in which alienation was a deeply felt reality. At North Grounds, students quickly adapted to their new circumstances and became ambivalent about fostering connection. Like the cloistered site plan of the new complex, North Grounds was inward-facing. As the *Cavalier Daily* concluded in its 1975 story on the new law school, "a move was necessary, and it was made. But not without its consequences."[59]

If North Grounds was an island, at least it needed to be a more homelike one. The Law School and the Graduate Business School (which opened its building in 1975) attempted to improve this "functional but sterile environment" through an investment in trees and flowers. Law professors Daniel Meador, John Jeffries, and Emerson Spies (who became dean in 1976) spearheaded efforts to beautify the site. Landscaping solved a number of problems: it brought some of the park-like beauty of Central Grounds to North Grounds, it made use of the outdoor spaces created by Stubbins, and it disguised the enormous size of the buildings. Jay Graham of the University Planning Committee had saved from the bulldozers a small grove of trees between the law and business buildings, a patch of greenery in front of the business building, and a cluster of trees near the front of the law building, but these were all second- and third-growth woodland that had grown up over the old fields of Sunnyside. None were giants of the forest. Much of the site was bare and covered in mud. The stark environment exaggerated the apparent size of the buildings and made them unwelcoming. As one Business School professor explained: "Our buildings are so very large. . . . The south rear portion of the Law School currently looks like Lenin's tomb in Red Square. Our goal is to bring the buildings to smaller scale, to humanize them." Meador, who had returned from the University of Alabama, wanted heavy planting to "avoid the appearance of the Law School looking like a battleship." In fact, the building very much resembled a ship due to its length, its stacked levels (which called to mind tiers of decks), and the stair towers, which projected up past the roofline like smokestacks. Meador articulated the new landscape committee's desire to "develop a setting and environment comparable to the central grounds of the University." The committee wanted to avoid replicating the Lawn with its central open green framed by rows of trees, but it did hope to emulate the pastoral, matured look of the older portion of Grounds. Comparisons to Lenin's tomb and a battleship reflected not just the bulk and length of the law building but the feeling of an impersonal, foreign, even hostile atmosphere that only heightened the disparity between old Grounds and new. Perhaps in response to the abundance of order and efficiency in the new building, the landscape committee kept the grove between the law and business buildings somewhat wild. This literal "grove of Academe" stood in the center of the complex, its romantic nature a foil to a preponderance of asphalt and concrete.[60]

The modern lines of the law building, slowly concealed by trees and shrubs, were not at fault for any lingering sense of anonymity and isolation at North Grounds. The problem was one of form, not style. Although the designers of North Grounds chose various elements of the Academical Village to reinforce a connection with the historic campus, the commuter campus much more heavily influenced the design program. Access, efficiency, and economy were top priorities, so much so that the new design overcorrected Clark Hall's faults. Mural Hall had been loud and crowded, but it acted as a city square for the Law School community. The murals, though faded and dated, undeniably lent character to the building. At North Grounds, the long parkway-like concourse, segregation of spaces, blank walls, and abundance of parking lots mirrored shopping-strip suburbia. If the new residents of North Grounds felt alienated and anonymous, this was more likely the result of layout, design, siting, and scale than the use of a cantilevered third floor, ribbon windows, or exposed concrete. Nevertheless, whatever its shortcomings, the new law building succeeded in its main goal of housing a growing, changing institution. It opened just in time to welcome the Law School's first African American professor, Larry Gibson, and its first female professor, Lillian BeVier. The new building's emphasis on accessibility, therefore, had a figurative value; its many doors could welcome in a more diverse population than had those of Clark or Minor Hall.

At the new law building there was not much time for gazing backward. There were classes to take, lectures to give, socializing to do. Life moved forward despite problems at the new site, and as improvements were made, trees grew, and classes of students moved through, the new building began to feel less alien. Clark Hall was not entirely forgotten, at least not by the students who had attended classes there. In January 1976, when the last class to remember Clark Hall was months away from graduation, the *Virginia Law Weekly* ran an update on the building. Clark Hall's new occupant, the Department of Environmental Sciences, had by that time adapted the building to its own purposes. The department preserved the facade and Mural Hall but made significant changes elsewhere. The library, although still used for that purpose, was somewhat bare, devoid of the overabundance of law books and the portraits of law deans that once lined the walls. Once notorious for its poor acoustics and rickety wooden seats, the West Hall lecture room now had a drop ceiling and plastic chairs. In the former student lounge, a wind tunnel and silt-depositing experiment replaced the familiar tables, sofas, and clutter. Though preserved, Mural Hall had changed, too, at least in feeling: "the murals now look down upon rock and mineral collections and not upon the masses of law students who congregate there every day." According to the writer, Clark Hall had "probably been adapted to its new function quite well" but "lost much of its charm in the transition." Thus Clark Hall, like the Law School, found itself altered in response to the needs of the present and future. These transformations helped assure the University's prominence in the world of higher education, even if it came at the price of disrupting, diminishing, or repurposing tradition.[61]

4

The Creation of Law Grounds

When the new buildings for the Graduate School of Business Administration and Judge Advocate General's School opened in 1975, the Hugh Stubbins–designed North Grounds complex was largely complete. Located across the central mall to the west of the law building, the new home of the Graduate Business School was smaller, lower, and of simpler design than its neighbor, but together they formed an impressive modern court of red brick and thick concrete lines. Standing to the east, somewhat hidden from view by the law building, the JAG building was the tallest and most contemporary of the three, with a long two-story block projecting out over a smaller two-story base. The trio represented an investment of over $12 million. While not luxurious, the complex was a substantial addition to the University and a respectable specimen of contemporary design in higher education. Yet the building garnering the most attention on Grounds at the time was not the law or JAG buildings or the new modern structure for the School of Architecture on the back slope of Carr's Hill. On April 13, 1976, a date of double significance as Jefferson's birthday and the bicentennial year of American independence, the University dedicated the newly restored Rotunda. This "return to the original" as the *Alumni News* called it had been in the works since the mid-1950s, but the project truly got off the ground in 1965 when President Shannon established the Rotunda Restoration Committee. The timing was no coincidence. This extensive restoration, which replaced Stanford White's interior with one simulating the original destroyed in the 1895 fire, was a strategic counterbalance to the distending force of the State U. By attempting to reproduce the lost original, the University reaffirmed the Rotunda as its physical and institutional core, making a powerful statement that this was still "Mr. Jefferson's University." Thus at a time when the iconic structure could have become little more than a photo in campus publications, its gravitational pull on the surrounding University only increased as the twentieth century wore on. In time, this force would have a profound impact on the look and layout of North Grounds.[1]

In the 1990s, both the Law School and the Graduate Business School embarked on ambitious building programs that sought to bring the Academical Village to North Grounds. While Hugh Stubbins had made subtle references to the Jefferson campus in his design, twenty years later these functional, largely ahistorical quarters satisfied neither school. Two forces aligned to make expensive, more traditional complexes possible. The advent of postmodern architecture, with its revival of interest in historic precedents, brought classicism back into fashion. No longer did columns and pediments appear incompatible with new campus architecture. Added to this was the fact that between the 1970s and 1990s, the Law School and the Graduate Business School developed much more sophisticated fundraising systems, which unshackled their building programs from state budgets. While both schools enjoyed fuller coffers than ever before, they took remarkably different approaches to bringing Central Grounds to North Grounds. For the Business School, renamed the Colgate Darden Graduate School of Business Administration in 1975, the reclamation of the Academical Village was a straightforward process. Decamping to an adjacent hillside, the Darden School indulged itself in a grandiose, mass-produced vision of the Academical Village. The Law School was left with the challenge of transforming the old law-business complex into the new "Law Grounds": a prestigious setting where it could freely indulge the memory of the Rotunda and Clark Hall. While the desire to embrace the past would not go uncontested, ultimately the design limits imposed by the 1970s buildings helped pull the new complex back from complete surrender to nostalgia. Rather than succumb to a full masking over, the modern design of the original law-business com-

The Law Grounds expansion of 1995–97 provided the Law School with a new "front door" in the form of Clay Hall with its central Caplin Pavilion.

plex, with its deliberate accessibility, functionality, and focus on the future, fused with and moderated the renewed Jeffersonian impulse.

After its doors opened in September 1974, the new law building was in a state of near-constant change. This lack of stasis was largely due to the fact that Stubbins purposefully designed it as an unfinished product. Unlike Minor and Clark Halls, which opened as complete buildings, the North Grounds law building immediately stood ready for additions. During the planning process, it became clear that the Law School needed more square footage than it could afford at one time. Therefore Stubbins planned the structure in two phases so that it could be expanded as funds allowed. Paid for by private funds, phase II went up in 1977–78, turning the new law building back into a construction site.

Named for Walter L. Brown, an alumnus who helped establish the Law School Foundation, the Law School's private fundraising organization, the new addition was the Law School's first effort to fix the problems of phase I. Brown Hall provided the added square footage the Law School desired as well as some of the polish that the original structure lacked. Facing east, it abutted the rear of the original building. Constructed in the now-familiar combination of brick and concrete, Brown Hall was three stories, built downhill so that it stood at a level lower than phase I. Five large projecting bays on the second level dominated the facade. While it had even less in common with the classical building tradition than did the original structure, Brown Hall had a symmetrical rhythm of juts and voids and a huge pseudo-entablature not antagonistic to the architecture of ancient Greece and Rome. Overall, Brown Hall complemented but did not copy phase I. In fact, its design more closely resembled Campbell Hall, the new home of the School of Architecture, with its facade of large window bays.

Given its location behind the original structure, Brown Hall did little to change the exterior appearance of the law building, but it alleviated some of the interior plainness that students and faculty disliked about "No Name Hall." When Brown Hall opened in January 1979, the *Virginia Law Weekly* considered it much

superior to its adjoining "homely cousin," noting that "visitors who enter the Law School through Brown Hall are struck by the rich looks and pleasing aesthetics of the entrance hall and auditorium." Not only was Brown Hall more handsomely appointed than its neighbor, but it housed many new spaces, including a media center, interview rooms, a periodicals reading room, space for the new Oceans Law and Policy Center, and a four-hundred-plus seat auditorium with movable interior walls that could reapportion the space as needed. One writer for the *Virginia Law Weekly* reported that "if the popularity of a building can be measured by the number of students who willingly make use of it, Phase II has already become a spectacular success. In only two months, students have adopted it as a favorite place for study, relaxation and special activities." The new lounge with its overstuffed chairs became a "snooze room" for drowsy students. The building also featured an open-air interior courtyard, Moyston Court. Fully paved, with trees

Relying on private donations, the Law School constructed phase II of its North Grounds law building in 1977–78. Named Brown Hall, the new building had a cantilevered top floor with ribbon windows, projecting window bays, and slender concrete pilotis.

Moyston Court, named for law alumnus and donor Roy C. Moyston. The addition of phase II (at right) created the court, which abutted phase I (left). Left to right are Polly Dulaney, law alumnus Bernard Chamberlain, and Dean Emerson Spies, photographed during the dedication of the court c. 1979. The Caplin Reading Room replaced the underused Moyston Court during the 1990s renovations.

planted in wooden box planters, this area provided space for outdoor gatherings of students and faculty.[2]

Although Brown Hall was a success, the Law School had little luck when it came to remodeling the interiors of its original building, finally named Withers Hall in 1983. In 1980, the Law School attempted to improve the looks of the central concourse and student lounge with fresh paint, new wall treatments and furniture, and a reorganization of locker and coatroom space, but these changes failed to impress everyone. Despite the facelift, the *Virginia Law Weekly* concluded that "the infernal, internal Edifice Lex is left without flair or personality." In 1984, a private donor offered to pay for a redesign of the student lounge, and the Law School commissioned a plan that included a new semicircular brick-walled outdoor terrace. Expressing his support for the lounge redesign, law professor Edmund Kitch made familiar critiques of the appearance and layout of Withers Hall, hoping that changes to its "strongly functional and bureaucratic style" would improve the building's "impersonal and alienating atmosphere." Kitch had joined the faculty in 1982, and he had heard colleagues reminisce about the now almost mythical Clark Hall, with its "large public entrance hall where members of the community naturally gathered." Ultimately a lack of consensus between students and administrators killed the student lounge remodel. Nostalgia for the old building, however, would not die. Although nostalgia was understandably stronger among faculty and alumni than the student body, an afternoon of exploring piles of back issues led the editors of the *Virginia Law Weekly* in 1985 to express regret that "the bland glass and concrete structure that is Brown/Withers Hall does little to remind us of what went on in Clark Hall or in Minor Hall before that." The Law School found itself with the perennial problem of trying to improve a building limited by its utilitarian design and inextricably connected to its inhabitants' fond memories of Clark Hall.[3]

On the other side of the central mall, which landscape planners divided between a tangle of trees and bushes to the north and a brick-paved plaza to the south playfully known as "Red Square," the Darden School also sought to improve its functional building. Like the Law School, Darden had felt some regret in leaving Central Grounds. From its opening in 1955 until its reopening at North Grounds in 1975, Darden had occupied Monroe Hall, the red brick U-shaped building designed by the University's Architectural Commission. In a 1964 report on its future space requirements, the Graduate Business School concluded "that among the various alternative means of expansion that have been suggested the one that appears quickest, easiest, and cheapest . . . would be to convert Monroe Hall into a quadrangle. . . . This alternative would obviate the necessity of a large scale move of the School from one building to another."[4] A smaller and less established program than the Law School, Darden's low, straightforward building marked its secondary status at North Grounds. Compared to the law building, with its broadly cantilevered third story and play of angled first-story walls, the Darden building was plain. It consisted of two parts: a three-story main structure that formed a hollow square, with an open-air courtyard in the void, and a long two-story abutment. On the main building, thick concrete bands and tiers of brick-veneered wall delineated its three low stories. Paired windows, placed at regular intervals, punctuated the facade. At each corner, a concrete stair tower anchored the building to the ground. The main entry, opening to the east and located across from the front doors of the law building, consisted of a double row of the familiar concrete pilotis, through which visitors passed to gain access to the courtyard and two-story lobby. It was a basic structure that matched the law building's style and palette; its simplicity exemplified the limits of $3.36 million in 1975. During the move to

"Red Square," the brick-paved recreational area between the entrances to the law and Darden buildings.

THE LAW SCHOOL AT THE UNIVERSITY OF VIRGINIA

North Grounds, Darden's Dean C. Stewart Sheppard remarked, "It's going to be a continuing challenge to maintain the Jeffersonian spirit." Like the Law School, Darden would struggle with the intangibility of "the Jeffersonian spirit" and how exactly to recapture it at the new location.[5]

Whatever reservations the Darden School had about its move to North Grounds, it grew spectacularly on its new plot of land. With eight sixty-person amphitheater-style classrooms, eighteen group study rooms, and ninety faculty and staff offices, the new Darden building dwarfed Monroe Hall and provided capacity for a larger number of students and professors and a wider range of pro-

Architectural rendering of the Graduate School of Business Administration building, completed in 1975 at the new North Grounds complex.

grams. In only a few years, enrollment increased from approximately 280 to 480 students. While state support made this initial growth spurt possible, continued expansion relied on Darden's ability to raise large amounts of money independently. As was also true for the Law School, fundraising proved essential to growth at Darden in the late 1970s and beyond. In 1979, private donations paid for a new complex to the west, Sponsors Hall, a zigzagging brick hotel and dining facility designed to accommodate the school's residential executive education programs. The enterprise paid off; demand for space led Darden to expand the hotel from thirty-six to sixty rooms in 1984. Like the Law School's Brown Hall, Sponsors Hall was the Darden School's first foray into the scale of fundraising needed for major building projects. Its success sparked greater ambitions.[6]

In the late 1980s, when Darden turned its attention to renovating its original 1975 building, it got the attention of its neighbor across Red Square. Conscious of its success, Darden was looking for a way to dress up its uninteresting structure, seeking an "enhancement of the aesthetics of the Darden School exterior to reflect the national prominence befitting the school." Thomas H. Jackson, dean of the Law School from 1988 to 1991, appointed professor and law librarian Larry Wenger to attend meetings of the Darden School Building Committee and provide updates on the project. In February 1989, Wenger shared with Jackson the unusual scheme Darden proposed to enlarge and alter the appearance of its building. Providing a sketch, Wenger reported that "it involves five cubes, four of which would be attached to the Darden School and one to Sponsors Hall. These would be two to three stories high, and contain offices, student space and the like. . . . The two cubes at the lower left hand side of the existing Darden building would be connected by an atrium or something similar, to make a large lobby/entry way." The four cubes attached to the Darden Building radiated out from it in an arc in the direction of Sponsors Hall, playfully turned askew rather than set at right angles to the main building. With its lighthearted use of simple geometric forms, the design was too much for the University. In June, Wenger updated Jackson with "something in the way of gossip, the University's Architectural Review Committee rejected the preliminary designs for the additions to Darden. Apparently they don't like the idea of angular walls, and sent the proposal back for redrawing so that all additions are parallel to or at right angles to the existing building." The Law School likely looked on the plan's rejection with some relief, as part of the new construction would protrude out into the central mall area, placing the building closer to the Law School. Not only did law faculty and students resist the idea of Darden encroaching on the shared park, but the Law School was beginning to contemplate where a future phase III of its own building could go.[7]

As both the Law School and Darden considered new construction in the late 1980s, they made choices informed by political, cultural, and economic circumstances that were markedly different from the late 1960s, when the schools had planned the original law-business complex. The law, business, and JAG buildings brought to an end the brief period of modern architecture at the University that began with Gilmer Hall in 1963. The optimism and desire for newness that made modern buildings so desirable in the 1950s and 1960s ebbed as the promises of modernity proved elusive in the wake of renewed global conflict and economic uncertainty. Even as the brick and concrete of the North Grounds buildings went up, postmodernism was emerging as a reaction against the theoretical and aesthetic limits imposed by modernists. Although postmodernism was a term of varied meanings applied to interrogative and experimental movements in such diverse fields as literature, philosophy, music, and urban planning, postmodernism in architecture described a preference for difference over unity, a willingness to insert humor into design, and a rediscovery of history and ornamentation. Robert A. M. Stern, a New York–born architect who pioneered the use of the term *postmodernism* in his field, described it as an acceptance of the contradiction that "ours is a culture torn between the urge to jettison the past and start anew and the urge to link up in as many ways as possible with the past in order to ameliorate the impact of the radical changes science and technology have thrust upon us."[8] The lighthearted use of form in Darden's abandoned plan to attach cubes to its building was a postmodernist reaction to the formalism of the original structure. While in this instance architects chose to experiment with geometry in a contemporary way rather than look back to historical precedents, postmodernism's rejection of ahistoricism made the past again accessible for use in commercial, civic, and educational buildings. In the United States, the political and social conservatism of the Reagan era coupled with a rebounding economy in the mid-1980s created the right conditions for postmodernism, which was malleable enough to express exuberance, skepticism, wit, and nostalgia.

The University of Virginia, which had never lovingly embraced its modern buildings, easily fell in line with the postmodern rediscovery of historical precedents. This new license to pursue a Jeffersonian revival would have a significant impact on the campus; after a lull in the 1980s, construction boomed at the University in the 1990s and 2000s. Anticipating an upswing in building projects, the Buildings and Grounds Committee of the Board of Visitors released "A Vision Statement for the Planning and Design of the University of Virginia Buildings and Grounds" in 1991. In it the visitors directed that "the architectural legacy of the University of Virginia embodied in the Historic Academical Village should be reflected in the architecture of the University as a whole." Rather than an explicit style dictum, the statement provided a vague set of guidelines aimed at making the University more of an "ensemble" in keeping with the design philosophy behind the Academical Village. Referring to the hierarchy of Rotunda, pavilions, ranges, and gardens, the visitors emphasized the use of spatial and visual cues that made each part of the University "distinct while also allowing it to appear part of the larger whole to which it belongs." Even though the visitors made no mention of red brick or white columns, this desire for cohesion and deference to the Academical Village promoted a return to more classically inspired buildings and traditional building materials. Thus even though postmodernism began as a rejection of the perceived constraints and forced orthodoxy of modernism, it empowered a traditionalist impulse at UVa that sought conformity. The University had never eschewed its beloved red brick, but trademark Jeffersonian architectural elements such as semicircular arches, Tuscan columns, and double-sash windows returned, sometimes in a scale and quantity eclipsing anything in the Academical Village.[9]

In 1990, the Darden School decided to abandon its 1975 building altogether, giving it and the Law School space to contemplate new construction in a postmodernist idiom. At first, the Law School entertained no grandiose schemes of its own; it simply purchased the soon-to-be-vacated Darden building rather than move forward with its proposed phase III addition. Dean Jackson of the Law School conceded that this unexpected expansion was ill-fitting, explaining, "It would take some getting used to having two separate buildings, and the form and quality of the space in Darden is not of the kind that we would build were we to design and build ourselves." Meanwhile, freed of its outdated edifice, Darden lost no time pursuing an audacious building scheme. The school succeeded in securing a prime location in the woodlands to the west of its present structure, a site that the University had planned to use as intramural fields. After considering proposals by three architectural firms (finalists from an initial pool of twenty), Darden chose the most traditional scheme, submitted by Robert A. M. Stern, the well-known purveyor of postmodern design. Stern had already been the principal architect for one University structure, the Observatory Hill Dining Hall addition, a small building with paired Tuscan columns, pyramidal roofs, and a brick arcaded foundation. The plans for the Darden School were anything but modest; just the first phase of the building program anticipated five buildings encompassing over two hundred thousand square feet. As Stern's designs for the proposed "Darden Grounds" circulated, outraged faculty in the School of Architecture protested. For them, this aping of the fanlights, classical porticos, and columned loggias of Central Grounds was a bland derivative of the Academical Village. For Darden, being explicit was the point, and it proudly advertised its planned Jefferson-inspired buildings in its fundraising literature. Highlighting white columns, sloping roofs, and manicured lawns, the school assured alumni that "the exterior details bespeak quality."[10]

The fact that Darden and ultimately the Law School contemplated new construction programs at all speaks to transformations in the scale of American buildings over the preceding two decades. The growth in the size of campus buildings in the United States paralleled the corresponding aggrandizement of nearly all types of buildings in the country in the late 1980s and 1990s. As houses, stores, and hospitals got bigger, so did college classroom buildings and dormitories. Even in their initial, more modest proposals of attaching annexes to the 1970s structures, both schools sought a significant increase in square footage without corresponding growth in the student body. This was a significant change from the first iteration of North Grounds, which the University constructed with the purpose of admitting more applicants to its professional schools. Neither school had any plans to grow much beyond its current enrollment. For the Law School, this was about 1,200 students; for Darden around 480. While both the Law School and Darden sought to advance curricular goals through their added space, including lowering the student-faculty ratio, they also needed to house offices for swelling bureaucracies and reception areas for entertaining alumni donors. Thus not only the traditional design but the size and spatial arrangement of these new buildings would reflect the centrality of fundraising and alumni support to their respective missions.[11]

Darden's grand plans likely influenced the new dean of the Law School, Robert E. Scott, to reconsider simply renovating the interior of the old Darden building. Like Dean Lile and Dean Dillard before him, Scott wanted his ambitions for the Law School rendered in brick and mortar. A member of the faculty since 1974, he experienced the move to North Grounds and the regret of leaving Clark Hall and Central Grounds. He likewise had heard for years from faculty and alumni who bemoaned the new building and its location. But unlike the Darden School with its greenfield site, the Law School had no blank slate on which to erect a Jeffersonian fantasy. Instead, the Law School now had yet another 1970s building, and any new construction faced the difficult task of linking Withers-Brown and the Darden building. In letters to architectural firms in 1991, the Law School wrote that it wanted the buildings joined with "an aura of cohesion, symmetry and integration."[12] Achieving these qualities meant overcoming a series of practical obstacles: not only were the buildings two-hundred feet apart, but Withers Hall was significantly taller and larger than the Darden building. Withers also stood farther forward on the site. Further, Withers Hall with its large cantilevered top story would be virtually impossible to mask if the Law School wanted a symmetrical composition.

Preliminary ideas for a scheme to join the buildings came from Alan Dynerman, a graduate of the School of Architecture and founding partner in the firm of Williams & Dynerman of Washington, D.C. Beyond simply linking the buildings, Dynerman had to come up with a central addition that acknowledged their modern lines while updating them in a postmodern way. Produced in February 1992, his proposal joined the buildings at the most logical point, their front entrances, which directly faced each other across Red Square. The connecting link was a raised terrace, partially covered by a pergola that alluded to classical precedents but used square piers modeled on the pilotis of the existing buildings. To handle the problem of changes in elevation and to provide the Law School with additional square footage ("permitting its curriculum to flower," as the Law School wrote in its letter to various architects), Dynerman situated the terrace on a cryptoporticus or semi-subterranean passageway.[13] This structure was similar in function, if not in appearance, to those at the Academical Village and Monticello. Across the south side of the cryptoporticus ran a series of shallow arches containing windows and doors. The design was balanced but not fully symmetrical. Keeping in mind the inherent imbalance between the original buildings, Dynerman inserted a bit of irregularity: as access to the buildings required that pedestrians easily reach the walkway atop the cryptoporticus, Dynerman provided two sets of front steps but with different orientations. While one set rose in a straightforward manner perpendicular to the walkway, the other ran parallel to it, splaying out as it descended to ground level. Altogether, the pergola was a modest solution to the problem of joining the buildings, leaving the original structures fully intact.[14]

Scott was unhappy with the Dynerman plan and began contemplating more costly and substantial schemes for uniting the buildings. Although rejected by

"Law Grounds" as imagined by architect Alan Dynerman consisted of a pergola atop a cryptoporticus that linked the original law and Darden buildings. Williams & Dynerman, architects, 1992.

the dean, the Dynerman plan did prove useful as the Law School initiated the substantial fundraising that an even grander expansion required. As law professor Kent Sinclair explained to his colleagues, the Dynerman renderings served an important purpose, "mainly to have something to show alumni . . . [including] some of the large potential donors. Essentially these drawings are intended to say that there are lots of possibilities for harmonizing the two buildings and making them work efficiently for the Law School." As was also true for Darden, fundraising proved essential to the Law School's building program. Private money allowed both schools to operate independently of limited (and possibly unavailable) state funds. As Darden considered the funding strategy for its new complex, it benefited enormously from a change in Virginia state law that allowed private firms to develop projects at state-owned colleges and universities. This meant that Darden's fundraising arm, the private Darden School Foundation, could act as the developer, directly funneling money from donors into the building program. The Law

THE LAW GROUNDS
THE UNIVERSITY OF VIRGINIA

WILLIAMS & DYNERMAN ARCHITECTS   JUNE 1992

The proposed "Law Grounds" pergola featured concrete pilotis in the style of those used by Hugh Stubbins on the 1970s buildings. Williams & Dynerman, architects, 1992.

School, which likewise handled its fundraising through the private Law School Foundation, planned the same course of action.[15]

Although the Law School had a long history of soliciting alumni donations, the large-scale fundraising that Dean Scott set out to accomplish now was unlike anything the school had done before. Fortunately for Scott, the Law School Foundation had become much more sophisticated in its fundraising abilities, as had fundraising throughout higher education. Prior to the establishment of the Law School Foundation in 1952, the University conducted all fundraising for the Law School. William Andrews Clark Jr.'s gift of $350,000 had come about through his personal exchanges with Dean Lile, but the transaction itself went through President Alderman. Following World War II, as the University's fundraising efforts became more organized, the new University of Virginia Development Fund included the million-dollar "Law Can Lead the Way" campaign, which the Law School hoped would fund a new wing at Clark Hall, a new professorship, scholarships, and fellowships. The limited success of University fundraising in providing aid to the Law School encouraged the school's alumni association to set up a private foundation, which gave the school a legal means to accept and administer gifts directly. At the time of its establishment, Dean F. D. G. Ribble lauded the foundation as "a trust utterly free from any state control." Even then, the Law School's fundraising tended to be somewhat haphazard. The foundation began its annual fund drives in 1965 to encourage continuous financial support, as opposed to seeking only occasional gifts or one-time bequests. In 1968, the Law School Foundation became a nonstock corporation, which provided a more versatile format for managing its leadership and investments. Each of these changes followed national trends in fundraising as universities and departments across the nation sought out better ways to secure alumni dollars. The Law School Foundation was unequipped to raise funds for the entire North Grounds project in the 1970s, but it did raise the $2.5 million needed for Brown Hall. A second campaign in the early 1980s raised $12.5 million. Even so, the scale of fundraising Dean Scott now considered in order to expand and beautify the law complex was unprecedented in the Law School's history.[16]

Given the importance of their donations, alumni's ideas, memories, and feelings about the Law School played an important role in this latest law building project. As architectural historian Daniel Bluestone has pointed out, the reliance on private donations, especially the large donations of a few very wealthy donors, had implications for the design of both the law and Darden complexes. Both schools recognized that their alumni tended to favor traditional buildings. In the case of the Law School, older alumni had fond memories of Clark Hall. The promotional text that accompanied the Dynerman renderings conveyed a raison d'etre for new construction that had broad appeal; this was not simply the practical union of two educational buildings but the symbolic reunion of the Law School and Central Grounds. The new "Law Grounds" would be a "contemporary academical village." Here was the chance to recover a lost "sense of place and beauty that Thomas Jefferson thought was so vital," to restore "the feeling of Clark Hall and the main grounds, a prospect that gives us all a sense of genuine excitement and urgency." Such nostalgic language accompanied all phases of the subsequent fundraising and building program and shaped the design process.[17]

While the importance of private fundraising distinguished Law Grounds from Minor, Clark, and Withers-Brown, the four projects shared the fact that with each, the Law School saw its new building as both a ladder to the future and an anchor to the past. This dichotomy was, of course, true of the University broadly. Harry W. Porter Jr., dean of the School of Architecture, recognized the importance of this binary when he wrote to Dean Scott with his ideas for the expansion: "The primary design objective is to achieve a setting for the School which signals its national prominence and which links it to the architectural traditions of the University of Virginia. As you know, the Board of Visitors has adopted a 'Vision Statement' for the buildings and grounds of the University which stresses the importance of creating conditions throughout the University which reflect the legacy of Mr. Jefferson's academical village (without copying)." This input, while providing no specifics on what exactly the Law School should build, reinforced the sense that a traditionalist approach was the right one to take, and that the

Law School's "national prominence" was once again at stake as it embarked upon another major building campaign.[18]

In early 1993, the Law School interviewed five architectural firms. Williams & Dynerman returned, along with several firms known for college architecture, including Perry Dean Rogers & Partners of Boston and Ayers Saint Gross Inc. of Baltimore. Ayers Saint Gross was already involved in the Darden project, hired by the building committee there to assist Stern. Their role in this large project, along with their work for the University on proposed renovations to Newcomb Hall, helped land them the Law School commission. The Law School was likely drawn to the firm partly because of their experience in updating aging educational facilities. At Delaware the firm overhauled the combined 152,000 square feet of the Colonial Revival Brown Laboratory and its 1973 Drake Hall annex and added a 65,000-square-foot wing, designed in a stripped red-brick, gabled-roof style sympathetic to the surrounding campus. At Johns Hopkins, they completed a huge new physics and astronomy building, which was likewise "built of materials familiar to the campus and used in a conventional fashion." Although not a revivalist building, the structure complemented the Classical Revival Homewood Campus with its historic Federal-style Homewood house. Ayers Saint Gross was part of the postmodern trend in college architecture of building huge structures designed to proclaim both an investment in the future and a reverence for the past. This was just what Dean Scott wanted for the Law School: a design that could do more than simply merge the 1970s law and Darden buildings in a practical way.[19]

In its planning, analysis, and programming report submitted during the interview process, Ayers Saint Gross argued that they could successfully cater to a sense of Central Grounds nostalgia while creating buildings that lacked nothing in space, shine, or convenience. This approach not only played to the Board of Visitors, who had made clear their desire to venerate Jefferson, but also to the Law School, where the denigration of Withers Hall had become something of an institutional pastime. Through their work at the Darden School and Newcomb Hall, the firm had "gained a great respect for the 'Founders Vision'" that would enable them to transfigure the Law School in a way "both modern in approach to the problems of our time, and traditional in adherence to the physical concepts which founded the University." Mindful of audience, Ayers Saint Gross vowed to achieve this proper balance between past and future; "only then, if Mr. Jefferson could look down from his mountain top at the School of Law, would he be proud." Of course it was impossible to know what Jefferson would think if he gazed down from Monticello some 166 years after his death and spied a campus full of the architectural fashions of a century and a half rendered in red brick and white trim. But this tactic of imagining what would please Mr. Jefferson was an easy sell. The firm was repeating a pitch that the University had made to itself and others many times before.[20]

The Ayers Saint Gross proposal acknowledged the specificity of the Law School's connection to Central Grounds. The Law School had a long history that Darden did not. Monroe Hall, Darden's original home on Central Grounds, had been built to house social sciences some twenty-five years before the new Graduate School of Business Administration moved in. The planned Darden complex communicated this reality; founded late in the history of the University, the Darden School established its connection to that history by appropriating the Academical Village. By comparison, the Law School was one of the original schools of the University, and it regarded its years in Clark Hall as its halcyon days. Recognizing this fact, Ayers Saint Gross held up Clark Hall alongside Jefferson's architecture as the Law School's gold standard. Forgotten were Clark Hall's cramped corners and echoes, its rats and fleshy murals. The firm argued that "for the School of Law, perhaps only during the period following 1932 with the dedication of Clark Hall and the move from Minor Hall, was there a 'coincidence of quality' among the academic curriculum, the faculty, and the physical facilities." Thus it was not simply the spirit of Central Grounds generally but Clark Hall specifically that needed to be conjured up at Law Grounds. The more recent past, with its regrettable architecture, would be hidden by new construction that recalled a golden age: "Symbolic and meaningful spaces such as Memorial Hall [Mural Hall] in Clark Hall . . . should replace those memories of 'Red Square' and 'Withers High.'" What Ayers Saint Gross offered the Law School was a way to recast its own history through the experience of space. Through architecture, the Law School could revisit an idealized past, seemingly stripped of its imperfections, and cast the less romantic sensibilities of Withers Hall to the shadows.[21]

Given the limitations imposed by the existing structures, bringing Central Grounds to North Grounds was a problem. Only at enormous expense could the architects have completely obscured the original buildings. The Law School's need to renovate classroom, office, and library spaces during the expansion precluded any possibility of this expensive folly. Yet given Scott's insistence on something larger than a pergola, the question of how to merge new and old was more challenging than ever. In early 1993, during the interview process for the Law Grounds project, Ayers Saint Gross submitted four studies for linking the buildings in ways that created a "memorable environment." The simplest resembled the Dynerman plan: a loggia crossed the site of Red Square and joined the buildings at their main entrances. This plan relied more on landscaping than architecture to achieve a Central Grounds–like atmosphere. The firm removed the driveway and motor court at the front of the building, replacing them with a hedge-lined lawn; to the rear of the connector, the wild assortment of trees and flowering shrubs known as the Spies Garden (named for Emerson Spies, dean of the Law School from 1976–80) became a more formal landscape with a wide lawn. A second plan likewise left the existing buildings largely as they were but bridged the gap between them with an enclosed connector, with a small pavilion topped with a pyramidal roof and lantern at its center. This walk-through linked the buildings at a point slightly behind their present entries. Again the driveway and motor court were removed and replaced with a lawn, though in this plan a U-shaped covered walkway connected the complex to Massie Road. Presumably this feature would have called to mind the covered walkways of the Academical Village, though Ayers Saint Gross did not press the point with chinoiserie railings.[22]

The third and fourth designs required more extensive changes to the buildings.

The "Spies Garden," named for Law School Dean Emerson Spies, consisted of the handful of trees that survived the construction of the complex and newly planted trees and shrubs. By the 1990s, large azalea bushes dominated the plantings. During the "Law Grounds" renovations of 1995–97 this area became a formal courtyard with few surviving remnants of its wilder days.

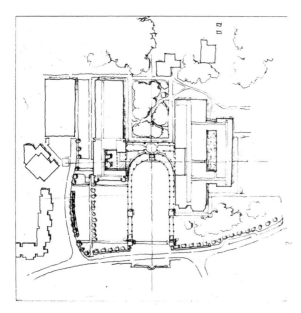

This proposal for a connecting link between the law and Darden buildings was the second of four designs produced by Ayers Saint Gross in early 1993. Ultimately this plan most closely resembled the final design for the expanded Law Grounds.

In both, the architects sought to correct the problem of the fronts of the buildings not lining up; Withers-Brown stood much closer to Massie Road than did the Darden building. In one design, new additions to the fronts of both buildings made them line up properly and look more alike. This also masked the bulbous protrusions on the south side of Withers Hall that Stubbins had used to express the presence of the irregularly shaped classrooms inside. As these modifications would be expensive, the architects linked the buildings with a simple U-shaped open-air walkway that ran alongside both buildings and connected in the rear, through the site of the Spies Garden. The fourth design was the most unusual. While leaving the exterior of Withers Hall largely the same, the plan gave the Darden building a front addition bringing it closer to the road and a fanciful stepped clock tower that resembled a miniature version of the famed Lighthouse at Alexandria. It was

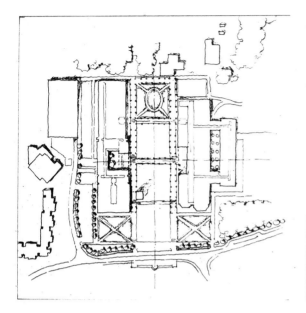

only this design that seemed to embrace the asymmetry of the complex. Similar to the third plan, this design also called for covered walkways between the buildings as well as a formal landscape of lawns and boxwood parterres. After winning the job, it was up to Adam Gross, the principal-in-charge; Luanne Greene, the project architect; and their team at Ayers Saint Gross to determine which of these solutions, if any, was the right one for the design problem.[23]

Perhaps because students often became vocal about building projects only after a planning stage was over, Dean Scott hoped to get them involved immediately. The student turnout to a design meeting arranged by Scott with Adam Gross, however, was "anemic." Although the students in attendance focused much of the discussion on concerns specific to them, such as interview rooms, parking, and lockers, they also offered ideas about the connecting link between the buildings. Ideally it

Another proposal for the Law School expansion by Ayers Saint Gross included a stepped clock tower and modest covered links between the buildings.

would not be simply a passage but a place of interaction, both among students and between students and faculty. Alcoves could facilitate "after-class exchanges and questions." Scott and Gross took notes of these suggestions, which supported the notion that the connecting link should be the new "front door" of the Law School rather than merely a passageway.[24]

In March 1993, the *Virginia Law Weekly* reported on the success of the Law School's new capital campaign, launched the previous July. Already the campaign had brought in enormous sums of money. In the 1980s and 1990s, the capital campaign grew in importance to become a primary fundraising tool of universities. They were useful in generating major gifts because they ran for a certain number of years, lending a sense of urgency to annual giving drives. Institutions usually tied to them to major initiatives. Capital campaigns also simplified fundraising by including all gifts given during the time of the campaign. Therefore, rather than raise money for numerous discrete causes, colleges and universities held years-long capital campaigns, with donors designating certain uses for funds. At the end of a capital campaign (the Law School's would run until 2000), institutions could tout an impressive lump sum of earnings rather than various smaller amounts. Thus the Law School's 1992–2000 capital campaign covered all types of donations and projects, though the Law Grounds project was the face and force behind the effort. Using Law Grounds promotional materials targeted at alumni who had attended classes in Clark Hall, the Law School outpaced fundraising benchmarks, amassing $16 million in pledges in nine months. The *Virginia Law Weekly* wrote that the success of the capital campaign "enlarge[d] the scope of possibilities" for expansion, reporting that "anything, in fact, everything can be changed in designing the new Law School, and absolutely nothing has been set in stone in terms of architectural plans."[25]

Indeed, the influx of funds meant that the Law School could pursue a more substantial building program, and over the course of 1993 the connecting link between Withers Hall and the Darden building became the centerpiece of the design and the primary vehicle for recovering the lost essence of Clark Hall and

Central Grounds. The Law School chose the second Ayers Saint Gross proposal, although the plan changed considerably with time. Gross and Greene moved the central pavilion forward, joining the older buildings at their current main entries. In the firm's master plan for Law Grounds, delivered to the Law School that September, the pavilion appeared as the new "front door" of the complex. The inspiration for the design of the new pavilion was Clark Hall, although there were also allusions to the Rotunda and Monticello. The pavilion was a boxy structure with a straightforward facade dominated by six square piers, a simplified interpretation of Clark Hall's Corinthian hexastyle portico. Reminiscent of Clark's classic entablature and marble attic, a heavy lintel topped the pavilion's piers. Set to the rear portion of the pavilion, an attic story rose to a pyramid roof, another allusion to Clark. Gross, however, chose to cap his pyramid with a lantern, which not only gave the structure additional height but provided a vague reference to the oculus of

This study by Ayers Saint Gross for the new structure connecting the law and the Darden buildings expanded on the firm's earlier proposal for a central pavilion linked to the older buildings with one-story hyphens. Although this version is more substantial than the previous conception, the final plan called for a still taller, more massive structure.

the Rotunda. As was true with the oculus, the lantern would light a lofty interior space. In this case, that space was a formal reception hall for alumni events. Thus spaces for entertaining alumni, unknown in the three previous Law School buildings, became the centerpiece of the donor-funded Law Grounds. On either side of the pavilion, low hyphens provided connections to the older buildings. This was a hierarchical, horizontal arrangement of spaces, again inspired by Clark Hall.[26]

Encouraged by David A. Harrison III, a major donor for Law Grounds, the central pavilion became an even more prominent feature of the design. When Scott presented the plan to the Law School Foundation Building Advisory Committee, the pavilion design garnered enthusiastic approval, particularly from Harrison, a member of the committee and a 1941 graduate of the Law School. A retired investment banker then living at his Flowerdew Hundred plantation on the James River, Harrison contributed $5 million to the building program in 1992. Scott assured Harrison in familiar language that his gift "could create the sense of 'place' which has been missing since the Law School left Clark Hall," and Harrison was one of the many alumni who fondly recalled the Law School's old home on Central Grounds. His gift not only prompted the Law School to attach his name to the Law Grounds project (as of 2017, the North Grounds law complex remains the David A. Harrison III Law Grounds), but it also gave Harrison much weight in the design process. Like William Andrews Clark Jr. before him, Harrison had a love of art and architecture, and his gift allowed the Law School to be as ambitious as he and Scott wanted. Harrison in particular wanted the pavilion made larger. In a subsequent redesign, which by summer 1994 emerged as the final drawing, the Ayers Saint Gross team made the pavilion heftier and more visually interesting. They gave the building a broader face, stepping back the ends of the portico to provide the facade a greater sense of depth. The attic and pyramid were set slightly higher so that the pavilion was clearly taller than both Withers Hall and the Darden building, commanding more attention. Even so, the architects were careful not to make the pavilion appear too massive; although tall, it read from the front as a single story (which, aside from utility spaces, it was). In this regard, the design drew inspiration from Monticello. The pyramidal top, set back on the building and easily reimagined as a dome, likewise invited comparisons to Jefferson's home and the Rotunda. Seeing the plans, a writer for the *Virginia Law Weekly* referred to the pavilion as "a Rotunda-like building."[27]

Using massing, symmetry, a central portico, and a pyramidal roof, Ayers Saint Gross had managed to design a new face for the Law School that referenced cherished buildings of the past. But the firm did so without ignoring the style and materials of the older structures. Gross credited the "benign" quality of Withers Hall and the Darden building with making this challenge less daunting; he shared his perspective that "there are more destructive examples of bad architecture that would have been more difficult to fix than these buildings." In their plainness, Withers Hall and the former Darden building were easy enough to push to the background, particularly as the new hyphens would plow into the original fronts to the buildings, disguising their central features and orientation. As both buildings were quite large, especially Withers, Gross and his team wisely chose not to "reface them in some kind of literal Jeffersonian garb," calling the potential effect "absurd." However, the firm acknowledged the existing buildings by avoiding a Tuscan-columned pavilion with white double-sash windows that appeared blithely unaware of its hulking neighbors. Rather, they let the horizontality and palette of the older buildings shape the expansion. The new construction was classical, but it was the stripped, blocky classicism of many 1930s commercial buildings

The final study for the expanded Law Grounds building.

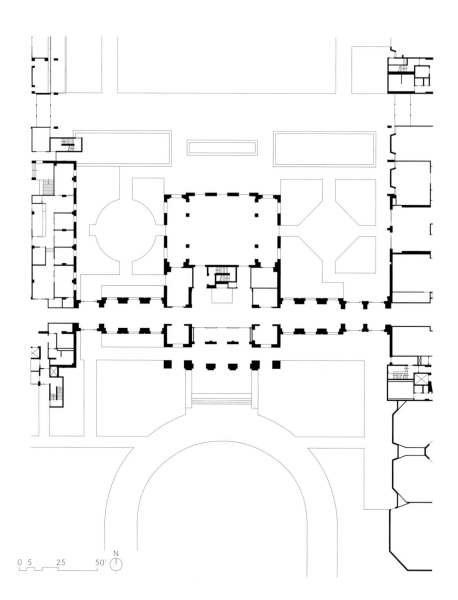

Floor plan, final
study for the Law
Forum (later Caplin
Pavilion) and South
Link (later Clay Hall)
in the expanded Law
Grounds building.

0 5   25   50'   N

(aside from Mural Hall, Clark Hall's interiors had been decorated in a similarly bare, functional classicism). There were no curves, decorative capitals, or dentils, and no white; instead the Ayers Saint Gross team chose smooth blocks and bands of cast gray limestone that complemented the stretches of concrete used by Stubbins. While a contrast in color and style would have called attention to the older buildings, the design subdued them by pulling the eye away from Withers and the Darden building and toward the central pavilion, which enabled the new structure to preside over Law Grounds like a diminutive Rotunda.[28]

Working through this balancing act of old and new, Ayers Saint Gross succeeded in conveying to its target audience an impending transfiguration of North Grounds, where the old would be made new and the past readily accessible. Writing with enthusiasm on the new master plan of the project, the *Virginia Law Weekly* asked students to "envision the new Law Grounds. Two tree-lined walkways leading north from Massie Road separated by a gently sloping lawn. The picture evokes The Lawn of the Central Grounds in its symmetry and proportions. And columns!" The new price tag was $26 million.[29]

Nearby, the Darden School was enjoying the abundant financial support of its alumni and other donors who were likewise taken with its own interpretation of Central Grounds and Jeffersonian classicism. By the time of its new building dedication in March 1996, the school's Campaign for Darden had raised $76.5 million. Completed in December 1995, the five buildings of the $37-million first phase of the project all displayed various configurations of Jeffersonian elements. The main building, Saunders Hall, was a cruciform structure dominated by a colossal portico made up of four Tuscan columns and a pediment with fanlight. Although the colors and details of the building looked much like those of Central Grounds, Saunders Hall bore a closer resemblance to James Madison's Montpelier (which also had a large Tuscan portico, likely suggested by Thomas Jefferson) than to Central Grounds. To the southwest, Saunders Hall opened onto a rectangular lawn lined with six identical pavilions, connected by open-air columned passageways. Here was a more obvious effort to convey the spirit of the Lawn, although

Flagler Academic Court, Darden School, 1995.

Stern bypassed porticos and pediments. Each pavilion had a large arched opening in front that framed an entryway with one-story Tuscan columns and an upper piazza with chinoiserie railings reminiscent of those used by Jefferson. Overhead were hipped roofs and dentil cornices. Yet the Flagler Academic Court, as Darden called its lawn, was not the point of arrival as Jefferson designed his Lawn to be; it was greenspace tucked to the side of the complex, invisible to passersby. As was true of the original law-business complex, Darden was an automobile campus; Saunders Hall's entry portico faced a driveway leading up from Massie Road. A gatehouse in red brick and white columns signaled an effort to make the long roadway more inviting and pedestrian. Critics lampooned the complex. Defending his creation, Stern countered: "We tried to make a deliberate Jeffersonian scheme here. If not here, where?"[30]

Although Law Grounds and Darden Grounds differed in their approach to historicism, both complexes took the open concept of the Academical Village and made it private. Darden did so by turning its new, treeless lawn to the side; the Law School did so by walling in its once open central mall. While the Law Grounds "south link" with its new pavilion closed the central mall in one direction, a simpler "north link" did so at the opposite end, uniting Withers Hall and the Darden building in the rear. This, Dean Scott said, would "serve the aesthetic function of 'closing' the outdoor 'room' that will consist of the reconfigured Spies Garden." Like Scott, Gross desired a more orderly and cloistered outdoor atmosphere; he called the Spies Garden "more of a dense garden or small forest" than a deliberate landscape. Further he described Red Square and the front approach to the complex as having "never been developed as spaces that have any kind of human scale or enclosure. They just bleed out." The architect turned to early plans of Oxford, Harvard, and Yale for ideas on how to design "a very clear, understandable outdoor space" and developed an interior courtyard with a central lawn surrounded by walks, which were in turn surrounded by walls. This alteration drew some parallels with the closing of the Lawn at Central Grounds in 1898, as both complexes had originally been designed to be physically and symbolically open and were now shut in. This pulling in was a continuation of the long trend in the history of the Law School. Even with their proximity to the Academical Village, both Minor Hall and Clark Hall had signaled the Law School's retreat into its own hallowed halls. Now at Law Grounds, with Darden removed to its Jeffersonian fantasy on an adjacent hilltop, the Law School could even consume the landscape, pulling lawns and trees behind closed doors.[31]

In the fall of 1995, Dean Scott hosted the "Last Party in Red Square," a send-off reminiscent of the "Last Tango in Mural Hall," before workers bulldozed the plaza into a construction site. Fliers invited students to "take one last look before

The Law Grounds pavilion under construction, from the *Virginia Law Weekly*, March 29, 1996.

Red Square is history!" Law Grounds was, in fact, a triumph of American capitalism: from the rubble of Red Square rose the framework of a multimillion-dollar building paid for by private donors, built to look something like the architectural works of a Founding Father. A year later, the *Virginia Law Weekly* exclaimed with unintentional irony "Eat Your Heart Out Frank Lloyd Wright" when it published a photograph of the "large Rotunda-esque" central pavilion under construction. Although observers may not have realized it, the rising form of the Rotunda-like pavilion made tangible the layering, masking, and retelling of history at the complex as it obliterated all traces of Red Square beneath its mass.[32]

Yet the history told by the new Clay Hall, as the Law School named the "south link," would not go entirely uncontested. Although Clay Hall was no Mural Hall, this new south link of Law Grounds had something in common with the older space: Clay Hall's builders designed it to showcase art. At first, the walls were bare. In December 1996, students and faculty could finally walk through the long, newly finished corridor of Clay Hall to either Withers Hall or the old Darden building (newly renovated and renamed Slaughter Hall). With its large windows on both the north and south sides, Clay Hall was "bright and sunny" and inviting, with "two mini-lounges and window benches where many law students have been seen pretending to study." Not until January 1997, however, was Clay Hall sufficiently complete to receive its long-intended fin-

The Law Grounds pavilion nearly completed, 1997.

ishing touch: the portraits of the former deans of the School of Law. During the planning stages of the expansion project, the Law School had decided to hang the eight oil paintings here, and Ayers Saint Gross designed the building with sizable bays between the windows to accommodate the portraits. The oldest of the paintings was the portrait of William Minor Lile, done in 1922 by Prince Pierre Troubetzkoy, a Russian-born aristocrat then living in Virginia; the remainder enjoyed less colorful histories. Together with paintings of other Law School notables, the early deans' portraits cycled through Clark Hall, mainly hung high on the walls of the library, before they were packed up, moved to North Grounds, and rehung in the new library. It was now a tradition that each dean be painted; the eighth por-

Clay Hall, 1997, showing the newly hung deans' portraits.

trait, of Thomas H. Jackson, arrived in 1992. Formerly hanging inconspicuously on a wall in the second floor library reading room, the portraits now enjoyed a place of honor in the new building.[33]

But not everyone was enthusiastic about this decorating scheme; controversy began as soon as the eight paintings went up in Clay Hall. Students assigned a variety of epithets to the space, including "Pale Male Hall" and "Dead White Male Hall," even though two former deans, Richard Merrill and Thomas Jackson, were still living and Merrill was teaching at the Law School. In a letter to the *Virginia Law Weekly,* law student Nina McAdoo opined that while "it is an historical fact that all of the Law School's deans have been white males . . . one is not sure that the focal point of the new entrance to our Law School should highlight that fact as if it were the defining characteristic of our Law School. . . . The point is that having portraits of a bunch of (mostly dead) white males on the wall of the grand new entranceway to the Law School sends a message that women and people of color are not really a part of U.Va. Law." In an op-ed, student Helen Wan recalled that she "felt physically sick" when she saw workers hanging the portraits. Wan was currently reading *Women Lawyers: Rewriting the Rules* by Harvard law alumna Mona Harrington, who recalled of her own law school environment: "Backing up the faculty as authority figures are the portraits. High on the walls of the classrooms, large oil paintings of legal luminaries stare down—bewigged English jurists, black-robed American judges, deans, professors, and other notable lawyers in three-piece suits, vests stretching across ample stomachs." Harrington told of one Harvard law alumna who, years after graduation, left a conference at her alma mater early, saying, "I could just feel the atmosphere closing in on me again. . . . I was just struck by the total maleness of the place." Inspired by Harrington to speak out, Wan used her legal training to argue against the placement of the portraits in Clay Hall: "To those who still remain unconvinced that the placement of these portraits in the main hallway is chilling, even downright offensive, to some inhabitants of our school, I would ask you to consider that even the law of sexual harassment explicitly acknowledges two forms of this discrimination: *quid pro quo* harassment and hostile environment harassment. If these portraits, placed front and center, don't contribute to such an environment at the Law School, I don't know what would." Wan, like other protesters, was not against the portraits themselves but their conspicuous placement; she wanted them returned to the library.[34]

The deans' portraits controversy of January and February 1997 was a battle over the memory enshrined in the new building and how that story of the past would shape the Law School's present and future. The number of women and minorities at the Law School, which had grown substantially since the Clark Hall days, meant that the school was no longer the place fondly remembered by many alumni. While some looked back warmly on the Law School of the 1940s, 1950s, and 1960s, others saw the Law School's past primarily as a time of white privilege. Considering that the designers of the 1970s law building had prioritized accessibility and modernity over history, some observers interpreted the Clay Hall portraits and surrounding architecture as the reintroduction of an elitist, exclusive past to the present-day facility. Writing in the *Virginia Law Weekly,* law student David Lieb argued, "Viewing the portraits in the context of the surrounding architecture may provide additional clues as to why those paintings have left some uneasy. . . . The invocation of the past does not stop with the paintings but extends to the whole architectural statement of the hall. The architecture in its precise symmetry implies an ordered world, and in its classical forms and proportions, a past order. That sense of past order is underscored by the presence of the paintings, which with their uniform and perfect fit to each wall space—it is as if the walls were designed with the portraits in mind—punctuate the statement with a sense of completeness."[35]

Not everyone agreed with this understanding of the portraits. Law student Paul McCoy told the Charlottesville *Daily Progress* that he found it "hard . . . to believe that people can genuinely be offended by any portraits of people sitting down fully clothed. . . . The reality is that these are people who did a lot of nice things for the school." He was among a number of people in the Law School community who voiced their disapproval of the protests. Law professor Earl C. Dudley Jr. wrote to the *Virginia Law Weekly* that while he took "a back seat to no one in the Law School on the question of commitment to racial, ethnic, and gender diversity," he thought students should remember that they "are all, in very personal ways, the beneficiaries of the work of each of the Deans whose portraits have been hung." Nevertheless the controversy continued into February; the *New York Times,* the

Chronicle of Higher Education, and the *Richmond Times-Dispatch* picked up the story. Some coverage, including that in the *New York Times,* pointed out that the Law School had not admitted women until the 1920s and African Americans until the 1950s. While hardly unique, these facts were not the information the Law School and University administration wanted attached to the impending debut of the multimillion-dollar expansion.[36]

Soon, however, these challenges to the hegemony of the Law School's architectural and decorative expression of its past came to an end. The strength of a golden age narrative proved more powerful than its detractors. Seeking a compromise, law student Christine Ellertson circulated a petition addressed to Dean Scott, asking "that you prominently display pictures, photographs or other signs in or around Clay/Buckner Link to show that more diverse populations have played important roles at UVA Law School." Ellertson raised concerns that "prospective students that wander the halls will wonder whether this school is an old boys' haven." Scott's response to the petition was gracious and conciliatory, though he refused to apologize for his historicist approach to Law Grounds. He was already working to add diversity to the portraits, commissioning a painting of the first female graduate of the Law School, Elizabeth Tompkins. The deans' portraits remained in Clay Hall. In his response to Ellertson, he used familiar language:

> The deans' portraits in Clay Hall are part of a wider effort to recover, through architecture, what was left behind when the Law School moved from Clark Hall to its present site in 1974. Many alumni who had spent their law school years in Clark Hall never felt a part of the North Grounds setting. The Law Grounds project is intended to reawaken a pride of place in our surroundings, to recapture something of the stirring architecture of Central Grounds. Clay Hall's facade is a postmodern interpretation of Clark Hall's entrance. The Holcombe Green Lawn now taking shape between Clay Hall and Massie Road will remind us of the Lawn that students once crossed daily. In these and other ways, those who have nurtured the current expansion and reno-

vation have sought to tie our physical surroundings to a great tradition that reaches back to the first law classes on the Lawn.

Noting on February 7 that the debate seemed to be "dying down," the *Virginia Law Weekly* concluded that "what remains . . . is the difficulty of creating an atmosphere in Clay Hall that combines the legacy of our past, and all it entails, with the reality of our present and vision of our future." Of course this had been a central problem at the University since the late nineteenth century.[37]

If the University of Virginia School of Law was guilty of attempting to shake off its midcentury modern lines in order to tell a different story about itself, it was not alone among law schools. Across the country in the 1990s, law schools replaced, defaced, or disguised the buildings of the 1960s and 1970s of which they had once been so proud. As new generations perceived this once contemporary architecture as ugly and old-fashioned, they looked for ways to reduce its visual impact in cities and suburbs and on college campuses. Between 1992 and 1999, the University of North Carolina School of Law expanded its building to hide the modern lines of Van Hecke-Wettach Hall. The new face of the school was a large symmetrical postmodernist building with an eight-columned circular temple as its entryway. In 1993–96, Columbia Law School sought to mitigate the aggressively midcentury modernist architecture of its building by adding a sleek aluminum-and-glass expansion that abutted the New York City sidewalk. The College of Law at Florida State University disguised its 1960s B. K. Roberts Hall with the surprising D'Alemberte Rotunda, a domed postmodernist play on Jefferson's famed building.

Regardless of one's perspective on the merits of the new Law Grounds complex, by the time the project was concluding in fall 1997 it would have been difficult not to be impressed with the scale of the renovation. The Law School building had doubled in size and now consisted of a quadrangle of 311,382 square feet. Withers Hall retained its long concourse and range of irregular octagonal classrooms, but nearly the entire structure had received a facelift. Perhaps the most striking change in the original Withers-Brown structure was the remodeling of the damp, underused Moyston Court into the Caplin Reading Room (see color gallery). Handsome, high-ceiled, and cherry-paneled, this new reading room helped relieve the library of evidence of its bare-bones origins. Extensive remodeling in the newly dubbed Slaughter Hall and the third floor of Withers, along with the new north and south links, created four new classrooms, four new seminar rooms, twenty-two new faculty offices, two new moot court rooms, over a thousand new full-size student lockers, and a variety of new study spaces. Outside, landscapers planted over four hundred new trees, including fifty-seven willow oaks, eighteen summit white ashes, eleven black gums, four Kentucky coffee trees, and four yellow woods. Lucky survivors of the expansion included nine old trees in the greatly changed Spies Garden that had survived the initial construction in the early 1970s. Removing the masses of azaleas and rhododendrons that characterized the irregular plantings of the first Spies Garden, the Landscape Committee created a much more formal outdoor area, with two geometric boxwood gardens on either side of the Caplin Pavilion (the new name of the center pavilion, which, like the eponymous reading room, was named for alumnus and donor Mortimer Caplin) and a rectangular fish pond. This and other areas around Law Grounds also boasted a total of over a thousand new shrubs and five thousand newly planted bulbs.[38]

In this radically altered environment, the Law School convened on Saturday, November 8, 1997, to dedicate the new Harrison Law Grounds, named for David A. Harrison III, who in total gave $8 million to the expansion. Over ten thousand alumni and friends had contributed funds to the project. The capital campaign was ultimately the most successful in the history of American legal education; the Law School raised $203 million between 1992 and 2000, surpassing the contemporaneous capital campaigns of Harvard and Yale. Over $30 million went into the Law Grounds building and landscape, evidence of the strong appeal of its historicist design program to alumni. Among the notables at the dedication was William H. Rehnquist, chief justice of the Supreme Court and a speaker at the ceremony, whose daughter had graduated from the Law School in 1985. As the band played "The Star-Spangled Banner," the crowd had an opportunity to contemplate the new Law Grounds. Just as the architects had joined Withers Hall and the Darden building to create a circular floor plan, so too, seemingly, had the Law School itself come full circle, arriving in a place purposefully suggestive of its earliest days on the Lawn. Taking the podium, Scott congratulated Adam Gross and Luanne Greene of Ayers Saint Gross for "hav[ing] forever dispelled the notion that you cannot make a sow's ear into a silk purse." For Scott, Law Grounds was about dreams brought to life. There were, of course, dreams of the future: "We dreamed that we could have the physical spaces to accommodate a newly enhanced academic program: one that places much greater emphasis on smaller classrooms, seminar rooms, places for the students to study together, spaces for student organizations." But, as had been true throughout the project, for those behind Law Grounds, dreams of the future were inseparable from visions of the past. "We dreamed," Scott continued, "that we could, through architecture, create a sense of place that would reunite the past, present and future of this institution and somehow embody and reinforce the values of civic virtue, community and engagement that uniquely characterize the School." For Scott, Harrison, and others, the move to North Grounds had severed not only the Law School's spatial relationship with the University but the school's grounding in its own history. This was a rebalancing, an effort to keep the forward-facing spirit of North Grounds and yet invite the spirits of Jefferson, Minor, Lile, Clark, and others to join the shadows produced by six new limestone piers and over four hundred newly planted trees. As Scott concluded, "We dreamed that we could reconnect the Law School to the University and, by creating a contemporary academical village here on the North Grounds, signal our enduring commitment to the University and its heritage."[39]

Trees, columns, and ghosts of the ancient past were not the only things to cast shadows on the proceedings. Although remade into the side wings of the new complex, the original law-business buildings still rose up and testified to an era not long past of cantilevered concrete, ribbon windows, and a lesser desire to venerate the old. In the end, Law Grounds was better for having them. Whereas the Darden School had been able to build on a vacant site and thus fully indulge its desire to reconnect with Jefferson's grounds, the Law School had been limited in its ability to do so by two modern buildings that architecturally and philosophically anchored the school to a less nostalgic frame of mind. The inability of the Law School to fully mask the buildings meant that the expansion would have to complement rather than condemn its older neighbors. The ghost of Jefferson could come in but not fully inhabit the building. And this is just as that gentleman would have had it—he had always been one to be off with the old and on with the new.

Conclusion

Although between 1995 and 1997 the Law School experienced a physical expansion unparalleled in its history, only a few years later the institution embarked on yet another construction project. The south link of Clay Hall and the Caplin Pavilion remained the "front door" of the Law School, but the administration hoped an expanded north link would become the heart of the structure. Named Hunton & Williams Hall for the Virginia-based law firm that provided financial support for the project, the existing north link served primarily as a corridor between Withers Hall and the former Darden building. Its redevelopment into a new Student-Faculty Center promised to be the "final step" in a re-creation of specific spaces and social behaviors associated with Clark Hall. In August 2000, the Law School demolished Café North, the humble dining hall built behind the law building in 1978, to make way for an enlarged and reconstructed Hunton & Williams Hall. Its centerpiece was a modified, reconstituted Mural Hall. Dean Scott hoped this new Student-Faculty Center would finally reverse the damage inflicted by the move to North Grounds. Scott explained that "by creating informal lounge and study space . . . together with faculty and student dining facilities, we hope that a 'Grand Central Station effect' will occur. I envision students and faculty passing through the area much as they did in the Mural Hall space in Clark Hall."[1] Appropriately, the Law School named this Mural Hall–like area Scott Commons after the dean who had done so much to bring Law Grounds to life.

This new Mural Hall did not have murals at all; rather, the space recalled its forebearer through its lines and uses. A long rectangular two-story room with a gabled roof and skylights, its proportions and essential features prompted those familiar with Clark Hall to immediately recall the former home of the Law School. In keeping with the postmodern classicism of Law Grounds, the new commons had plain wooden pediments and pilasters instead of the marble and decorative plaster work of its historic counterpart. Located away from offices and classrooms, the commons could fill with conversation, and in fact its echoing design seemed to encourage the same clamor of voices that Mural Hall had radiated throughout Clark Hall. As it had before, the Law School used the architecture of the Student-Faculty Center in an effort to employ the past, modifying it as needed for the present and future. The bare classicism and scant decor of the commons epitomized the school's approach to history in its buildings: in varying degrees, these buildings all made selective use of the past, evoking through space and material a stripped-down, amorphous recollection of history.

In this regard the Law School's architectural career aligned with that of the University as a whole. At a place so determined to look forward and backward at the same time, historicist architecture has been a primary means of reconciling progress and tradition. In particular, the University has reduced Jefferson's architecture in many cases to red bricks and white, unfluted columns, simplifying the past and making it more accessible. A survey of the University of Virginia shows buildings of a remarkable variety of sizes, uses, and styles that through materials, color, massing, and a few key architectural elements pay homage to a common heritage that is at once specific and nebulous. Together, the University's buildings provide a remarkable narrative of the flexibility of the "Jeffersonian" paradigm.

More broadly, they show how buildings that reference the past often serve to miti-gate the need and desire for change.

The buildings of the Law School tell this story well. The red brick, classicism, and fanlights of the Colonial Revival Minor Hall satisfied the layperson's desire for a veneer to a modern academic building that matched the original, adjacent cam-pus. Likewise Clark Hall evoked the Academical Village, a venerable courthouse, and an ancient mausoleum while nevertheless presenting its home department as an up-to-date national institution. The first North Grounds building made the greatest break with the past, but even here historical precedent was at work, sub-duing a modern design through the imposition of a palette and spatial arrange-ment that referenced the older campus. Finally the Law Grounds project, the most clearly derivative of the four, sampled the Rotunda, Monticello, and Clark Hall, conflating Jefferson, the Academical Village, and the Law School's institutional history into one usable past. At this expanded complex, explicit references to a prestigious legacy offered assurances of an equally bright future.

While the architectural history of the Law School presents an illustrative case study in the evolution of the University of Virginia campus, it also tells its own story, one of an institution within an institution. As much as the Law School has been central to the University, it has also been peripheral, and its history is one of constant effort to both connect with and remain distinct from the larger insti-tution. The Law School's dual identity as an academic department and a profes-sional school made it different almost from the very beginning; its status as the only income-generating department at the University in the late nineteenth and early twentieth centuries made it stranger still. The Law School's buildings demon-strate their connection to the University, but they also show how the department set itself apart. Minor Hall's physical placement let the Law School peer at the University while standing away from it; Clark Hall distinguished the school as having the finest departmental building on Grounds. In 1974, the move to North Grounds geographically isolated the school, while in the 1990s the Law School's highly successful fundraising machine created Law Grounds and announced the department's ability and desire to stand apart from its home institution. While the Law School used red bricks and lofty pillars as threads to tie itself to the rest of the University, it increasingly relied on references to its own distinctive past to make clear its self-reliance. As a silhouette of Mural Hall, Scott Commons in the new Student-Faculty Center at Law Grounds served these two purposes. It linked the Law School to Central Grounds and the University, but by making a specific allusion to a beloved former law building, it also spoke to the Law School's unique institutional and architectural history.

The history of the buildings of the Law School is an apt reminder that these often forgotten heirs to the Academical Village should not be dismissed as merely the predictable work of unimaginative building committees. The products of fraught, labored, and lengthy design processes, the law buildings were anything but inevitable architectural outcomes. Each came about through the negotiations of key individuals with a host of powerful but more diffuse forces, such as pressure from students and faculty, alumni expectations, changing academic and professional standards, and demographic and cultural transformations. Further, as successive law buildings arose, they did so within the context of their predecessors, rising up on foundations poured by previous generations. Rather than starting with blank canvases, the designers of each new building imitated, adapted, or rejected values and features prized by those before them. Thus the homes of the Law School are best understood not as freestanding manifestations of a particular time period but as chapters in a layered history. Together they tell a compelling story of a place that in changing has tried to remain the same.

As the University and Law School approach their two-hundredth anniversary in 2019, new opportunities will arise for the school to engage with the University and its past. Will this spark a richer engagement with the Law School's early history and invigorate connections between the school and the University? It is intriguing to imagine whether a new law building in 2025, 2050, or 2100 would look like the Rotunda, Minor Hall, Clark Hall, or even Withers Hall—or none of them. It seems impossible that the University of Virginia School of Law would ever inhabit a building without references to history, especially to its famous founder. As the Law School learned in 1974, one and a half miles is not nearly far enough to escape Jefferson's shadow. Like distance, time may also fail to shake off the spirit that lingers over the University. As decades pass and new modes of academic life challenge how students and faculty conceive of physical space, curricula, and community, the pull of Jefferson and his Academical Village may only become stronger.

Notes

ABBREVIATIONS

CD   *Cavalier Daily*

CT   *College Topics*

ESCP   Papers of Edmund S. Campbell, SSCL

PoP   Papers of the President, SSCL

LLSC   Law Library Special Collections, University of Virginia

LSBP   Law School Building Project, LLSC

RFBC   Records of the Faculty Building Committee, LLSC

SSCL   Albert and Shirley Small Special Collections Library, University of Virginia

VLW   *Virginia Law Weekly*

INTRODUCTION

1. "Why Come Back at Finals?," *University of Virginia Alumni News* 4, no. 19 (14 June 1916): 217–18.

2. The United Nations Educational, Scientific and Cultural Organization (UNESCO) World Heritage Committee named Monticello and the Academical Village together as a World

Heritage site in 1987. The committee recognized that Monticello and the Academical Village "represent a masterpiece of human creative genius." Given its recognized importance to world architecture, the number of works focused on the design of the Academical Village and subsequent development at the University of Virginia is surprisingly small. See John Kevan Peebles, "Thos. Jefferson, Architect," *Alumni Bulletin* 1, no. 3 (November 1894): 74; William Alexander Lambeth and Warren H. Manning, *Thomas Jefferson as an Architect and a Designer of Landscapes* (Boston: Houghton Mifflin, 1913); Fiske Kimball, *Thomas Jefferson, Architect: Original Designs in the Collection of Thomas Jefferson Coolidge, Junior* (Boston: Riverside Press, 1916); Frederick Doveton Nichols and Ralph E. Griswold, *Thomas Jefferson, Landscape Architect* (Charlottesville: University Press of Virginia, 1978); Joseph Lee Vaughan and Omer Allan Gianniny Jr., *Thomas Jefferson's Rotunda Restored, 1973–76: A Pictorial Review with Commentary* with a foreword by Frederick Doveton Nichols (Charlottesville: University Press of Virginia, 1981); George Humphrey Yetter, "Stanford White at the University of Virginia: Some New Light on an Old Question," *Journal of the Society of Architectural Historians* 40, no. 4 (December 1981): 320–25; Mary N. Woods, "Thomas Jefferson and the University of Virginia: Planning the Academic Village," *Journal of the Society of Architectural Historians* 44, no. 3 (October 1985): 266–83; Richard Guy Wilson, ed., *Thomas Jefferson's Academical Village: The Creation of an Architectural Masterpiece* (Charlottesville: Bayly Art Museum of the University of Virginia, 1993); Daniel Bluestone, "Captured by Context: Architectural Innovation and Banality at Thomas Jefferson's University" in *Buildings, Landscapes, and Memory: Case Studies in Historic Preservation* (New York: W. W. Norton, 2011), 40–77; Richard Guy Wilson, David J. Neuman, and Sara A. Butler, *University of Virginia: An Architectural Tour*, 2nd ed. (New York: Princeton Architectural Press, 2012).

3. "Report of the Board of Commissioners for the University of Virginia to the Virginia General Assembly, [4 August] 1818," in *The Papers of James Madison,* Retirement Series, vol. 1, 4 March 1817–31 January 1820, ed. David B. Mattern, J. C. A. Stagg, Mary Parke Johnson, and Anne Mandeville Colony (Charlottesville: University of Virginia Press, 2009), 326–40.

4. For the history of American campus planning, see Paul Venable Turner, *Campus: An American Planning Tradition* (New York: Architectural History Foundation, 1984), and Stefan Muthesius, *The Postwar University: Utopianist Campus and College* (New Haven: Yale University Press, 2000). Some more recent titles in the expansive historiography of American higher education include Christopher J. Lucas, *American Higher Education: A History* (New York: St. Martin's, 1994); Hugh Davis Graham and Nancy A. Diamond, *The Rise of American Research Universities: Elites and Challengers in the Postwar Era* (Baltimore: Johns Hopkins University Press, 1997); Roger L. Geiger, *The American College in the Nineteenth Century* (Nashville: Vanderbilt University Press, 2000) and *The History of American Higher Education: Learning*

and Culture from the Founding to World War II (New York: Oxford University Press, 2015); and John R. Thelin, *A History of American Higher Education* (Baltimore: Johns Hopkins University Press, 2004).

5. The University of Virginia School of Law is generally considered the fourth oldest active law school in the United States after the law schools at the College of William and Mary, the University of Maryland, and Harvard University. William and Mary and Maryland went through periods where they did not have law professors or offer law classes, making the University of Virginia School of Law the second oldest continuously operating law school in the United States. Because law schools as they exist today evolved gradually from single law professorships at early American universities, law schools have not always agreed as to which institution was oldest. See Henry D. Gabriel, "America's Oldest Law School," *Journal of Legal Education* 39, no. 2 (June 1989): 269–74.

6. For the history of the University of Virginia School of Law, see John Ritchie, *The First Hundred Years: A Short History of the School of Law of the University of Virginia for the Period 1826–1926* (Charlottesville: University Press of Virginia, 1978); Marsha Trimble, "A Genealogy: From Pavilion III to Walter L. Brown Hall," *Virginia Law School Report* 3, no. 3 (Summer 1979), 8–11, "Early Law Professors and Twentieth Century Deans," *Virginia Law School Report* 10, no. 1 (Winter 1986), 20–23, "Attending the Lectures of Law: A Perspective on the 19th Century Law School Experience," *UVA Lawyer* 20, no. 2 (Spring 1996), 34–47, and "The Legacy of Clark Hall," *UVA Lawyer* 21, no. 3 (Fall 1997), 41–47; and Kristin H. Jensen, ed., *The Diary of a Dean: Excerpts from the Private Journal of William Minor Lile* (Charlottesville: University of Virginia Law Library Special Collections, 2011).

7. For comprehensive histories of American legal education, see Alfred Zantzinger Reed, *Training for the Public Profession of the Law: Historical Development and Principal Contemporary Problems of Legal Education in the United States, with Some Account of Conditions in England and Canada* (New York, Carnegie Foundation for the Advancement of Teaching, 1921); Robert Stevens, *Law School: Legal Education in America from the 1850s to the 1980s* (Chapel Hill: University of North Carolina Press, 1983); and William P. LaPiana, *Logic and Experience: The Origin of Modern American Legal Education* (New York: Oxford University Press, 1994).

THE ACADEMICAL VILLAGE, THE ROTUNDA ANNEX, AND MINOR HALL

1. "New Law Building Climbing Upward," *CT,* 23 October 1909, 1.

2. Letter from Thomas Jefferson to Littleton Waller Tazewell, 5 January 1805, Thomas Jefferson, Correspondence, 1775–1826, MSS 38-755, SSCL.

3. For a discussion of the possible inspirations for Jefferson's architectural design of the University of Virginia, see Michelle Benoit and Richard Guy Wilson, "Jefferson and Marly: Complex Influences," *Bulletin du Centre de Recherche du Château de Versailles,* 2012, http://crcv .revues.org/11936.

4. Wilson, Neuman, and Butler, *University of Virginia,* 17, 40–41; "Law Building Taking On Its Final Form," *CT,* 8 January 1910, 1. Although white columns became ubiquitous at the University as it sought to construct buildings in harmony with the Academical Village, the columns of the original Jefferson buildings were initially painted a light tan color rather than white.

5. Craig Evan Klafter, "The Influence of Vocational Law Schools on the Origins of American Legal Thought, 1779–1829," *American Journal of Legal History* 37, no. 3 (July 1993): 312–16, 322–26; Stevens, *Law School,* 3–5; Ritchie, *First Hundred Years,* 4–5; J. Gordon Hylton, "Beyond the Shadow of Langdell: William Minor Lile and the Transformation of Legal Education at the University of Virginia, 1890–1920" (unpublished manuscript), 8.

6. Ritchie, *First Hundred Years,* 9–10.

7. Jefferson identified the pavilion as "Pavilion No. III W. Corinthian Palladio" on an 1818 drawing now housed at SSCL. See Mesick Cohen Wilson Baker Architects, *Pavilion III: University of Virginia, Historic Structure Report* (Albany, N.Y.: printed by the author, 2006), 3.

8. Mesick Cohen Wilson Baker Architects, *Pavilion III,* 12, 20–21, 24–28, 99.

9. For floor plans and room uses of Pavilion III, see Mesick Cohen Wilson Baker Architects, *Pavilion III,* 111–12, 130–32, 147–48. For the children of John Tayloe Lomax, see Edward Lloyd Lomax, *Genealogy of the Virginia Family of Lomax* (Chicago: Rand McNally & Co., 1913), 24.

10. University of Virginia, *A Catalogue of the Library of the University of Virginia . . .* (Charlottesville, 1828); Gaillard Hunt, ed., *The First Forty Years of Washington Society: Portrayed by the Family Letters of Mrs. Samuel Harrison Smith (Margaret Bayard) . . .* (New York: Charles Scribner's Sons, 1906), 226. For more information on the opening of the Rotunda as the University library, see John G. Waite Associates, Architects, *The Rotunda, University of Virginia: Historic Structure Report* (Albany, N.Y., printed by the author, 2008), 47.

11. Ritchie, *First Hundred Years,* 15–16; Lomax, *Genealogy of the Virginia Family of Lomax,* 31.

12. Rex Bowman and Carlos Santos, *Rot, Riot, and Rebellion: Mr. Jefferson's Struggle to Save the University That Changed America* (Charlottesville: University of Virginia Press, 2013), 123; Mesick Cohen Wilson Baker Architects, *Pavilion III,* 35–36, and *Pavilion X, University of Virginia: Exterior Restoration Plan* (Albany, NY: printed by the author, 2007), 24.

13. University of Virginia Faculty Minutes, 17 July 1832, Transcript, Vol. III, 870, RG-19/1/ 1.461, SSCL.

14. Peter Carr to Warwick Miller, MSS 10984, SSCL; Bowman and Santos, *Rot, Riot, and Rebellion,* 123–24.

15. Bowman and Santos, *Rot, Riot, and Rebellion,* 151; Virginius Dabney, *Mr. Jefferson's University: A History* (Charlottesville: University Press of Virginia, 1981), 22; Henry D. Reck, "John Barbee Minor: The Early Years," *Magazine of Albemarle County History* 12 (1951–52): 25, 28, 30, 32.

16. Hylton, "Beyond the Shadow of Langdell," 9–10; Ritchie, *First Hundred Years,* 19–20.

17. Minutes of the Board of Visitors, 25 September 1850, Transcripts of the Minutes of the Board of Visitors, 1817–1855, box 1, folder "Vol. III, Minutes—Public (2 of 3)," 174, SSCL.

18. John M. Bryan, *Robert Mills: America's First Architect* (New York: Princeton Architectural Press, 2001), 149.

19. Andrew Stevenson to Joseph C. Cabell, 3 January 1851, Cabell Family Papers, MSS 38-111, box 38, SSCL.

20. Minutes of the Board of Visitors, 29 June 1852, Transcripts of the Minutes of the Board of Visitors, 1817–1855, box 1, folder "Vol. III, Minutes—Public (3 of 3)," 207, SSCL; James P. C. Southall, *In the Days of My Youth, When I Was a Student in the University of Virginia, 1888–1893* (Chapel Hill: University of North Carolina Press, 1947), 93.

21. The main staircases for the Annex were just inside the entry points on the building's south side, where it abutted the Rotunda, although stairs in central transverse passages provided communication between the lower two floors. A photograph of the Annex ruins provides evidence that another set of interior stairs existed in the northeast corner of the building; it is unclear if these steps communicated with all floors. Morgan Poitiaux Robinson, in his 1905 history of the fire, referred to "the high narrow stairs leading to the rear door of the stage in the Public Hall," but these likely were the exterior stairs, not part of the original Mills design, which appear in a photograph of the Annex and provided access to the building's north portico. See Robinson, *The Burning of the Rotunda: Being a Sketch of the Partial Destruction of the University of Virginia* (Charlottesville, 1905), 5. Architectural drawings of the Annex survive in the papers of Montgomery C. Meigs at the Winterthur Library, but these drawings likely differ from the Annex as it was constructed. For more information on the Annex see John G. Waite Associates, *The Rotunda,* 57–61.

22. Philip Alexander Bruce mentioned "the engineering drawing-room, which was situated immediately above the public hall" in *History of the University of Virginia, 1819–1919: The Lengthened Shadow of One Man* (New York: MacMillan, 1920), 4:255. A contemporaneous article in the *Alumni Bulletin* places the Engineering Department's instrument room in the northwest corner

of the Annex, where the fire started. "The University Ablaze," *Alumni Bulletin* 2, no. 3 (November 1895): 67.

23. Southall, *In the Days of My Youth,* 93. The *Alumni Bulletin*'s column about the Rotunda fire confirms Southall's description: "Below the Public Hall were the laboratories and lecture room of the School of Physics, and under these the lecture room and library of the Law Department and the lecture room and shops of the Engineering Department" (67–68).

24. Andrew Stevenson to Joseph C. Cabell, 3 January 1851, Cabell Family Papers, MSS 38-111, box 38, SSCL.

25. Francis Henry Smith, "The Rotunda," *Alumni Bulletin* 2, no. 3 (November 1895): 85.

26. Minutes of the Board of Visitors, 29 June 1853, Transcripts of the Minutes of the Board of Visitors, 1817–1855, box 1, folder "Vol. III, Minutes—Public (3 of 3)," 221, SSCL.

27. Walter Scott Hancock Journal, 3 November 1895, MSS 7961, SSCL; Robinson, *Burning of the Rotunda,* 4–5.

28. Margaret Bell Dunnington to Sadie Dunnington, 28 October 1895, MSS 10647, SSCL; Hancock Journal, 3 November 1895; John T. Thornton to Mrs. E. Rosalie Thornton, 27 October 1895, transcription, University of Virginia Library Online Manuscripts, https://explore.lib .virginia.edu/exhibits/show/rotunda/fire/firsthand-accounts/thornton.

29. "The Law Library," *Alumni Bulletin* 1, no. 3 (November 1894): 88; Hancock Journal, 3 November 1895; *University of Virginia Catalogue 1895–'96, Announcements 1896–'97,* 1, LLSC; *University of Virginia Catalogue 1894–'95, Announcements 1895–'96,* 53, LLSC. An article in the *Alumni Bulletin* recorded that whereas the library had held 56,733 entries at the time of the fire, post-fire there were only 17,194 books, including 5,000 law books. "A Further Note on the Library," *Alumni Bulletin* 2, no. 3 (November 1895): 101.

30. "Unveiling of the Bust of Prof. John B. Minor," *Alumni Bulletin* 2, no. 2 (July 1895): 41–42.

31. "Funeral of Prof. John B. Minor," *Washington Post,* 1 August 1895, 4; Robinson, *Burning of the Rotunda,* 10. The 1896 *Corks & Curls,* the University yearbook, reported "all of the readily portable philosophical apparatus, the engineering instruments, the department library of the Law School, the furniture and records of the Chairman's office, most of the books on the first floor of the library, all of the portraits, the Lee papers, the interesting framed original letters and documents, the Minor bust with its pedestal, and the life-size statue of Jefferson were saved." *Corks & Curls* (Charlottesville, 1896), 18.

32. Washington Hall was home to the Washington Debating Society. An article from the 1897 *Corks and Curls* provides a sense of the improvised space: "Wash Hall, which owing to the recent fire had been assigned to the law department for the conduction of its lectures, was the same in

which Henry W. Grady and John W. Daniels learned that eloquence which has so distinguished them in after life. But now the building was entirely given over to the law department and its cases of books lined the walls on every side. In front of me and to my right were the 'American Reports' with their cumbersome digests, while to the left were the 'United States Reports,' and further down were the reports of the several states, 'The American Decisions' and the 'Virginia Law Reviews.'" "The Law Class," *Corks & Curls* (Charlottesville, 1897), 37. Walter Scott Hancock noted "the Law Class use[s] the 'Wash' Hall" in his journal entry for 3 November 1895.

33. Report of the Faculty to the Rector and Visitors, 31 October 1895, printed in "The University Ablaze," *Alumni Bulletin* 2, no. 3 (November 1895): 72–73.

34. John H. Langbein, "Law School in a University: Yale's Distinctive Path in the Later Nineteenth Century," in *History of the Yale Law School: The Tercentennial Lectures,* ed. Anthony T. Kronman (New Haven: Yale University Press, 2004), 61–62; George E. Nitzsche, *University of Pennsylvania, The Proceedings at the Dedication of the New Building of the Department of Law, February 21st and 22nd, 1900* (Philadelphia: Press of International Printing Company, 1901), 235–36, 241.

35. For a history of the construction of Austin Hall, see Charles Warren, *History of the Harvard Law School and of Early Legal Conditions in America* (New York: Lewis Publishing, 1908), 2:432–37. For floor plans of the building see "Austin Hall, Harvard Law School," *The Builder* 49, no. 2237 (19 December 1885), 858.

36. Ritchie, *First Hundred Years,* 35–36, 45, 54–56; Hylton, "Beyond the Shadow of Langdell," 12, 19–23, 37–47.

37. Wilson, Neuman, and Butler, *University of Virginia,* 65–66.

38. For Columbia University, see Richard Guy Wilson, *McKim, Mead & White, Architects* (New York: Rizzoli International Publications, 1983), 172–77; for New York University, see Samuel G. White and Elizabeth White, *Stanford White, Architect* (New York: Rizzoli International Publications, 2008), 326–30.

39. Charles C. Baldwin, *Stanford White* (New York: Dodd, Mead & Co., 1931), 222.

40. Wilson, Neuman, and Butler, *University of Virginia,* 80–82.

41. Annual Report of the Faculty of Law for 1904, Dean's Papers, RG 100-78, box 47, 1904–1947, 5, LLSC.

42. Lile to Alderman, 23 February 1908, Alderman to Lile, 10 March 1908, and Lile to Alderman, 26 March 1908, PoP, RG-2/1/2.472 I, box 15, folder "Law Building."

43. Alderman to Lile, 10 March 1908, Alderman to McKim, Mead & White, 16 March 1908 and 22 May 1908, and McKim, Mead & White to Alderman, 17 March 1908 and 26 May 1908, ibid.

44. R. M. Price, Office of the President, to Building Committee, Board of Visitors, 30 May 1908, Carpenter & Blair to Alderman, 25 May 1908, J. K. Peebles to Alderman, 27 May 1908, and Taylor & Hepburn to Alderman, 27 May 1908, ibid.

45. Alderman to Manning, 23 May 1908, and Manning to Alderman, 10 October 1908, ibid.

46. Alderman to Manning, 12 October 1908 and 16 October 1908, and R. H. Whitehead, Dean, Department of Medicine, to Alderman, 9 September 1908, ibid.

47. Alderman to Manning, 12 October 1908 and 16 October 1908, and Manning to Alderman, 21 October 1908, ibid.

48. Taylor & Hepburn, Report, "Law Building for the University of Virginia," and Walter D. Blair, "Description of the Law Building for the University of Virginia," ibid. Peebles' original proposal likely survives in an undated study for Minor Hall in the Small Special Collections Library. In this study, the law building is an elongated and more embellished version of the structure as built, with a nine-bay (as opposed to seven-bay) central block and four-bay (rather than three-bay) wings. A small site plan included in the drawing shows the building along the "long walk" that ran near the hospital. On November 5, 1908, when the Board of Visitors hired Peebles, they directed him to alter his plans to fit the new site. He changed the plans to make Minor Hall more square in shape. See Minutes of the Board of Visitors, 5 November 1908, Transcripts of the Minutes of the Board of Visitors, June 1903–March 1915, box 4, folder "Vol. VIII, Minutes—Public (3 of 7)," 356, SSCL.

49. Peebles, "Thos. Jefferson, Architect," 74; Wilson, Neuman, and Butler, *University of Virginia,* 163.

50. John E. Wells and Robert E. Dalton, *The Virginia Architects, 1835–1955: A Biographical Dictionary* (Richmond: New South Architectural Press, 1997), 75–76, 344–47.

51. John K. Peebles to Edgar A. Anderson and William M. Lile, 15 January 1909, PoP, RG-2/1/2.472 I, box 15, folder "Law Building"; George E. Thomas, *University of Pennsylvania: An Architectural Tour* (New York: Princeton Architectural Press, 2002), 130–31.

52. "New Law Building Climbing Upward," *CT,* 23 October 1909, 1.

53. "Law Building Taking On Its Final Form," *CT,* 8 January 1910, 1; "Law School Moves First of the Year," *CT,* 22 October 1910, 1; "New Law Building Nearly Completed," *CT,* 29 April 1911, 3; "Law School Now in Handsome Home," *CT,* 22 September 1911, 5.

2. CLARK MEMORIAL HALL AND THE ALLYN COX MURALS

1. Ayers Saint Gross, Process Journal, 22 February 1993, Section 4, LSBP, RG 313-05, box 5, folder 3.

2. Diaries of William Minor Lile, Diary 8, 10 July 1923, Diary 10, 2 December 1929, MSS 89-1, LLSC.

3. Ibid., Diary 10, 14 November 1929.

4. *University of Virginia Record, Department of Law Announcements 1930–1931,* New Series 16, no. 2, 29.

5. Hylton, "Beyond the Shadow of Langdell," 54–55, 60; Ritchie, *First Hundred Years,* 92, 101.

6. Lile Diaries, Diary 10, 2 December 1929; "Suggestions Regarding the Design of the Library Addition to the Present Law School Building," 18 February 1930, PoP, RG-2/1/2.491 I, box 14, folder "1930–1931, Department of Law—Clark Hall Furnishings (2)"; Alderman to Clark, 22 February 1930, PoP, RG-2/1/2.491 I, box 13, folder "1930–1932, Department of Law—Clark Hall Correspondence"; Taylor to Campbell, 4 January 1930, ESCP, MSS 3505, box 9, folder "1929–1930, Board of Architects—U.Va.—Correspondence from R. E. Lee Taylor."

7. "Suggestions Regarding the Design of the Library Addition to the Present Law School Building," 18 February 1930, PoP, RG-2/1/2.491 I, box 14, folder "1930–1931, Department of Law—Clark Hall Furnishings (2)"; Alderman to Clark, 22 February 1930, PoP, RG-2/1/2.491 I, box 13, folder "1930–1932, Department of Law—Clark Hall Correspondence."

8. Clark to Alderman, 8 March 1930, PoP, RG-2/1/2.491 I, box 13, folder "1930–1932, Department of Law—Clark Hall Correspondence"; Lile Diaries, Diary 10, 11 March 1930; Alderman to Clark, 11 March 1930, PoP, RG-2/1/2.491 I, box 13, folder "1930–1932, Department of Law—Clark Hall Correspondence."

9. John R. Thelin and Richard W. Trollinger, *Philanthropy and American Higher Education* (New York: Palgrave Macmillan, 2014), 20; L. Moody Simms Jr., "Du Pont's Bequest to the Future of the University," *University of Virginia Alumni News* 53, no. 2 (November–December 1964): 10–11; Dabney, *Mr. Jefferson's University,* 63–64, 84, 105.

10. Clark to Alderman, 8 March 1930, 1 May 1930, PoP, RG-2/1/2.491 I, box 13, folder "1930–1932, Department of Law—Clark Hall Correspondence"; William E. Conway, "Books, Bricks, and Copper: Clark and His Library," in *William Andrews Clark, Jr., His Cultural Legacy: Papers Read at a Clark Library Seminar, 7 November 1981,* eds. William E. Conway and Robert Stevenson (Los Angeles: William Andrews Clark Library, 1985), 4; Clark to Alderman, 1 May 1930, PoP, RG-2/1/2.491 I, box 14, folder "1930–1931, Department of Law—Clark Hall Furnishings (2)"; Peebles to Taylor, Blair, and Campbell, 8 December 1930, ESCP, MSS 3505, box 9, folder "1930, Board of Architects—Correspondence."

11. Conway, "Books, Bricks, and Copper," 3. For an account of William Andrews Clark Sr.'s business affairs see Michael P. Malone, *The Battle for Butte: Mining and Politics on the Northern Frontier, 1864–1906* (Seattle: University of Washington Press, 1981).

12. William D. Mangam, *The Clarks: An American Phenomenon* (New York: Silver Bow Press, 1941), 54–55, 189; Wayne Craven, *Gilded Mansions: Grand Architecture and High Society* (New York: W. W. Norton & Co., 2009), 361.

13. National Register of Historic Places, W. A. Clark Mansion, Butte, Silver Bow County, Montana, National Register #70000366; Mangam, *Clarks,* 54–55; Craven, *Gilded Mansions,* 359–61. The Senator William Andrews Clark house was demolished in 1927 to make way for the apartment building still standing at 960 Fifth Avenue. In a series entitled "Architectural Aberrations," *Architectural Record* said of the house that "the Copper King and his architect seem unaware that boldness and brassiness are going out of fashion in house building," castigating in particular the enormous cupola with its "ferociously corbelled balcony." "The House of Senator Clark," *Architectural Record* 19, no. 1 (January 1906): 30.

14. Conway, "Books, Bricks, and Copper," 5; Mangam, *Clarks,* 199, 208.

15. Lile Diaries, Diary 10, 2 December 1929; Clemons to Clark, 21 July 1930, PoP, RG-2/1/2.491 I, box 14, folder "1930–1931, Department of Law—Clark Hall Furnishings (2)." For additional information on Clark's gift of *Notes on the State of Virginia* see Clark to Alderman, 7 July 1930, ibid.

16. Robert D. Farquhar, "The Building," in *Williams Andrews Clark Memorial Library: Report of the First Decade, 1934–1944* (Berkeley: University of California Press, 1946), 21.

17. Allyn Cox painted the vestibule of Clark's library in 1925 and worked on the other rooms until 1927. In 1930, Cox created murals for Clark's Paris apartment. Around the same time, Clark contributed $15,000 to the refurbishment of Pershing Hall, the American Legion Building at 49 Rue Pierre Charron in Paris, plus additional funds for the furnishing and decoration of a memorial room to soldiers of the Great War who had attended the University of Virginia. Clark commissioned Allyn Cox to create murals for the room, including one of a view of the Rotunda and one of Monticello; as of 2015, these murals are on loan from Pershing Hall (now a hotel) to the Musée Franco-Américain du Château de Blérancourt. See inventory of Cox's works, Allyn Cox Papers, Archives of American Art, Smithsonian Institute, microfilm roll 3108; "American Legion Memorial, Paris, France" (Washington: U.S. Government Print Office, 1935), 37. For references to the Virginia memorial room at Pershing Hall in UVa correspondence see Francis E. Drake to Clark, 20 March 1931, and Alderman to Clark, 14 April 1931, PoP, RG-2/1/2.491 I, box 14, folder "1930–1931, Department of Law—Clark Hall Furnishings (2)"; Clark to Newcomb, 22 January 1932, PoP, RG-2/1/2.491 I, box 13, folder "1930–1932, Department of Law."

18. William M. Fontaine, *Introductory Lecture by Wm. M. Fontaine, M. A., Professor of Geology and Natural History, University of Virginia: With a Short Account of the Lewis Brooks' Museum of Natural History* (Charlottesville, 1879), 2; Wilson, Neuman, and Butler, *University of Virginia,*

90; "The Jarring Discord," *CT*, 7 April 1909, 4; Lile Diaries, Diary 10, 11 March 1930; Architectural Commission, Development of the University of Virginia, Recommendations, Sites for Law and Engineering Buildings, etc., 1 April 1930, PoP, RG-2/1/2.472 IX, box 3, folder "April–June 1930, Buildings and Grounds."

19. Alderman to Lile, 14 March 1930, PoP, RG-2/1/2.491 I, box 13, folder "1930–1932, Department of Law"; Lile Diaries, Diary 10, 18 March 1930; University of Virginia, Clark Memorial Law Building, Memoranda for Architects, 1 April 1930, PoP, RG-2/1/2.472 IX, box 3, folder "April–June 1930, Buildings and Grounds."

20. Wilson, Neuman, and Butler, *University of Virginia,* 95–100, 104, 115–17, 142–43, 163–64.

21. Lile Diaries, Diary 10, 31 May 1930; Architectural Commission to Alderman, "Suggestions Regarding the Design for a New Law School Building," 18 February 1930 (handwritten date at bottom of first page), PoP, RG-2/1/2.491 I, box 14, folder "1930–1931, Department of Law—Clark Hall Furnishings (2)"; Taylor to Peebles, 3 January 1930, Taylor to Campbell, 4 January 1930, ESCP, MSS 3505, box 9, folder "1929–1930, Board of Architects—U.Va.—Correspondence from R. E. Lee Taylor"; Campbell to Taylor (n.d.), ESCP, MSS 3505, box 9, folder "1930, Board of Architects—U.Va.—Correspondence to R. E. Lee Taylor"; Newcomb to Lile, 25 October 1930, PoP, RG-2/1/2.472 IX, box 7, folder "1929–1930, Li–Ly (misc)."

22. Taylor to Peebles, 15 October 1930, ESCP, MSS 3505, box 9, folder "1929–1930, Board of Architects—U.Va.—Correspondence from R. E. Lee Taylor"; Campbell to Blair, Peebles, and Taylor, 24 October 1930, ESCP, MSS 3505, box 9, folder "1930, Board of Architects—Correspondence."

23. Minutes of Architectural Commission Meeting, 9 September 1930, and Taylor to Blair, Peebles, and Campbell, 27 August 1930, ESCP, MSS 3505, box 9, folder "1929–1930, Board of Architects—U.Va.—Correspondence from R. E. Lee Taylor." For the Franklin National Bank of Philadelphia, see Richard Guy Wilson and McKim, Mead & White, *The Architecture of McKim, Mead & White in Photographs, Plans and Elevations* (New York: Dover Publication, 1990), plates 395–96. For the Architectural Commission's drawings for a grander Mural Hall, see RG 100-78, box 6, folder 6, LLSC; this folder also includes a study for incorporating the murals into the library. For Taylor's rejected plan for Clark Hall, see Clark Hall blueprints, RG-31/1/2:3.051, SSCL.

24. Taylor to Peebles and Campbell, 6 October 1930, ESCP, MSS 3505, box 9, folder "1929–1930, Board of Architects—U.Va.—Correspondence from R. E. Lee Taylor"; Campbell to Blair, Peebles, and Taylor, 10 October 1930, ESCP, MSS 3505, box 8, folder "Board of Architects—Correspondence to John K. Peebles."

25. Lile Diaries, Diary 10, 31 May 1930; Lile to Newcomb, 23 October 1930, PoP, RG-2/1/2.472 IX, box 7, folder "1929–1930, Li–Ly (Misc)."

26. Taylor to Peebles, 15 October 1930, ESCP, MSS 3505, box 9, folder "1929–1930, Board of Architects—U.Va.—Correspondence from R. E. Lee Taylor"; Lile Diaries, Diary 10, 29/30/31 October 1930.

27. Campbell to Blair, Peebles, and Taylor, 24 October 1930, ESCP, MSS 3505, box 9, folder "1930, Board of Architects—Correspondence"; Lile Diaries, Diary 10, 29/30/31 October 1930.

28. Taylor to Peebles, Blair, and Campbell, 27 August 1930, 3 September 1930, ESCP, MSS 3505, box 9, folder "1929–1930, Board of Architects—U.Va.—Correspondence from R. E. Lee Taylor."

29. Lile Diaries, Diary 11, 6 April 1931, 3 July 1931, 18 July 1931, 22 July 1931, 3 September 1931, 28 November 1931; "New Law Building Nears Completion," *CT,* 9 May 1932, 1–2. Clark's companion was Raymond Lemire, who was orphaned in World War I and afterward received financial support from Clark. Mangam identified Lemire as one of Clark's lovers. See Mangam, *Clarks,* 214–15.

30. "Clark Memorial Dedication Nears," *Washington Post,* 2 October 1932, M8; "New Law Building Will Be Dedicated Wednesday, Oct. 5," *CT*, 16 September 1932, 5; "Announcements," *Virginia Law Review* 19, no. 1 (November 1932): 61; "New Law Building Nears Completion," 2. For a detailed description of Clark Hall, including references to furniture and paintings, see "Alumni Invited to Law Dedication," *University of Virginia Alumni News* 21, no. 1 (September 1932): 2–6. The September and October 1932 issues of the *Alumni News* also include a variety of photographs of the interior and exterior of Clark Hall.

31. "Clark Memorial Dedication Nears," M8; Armistead M. Dobie, "Address of Acceptance," *University of Virginia Alumni News* 21, no. 2 (October 1932): 34.

32. "Charlottesville," *Washington Post,* 9 October 1932, 20.

33. Clark to Newcomb, 7 October 1932, PoP, RG-2/1/2.491 I, box 13, folder "1930–1932, Department of Law—Clark Hall Correspondence."

34. For history of the New Deal murals see Sara Amelia Butler, "Constructing New Deal America: Public Art and Architecture and Institutional Legitimacy" (PhD diss., University of Virginia, 2001); Martin R. Kalfatovic, *The New Deal Fine Arts Projects: A Bibliography, 1933–1992* (Metuchen, N.J.: Scarecrow Press, 1994); A. Joan Saab, *For the Millions: American Art and Culture Between the Wars* (Philadelphia: University of Pennsylvania Press, 2004); Ann Prentice Wagner, *1934: A New Deal for Artists* (Washington, DC: Smithsonian American Art Museum, 2009).

35. The new copy of *The School of Athens,* painted by George W. Breck, arrived at the Univer-

sity in March 1902 and was installed in Cabell Hall by mid-April. See "New 'School of Athens,'" *CT*, 13 November 1901, 1, and "School of Athens," *CT*, 22 March 1902, 4.

36. Lile Diaries, Diary 11, 8 February 1931.

37. H. Wayne Morgan, *Kenyon Cox, 1856–1919: A Life in American Art* (Kent, OH: Kent State University Press, 1994), 19, 24–28, 124–26, 132–35, 137–38, 144–48, 153–58, 170–74, 182.

38. Robert Schwengel, *The American Story in Art: The Murals of Allyn Cox in the U.S. Capitol* (Washington, D.C.: National Society of the Daughters of the American Revolution, 1986), 4–5; Bailey Van Hook, *The Virgin & the Dynamo: Public Murals in American Architecture, 1893–1917* (Athens, OH: Ohio University Press, 2003), 183–89. For the Anne Harriman Vanderbilt commission, see "A Decorated Entrance Hall," *House & Garden* 42, no. 2 (August 1922): 41, and Ruby Ross Goodnow, "Pages from a Decorator's Diary," *House & Garden* 42, no. 5 (November 1922): 84; Katrina Ely Tiffany: Caroline Duer, "The Painted Hallway: Murals in the 17th Century Italian Style Have Been Used in this Remodeled New York Home," *House & Garden* 42, no. 6 (December 1922): 47; Helen Huntington Astor: *House & Garden* 59, no. 3 (March 1931): 68–69; City Bank-Farmers Trust Company: Elisabeth Luther Cary, "Freedom in Decoration," *New York Times*, 28 April 1929, 124, and "Downtown Structure Ready for Tenants," *New York Times*, 19 February 1931, 45; Continental Bank: "New Bank Edifices in Downtown Area," *New York Times*, 1 May 1932, RE1, and "Continental Moves to Skyscraper Home," *New York Times*, 9 May 1932, 27; Atlanta houses: Elizabeth Meredith Dowling, *American Classicist: The Architecture of Philip Trammell Shutze* (New York: Rizzoli, 1989), 70–71, 76, 154–57.

39. Clark to Alderman, 8 March 1930, PoP, RG-2/1/2.491 I, box 13, folder "1930–1932, Department of Law—Clark Hall Correspondence"; Cox to Alderman, 17 March 1930, PoP, RG-2/1/2.491 I, box 14, folder "1930–1931, Department of Law—Clark Hall Furnishings (2)."

40. Cox to Alderman, 20 December 1930, Alderman to Clark, 6 August 1930, and Cox to Alderman, 13 March 1931, PoP, RG-2/1/2.491 I, box 14, folder "1930–1931, Department of Law—Clark Hall Furnishings (2)."

41. Cox to Alderman, 20 December 1930, ibid.

42. Lile Diaries, Diary 11, 18 February 1931.

43. In January 1932, the State Art Commission consisted of Governor John Garland Pollard, Edmund S. Campbell, artist Gari Melchers, and architects Wickham C. Taylor and Philip N. Stern.

44. Taylor to Campbell, 1 February 1932, PoP, RG-2/1/2.491 I, box 13, folder "1932–1933, Department of Law—Clark Hall Furnishings"; Melchers to Campbell, 3 February 1932, ESCP, MSS 3505, box 25, folder "1930–1932 Gari Melchers"; Campbell to Cox, 20 April 1933, Cox to Newcomb, 21 April 1933, and Cox to Newcomb, 29 April 1933, PoP, RG-2/1/2.491 I, box 13,

folder "1932–1933, Department of Law—Clark Hall Furnishings"; Campbell to Cox, n.d. (after 18 April 1933), ESCP, MSS 3505, box 14, folder "1930–1933 Allyn Cox."

45. Newcomb to Campbell, 23 August 1932, PoP, RG-2/1/2.491 I, box 3, folder "1930–1933, Art and Architecture and Music." Lile recorded in his diary on November 28, 1931, that Clark had left him "a copy of the lettering he desired for the bronze memorial tablet to his wife," the text of which Lile recorded in his diary: "This building was erected in loving memory of his wife, Mabel Foster Clark (1880–1903), and (is?) dedicated to the University of Virginia and the students of its Law School, present, past and future, by William Andrews Clark, Jr.—1932. LLB., Class of 1899." Lile confessed in his journal, "I do not wholly like the wording of the tablet as Clark had drawn it," and as Clark had given Lile "some discretion in the matter of alterations," he altered it to read: "This building was erected by William Andrews Clark Jr LL B Class of 1899 in loving memory of his wife Mabel Foster Clark 1880–1903 and is dedicated to the Faculty Alumni and Students of the Law School University of Virginia." See Lile Diaries, Diary 11, 28 November and 4 December 1931. Lile proposed the changes to Clark, to which Clark responded with his usual amiability: "I felt that there was something wrong in the original version, and I think your substitution fits to a tee." Lile to Clark, 4 December 1931, and Clark to Lile, 14 December 1931, PoP, RG-2/1/2.491 I, box 14, folder "1930–1931, Department of Law—Clark Hall Furnishings (2)."

46. Cox to Newcomb, 26 September 1932, PoP, RG-2/1/2.491 I, box 13, folder "1932–1933, Department of Law—Clark Hall Furnishings."

47. A. T. Murray, trans., *The Iliad* (New York: G. P. Putnam's Sons, 1924–25), 2:325, 327. A copy of this excerpt can be found in PoP, RG-2/1/2.491 II, box 15, folder "1934–1936, School of Law, General."

48. Kenyon Cox to Allyn Cox, 7 January 1918, Kenyon Cox Papers, Avery Architectural and Fine Arts Library, Columbia University, quoted in Morgan, *Kenyon Cox,* 97.

49. Cox to Campbell, 11 April 1933, ESCP, MSS 3505, box 14, folder "1930–1933 Allyn Cox."

50. Architectural League of New York, *Year Book of the Architectural League of New York and Catalogue of the 49th Annual Exhibition* (New York: Architectural League of New York, 1934), 5, 60–63; Cox to Newcomb, 11 April 1934 and 12 April 1934, PoP, RG-2/1/2.491 II, box 15, folder "1934–1936, School of Law—General," SSCL; Peter A. Juley & Son, *Moses Proclaiming the Law* by Allyn Cox, *New York Times*, 27 May 1934, RP4; Clark to Newcomb, 20 April 1934, PoP, RG-2/1/2.491 II, box 15, folder "School of Law—General"; Cortissoz to Cox, 21 April 1934, Reel N69-10, Allyn Cox Papers, Archives of American Art, Smithsonian Institution; Carlyle Burrows, "The Architectural League Exhibition," *New York Herald Tribune*, 20 May 1934, V8. For more on Royal Cortissoz, see H. Wayne Morgan, *Keepers of Culture: The Art-Thought of Kenyon Cox,*

Royal Cortissoz, and Frank Jewett Mather, Jr. (Kent, OH: Kent State University Press, 1989). The Architectural League exhibit ran from May 22 to June 2.

51. Harry Haller, "Cox Murals at Virginia University Recall History of Law School's Clark Memorial," *Washington Post,* 19 November 1934, 6; Cox to Newcomb, 21 April 1934, PoP, RG-2/1/2.491 II, box 15, folder "1934–1936, School of Law—General," SSCL.

52. Cox to Newcomb, 24 January 1934, PoP, RG-2/1/2.491 II, box 15, folder "1934–1936, School of Law—General," SSCL.

53. Haller, "Cox Murals," 6.

54. Cox to Newcomb, 29 January 1935, Newcomb to Cox, 4 February 1935, Cox to Newcomb, 4 November 1935, and Newcomb to Cox, 8 November 1935, PoP, RG-2/1/2.491 II, box 15, folder "1934–1936, School of Law—General," SSCL.

55. Wilson, Neuman, and Butler, *University of Virginia,* 26–29.

56. Haller, "Cox Murals," 6.

57. "W. A. Clark, Jr., Summoned by Death," *Los Angeles Times,* 15 June 1934, A1; "Clark Rites Conducted," *Los Angeles Times*, 20 June 1934, A1; Armistead Dobie, "William Minor Lile (1859–1935)," *Virginia Law Review* 22, no. 8 (June 1936), 851.

3. THE MOVE TO NORTH GROUNDS

1. Muthesius, *The Postwar University,* 14.

2. Enrollment figures provided by George A. Stovall, director of institutional assessment and studies, University of Virginia; Dabney, *Mr. Jefferson's University,* 330.

3. Gregory Swanson was the first African American student admitted at UVa but not the first enrolled. The success of Swanson's suit against the University allowed Walter N. Ridley to enroll in the doctoral program in education in January 1950. Dabney, *Mr. Jefferson's University,* 379–80. Swanson, a graduate of Howard University, entered the University of Virginia School of Law as a graduate student, pursuing an LL.M. (Master of Laws). He did not receive his LL.M., making John F. Merchant, who completed his J.D. in 1958, the first African American graduate of the Law School.

4. Dabney, *Mr. Jefferson's University,* 67–68, 380, 490; Ritchie, *First Hundred Years,* 98; enrollment figures per Stovall.

5. Steve Hopson, "Shannon Gives Views on Growing University," *CD,* 21 November 1963, 1.

6. Enrollment figures provided by Stovall.

7. For the introduction of modern architecture to the University of Virginia, see Bluestone, "Captured by Context," 61–69.

8. Ken Lucas, "Gilmer Hall Facilities Termed 'Most Modern in the Country,'" *CD,* 15 October 1963, 2; Kit Williams, "Chaotic or Desirable? New Architectural Trend Viewed," *CD,* 9 October 1963, 1.

9. Williams, "Chaotic or Desirable?," 1; "'State-U' Defined," *CD,* 16 May 1967, 2.

10. "Eleventh Hour Plea," *CD,* 29 October 1965, 2; Fourth-Year Class, School of Architecture, letter to the editor, *CD,* 4 November 1965, 2.

11. Paul Saunier Jr., "Plans for the Future of the University," *University of Virginia Alumni News* 50, no. 7 (May–June 1962): 41; Bluestone, "Captured by Context," 65–66; "New Chemistry Building Plans," *University of Virginia Alumni News* 53, no. 3 (January–February 1965): 15; Betty B. Lanham, letter to the editor, *University of Virginia Alumni News* 53, no. 4 (March–April 1965): 40.

12. *University of Virginia Record, Department of Law, Announcements 1933–1934* (Charlottesville: University of Virginia, 1933), 30; 1960 enrollment figures provided by Stovall.

13. Crosby Wells, letter to the editor, *VLW,* 5 May 1949, 2.

14. The Judge Advocate General's School initially occupied space in both Clark Hall and Hancock House, one of the dormitories across McCormick Road from Clark. In 1956 the JAG School moved into a new Colonial Revival building (now known as Kerchof Hall) to the rear of Clark Hall, although it continued to use classrooms and offices in the law building. See "Judge Advocate School to Open at U. of Virginia," *Washington Post,* 9 September 1951, C6; "University of Virginia Law School, Annual Report of the Dean," *VLW,* 21 November 1951, 6; "New JAG Building Dedicated," *VLW,* 4 October 1956, 3.

15. *University of Virginia Record, Department of Law, Announcements 1933–1934,* 7; Irwin T. Zooker II, letter to the editor, *VLW,* 17 November 1960, 2; "Reed Presents 100,000th Book to Law School," *VLW,* 19 February 1953, 1.

16. Zooker, letter to the editor, 2; Lindsey Cowen to Law School Student Buildings and Grounds Committee, 15 September 1959, RG 100-78, box 6, folder 5, LLSC; "Clean-up Drive, New Proposals Aid Clark Hall," *VLW,* 15 October 1959, 4; "A Thousand Words," *VLW,* 23 February 1961, 2; "The Lounge," *VLW,* 24 October 1963, 2; "Pigsty," *VLW,* 25 February 1965, 2.

17. B. S. Warren III, "Third Floor Construction Completed; Official Opening Scheduled Saturday," *VLW,* 2 November 1961, 1; Douglas A. Nelson, "Formerly Drab Ladies' Lounge Now Cheerier," *VLW,* 8 November 1962, 3; "Kelly Memorial Lounge Opening Set," *VLW,* 11 November 1965, 1; "Lunchroom Begins Operation; Carpeted Lounge Opens Soon," *VLW,* 21 October 1965, 3; "Moot Court Room to Be Remodeled by Class of 1962," *VLW,* 29 November 1962, 4. In November 1965, the Law School dedicated the refurbished student lounge to the late Edward J. Kelly Jr., a third-year student who had been killed in a car accident the previous March

while serving as student body president. The Law School dismantled the moot court room in 1971 and converted the space into offices. See "Moot Court Room Is Quietly Buried," *VLW*, 8 October 1971, 4.

18. Stevens, *Law School,* 205–9; "Special Report" attached to Dillard to Shannon, 19 February 1963, Dillard Manuscripts, MSS 84-8, box 21, folder 11, LLSC.

19. William Chapman, "Virginia Senate Leaders Seek to Limit Out-of-State Students," *Washington Post,* 17 January 1964, C1; "Visitors State Policy: University a National Institution," *University of Virginia Alumni News* 53, no. 4 (March–April 1965), 12–13, 35, 37, 39; "University President Criticizes Plan to Take Only Virginians," *Washington Post*, 19 January 1964, B1; Report on the Size of the Law School, 17 November 1965, PoP, RG-2/1/2.681, box 24.

20. Dillard to Cowen, 28 January 1963, and Cowen to Dillard, 6 February 1963, Dillard Manuscripts, MSS 84-8, box 21, folder 11, LLSC; Dillard, letter to alumni, 20 November 1964, Dillard Manuscripts, MSS 84-8, box 78, folder "Alumni."

21. Shannon to Thomas K. Fitzpatrick, Chairman, Architectural Advisory Committee, 19 December 1963, PoP, RG-2/1/2.671, box 21, folder "Law General"; Sasaki, Dawson, DeMay Associates, Inc., *The University of Virginia Development Plan* (Watertown, Mass.: 1965), 53–55.

22. Memorandum of Meeting, Master Plan Committee, 17 January 1963, PoP, RG-2/1/2.661, box 8, folder "Committee on Master Plan"; Peter Walker and Melanie Simo, *Invisible Gardens: The Search for Modernism in the American Landscape* (Cambridge: MIT Press, 1994), 228, 234.

23. Richard P. Dober, *Campus Planning* (New York: Reinhold, 1963), 3, 57–62, and "Form and Style in Campus Design," *Progressive Architecture* 41, no. 9 (September 1960), 130.

24. Sasaki, Dawson, DeMay Associates, Inc., *The University of Virginia Development Plan,* 31–32, 53–55; Dan Shipp, "Five 'Academic Areas' Planned: Master Plan Provides for Future Growth," *CD*, 29 March 1966, 1; Charlie Calhoun, "Master Plan for University Growth Described to Council by Saunier; Expansion Blueprint Seeks to Keep Remarkable Heritage," *CD*, 10 February 1966, 1.

25. Meador to Dillard, 24 February 1965, RFBC, RG 301-78, box 1, folder 1.

26. Daniel J. Meador, ed., *Hardy Cross Dillard: Writings and Speeches* (Charlottesville: University of Virginia Law School Foundation, 1995), 15.

27. In a draft of a letter written in 1997, Robert E. Scott, dean of the Law School (1991–2001), referred to "a breach made in 1974 when the Law School was evicted from Clark Hall and moved to North Grounds." See Robert E. Scott to Deans' Portraits Controversy Petitioners, LSBP, RG 313-05, box 8, folder 9. There is some evidence to support this feeling; in April 1974, prior to the move, a self-study report for the Law School stated "some members of the faculty feel, rightly or wrongly, that the decision to move was made for the Law School by the University—that over

time the Law Faculty was 'locked into' the move without the full and mature consideration of the wisdom of moving away from the Grounds." Law School Self-Study Steering Committee, *Self Study Report of the University of Virginia School of Law* (Charlottesville: The Law School, 1974), 64–65.

28. Dillard and Brown to Frank E. Maloney, Dean, University of Florida College of Law, 7 February 1964, Dillard Manuscripts, MSS 84-8, box 10, folder "1964 AALS—Florida Inspection," LLSC.

29. Memorandum, Minutes of Meeting, 9 December 1966, Board of Visitors of the University of Virginia Committee Records, RG-1/1/3, box 11, folder "1965–1968," SSCL.

30. Werner Sensbach, conservation with the author, July 2014.

31. Memorandum of Understanding, attached to letter, Abbott to Edgar F. Shannon, 15 May 1967, RFBC, RG 107-80, box 13, folder 4.

32. Benjamin Jean Carstoiu, *Sunny Side: The Duke House, Barracks Road, Charlottesville,* Architecture in Virginia no. 167 (Charlottesville: School of Architecture, University of Virginia, 1995), n.p.; K. Edward Lay, *The Architecture of Jefferson Country: Charlottesville and Albemarle County, Virginia* (Charlottesville: University of Virginia, 2000), 227.

33. "University Expansion Plan Revised; 91.8 Million Dollars Requested," *CD,* 4 April 1967, 1; "Officials Disclose New Law Building Construction Plan," *VLW,* 6 April 1967, 4.

34. Rogers to Shannon, 17 April 1967, Board of Visitors of the University of Virginia Committee Records, RG-1/1/3, box 11, folder "1959–1971, Buildings & Grounds Committee Correspondence," SSCL; Memorandum, Minutes of Meeting, 31 May 1967, Board of Visitors of the University of Virginia Committee Records, RG-1/1/3, box 11, folder "1965–1968, Buildings & Grounds Committee Minutes," SSCL; Rogers to J. Sloan Kuykendall, Board of Visitors of the University of Virginia Committee Records, RG-1/1/3, box 11, folder "1959–1971, Buildings & Grounds Committee Correspondence," SSCL.

35. R. Vernon Swartsel Jr., letter to the editor, *VLW,* 26 February 1970, 2; "Law Students Concerned over Move to Copeley Hill," *CD,* 2 March 1970, 1; Matt Pirrung, "Law Students Approve Copeley Plan," *CD,* 4 March 1970, 1.

36. "New Law School," *CD,* 15 November 1973, 1; Barbara Brownell and Buck Cole, "Sprawling Developments Threaten 'Community,'" ibid., 3.

37. John S. Chapman Jr., letter to the editor, *VLW,* 5 March 1970, 2.

38. Alford to Thomas K. Fitzpatrick, 10 March 1967, RFBC, RG 301-78, box 3, folder 13.

39. Ronald D. Castille, "Budget Cuts Endanger Law Complex," *VLW,* 12 February 1970, 1.

40. "Officials Disclose New Law Building Construction Plan," *VLW,* 6 April 1967, 4.

41. Hugh Stubbins and Associates, "Master Plan for School of Law, Judge Advocate General's

School, Graduate School of Business Administration, and Coordinate Facilities," 1968, RFBC, RG 301-78, box 3, folder 11.

42. Ibid.

43. Robert P. Kyle, "Present Inadequacies Require Large Modern Law Facilities," *VLW,* 2 May 1968, 1; Hugh Stubbins and Associates, Conference Report, 28 February 1968, RFBC, RG 301-78, box 1, folder 3.

44. Alford to Hunt, 29 November 1967, RFBC, RG 301-78, box 2, folder 22; Project Criteria for the Law School, November 1967 revision, RFBC, RG 301-78, box 4, folder 10.

45. Bergin to Alford, n.d. (1967), RFBC, RG 301-78, box 4, folder 2; Paul Spencer Byard, *The Architecture of Additions: Design and Regulation* (New York: W. W. Norton & Co., 1998), 169–70; Charles D. Kelso, *The Planning and Design of Law Buildings* (Indianapolis: Indiana University School of Law, 1966).

46. Alford to Maloney, 25 April 1967, and Maloney to Alford, 25 May 1967, RFBC, RG 301-78, box 3, folder 10. The new law building of the University of Florida opened in 1968 as the Spessard L. Holland Law Center.

47. Alford to Kelso, 25 April 1967, and Kelso to Alford, 1 May 1967, RFBC, RG 301-78, box 3, folder 5; Charles D. Kelso, "Planning and Design of Law Buildings, A Color-Slide Presentation," 1965, RFBC, RG 301-78, box 3, folder 6.

48. Minutes, General Committee Meeting for School of Law and GSBA Complex, 28 February 1968, PoP, RG-2/1/2.711, box 14, folder "Spc. Committee—Law & Graduate Business Complex, Copeley Hill, 1967–68"; Stubbins and Associates, Conference Report, 28 February 1968, RFBC, RG 301-78, box 1, folder 3.

49. In the Conference Report for the law-business complex, 28 February 1968, Charles C. Abbott, dean of the Business School, "expressed some concern of the vertical scale." Stubbins "explained that it was inesthetic [in aesthetic] harmony and also affords certain economy of land use." At this point Stubbins envisioned several "high-rise developments" for the complex, including the faculty office towers for the Law School and the Graduate Business School, the shared law-business dormitory, and the JAG School dormitory. In March 1968, Waller Hunt of the UVa Planning Department wrote to Stubbins that the Board of Visitors' Buildings and Grounds Committee "does wish to suggest that the School purpose will be better served by a faculty building with fewer floors, perhaps three." The memorandum of the building committee meeting held 11 April 1968 reports that the business building had at that point dropped from seven to four floors. See Hugh Stubbins and Associates, Conference Report, 28 February 1968, RFBC, RG 301-78, box 1, folder 3; Hunt to Stubbins, 8 March 1968, PoP, RG-2/1/2.711, box 14, folder "Spc. Committee—Law & Graduate Business Complex, Copeley Hill, 1967–68"; Memorandum of

Meeting, 11 April 1968, RFBC, RG 301-78, box 1, folder 3; Kyle, "Present Inadequacies Require Large Modern Law Facilities," 1, 3.

50. Alford to Stubbins, 20 July 1968, RFBC, RG 301-78, box 3, folder 11.

51. Hugh Stubbins and Associates, Conference Report, 28 February 1968, RFBC, RG 301-78, box 1, folder 3.

52. Alford to Meador, 2 September 1968, RFBC, RG 301-78, box 1, folder 8; Douglas Hamner to Vincent Shea, 20 August 1969, RFBC, RG 301-78, box 5, folder 10; J. S. Barret and H. Douglas Hamner Jr., Review of Project Criteria, attached to letter, Barret and Hamner to Werner Sensbach, 18 March 1969, RFBC, RG 301-78, box 4, folder 14.

53. Alford to Sensbach, 28 March 1969, RFBC, RG 301-78, box 4, folder 14; Bernstein to Law School Building Committee, 13 December 1971, RFBC, RG 301-78, box 1, folder 6; Law School Self-Study Steering Committee, *Self Study Report of the University of Virginia School of Law*, 65. According to Garth Anderson, the University's facilities historian, the law building included plumbing for a separate dean's toilet but the space was not fitted out as a restroom.

54. "Nostalgic Law Council Reveals 'Last Tango' for Mural Hall," *VLW,* 29 March 1974, 4; Katherine Ann Graham, "First Year Class Inaugurates Building as Remainder Plan Move on Monday," *VLW*, 20 September 1974, 1; "On Life after Clark," *VLW*, 20 September 1974, 2; Katherine Ann Graham, "A Clark Hall Reminiscence," *VLW*, 27 September 1974, 2.

55. "A Bill of Particulars," *VLW,* 3 October 1975, 2. There were a number of suggestions for names for the new building after its completion; law student George W. C. McCarter suggested the "magnificent new temple" be named "McReynolds Hall" for UVa law alumnus and Supreme Court justice James Clark McReynolds. See letter to the editor, *VLW*, 11 October 1974, 2. In 1982, the editors of the *Virginia Law Weekly* suggested the building and the school itself be named after former dean Hardy Dillard. See "The Dillard School," *VLW*, 22 October 1982, 2. The choice of "Withers Hall" came about through the donation of $2.8 million from a private trust established by the estate of Lacy Withers Armour, daughter of Henry Malcolm Withers, who attended law classes at the University in 1868–69. See "School Receives $2.8 Million Grant," *VLW*, 23 September 1983, 1. The name "Withers Hall" did not meet with universal approval. For example, law alumnus Jim O'Reilly wrote in 1984 that he and his Clark Hall classmates "often discussed what the new lump of red clay on North Grounds should be like. Had we been able to guess, I regret to say, H. M. Withers would not have leapt to mind as the natural choice for inspiration, but in the obscurity and wealth which the name carries, the tradition of Clark Hall [named for millionaire donor and alumnus William Andrews Clark Jr.] is carried on." See letter to the editor, *VLW*, 3 February 1984, 2.

56. "Mudhole North," *VLW,* 10 February 1978, 2; "Phase II's Poor Cousin," *VLW,* 19 October 1979, 2; Robert M. Simms, letter to the editor, *CD,* 4 October 1974, 3.

57. Lenny Marsico, "New Law School: Not as 'Conducive to Interaction,'" *CD,* 1 May 1975, 11; Blair M. Gardner, "Farmer Recalls Early Years; Remembers Faculty, Alumni," *VLW,* 30 April 1976, 4; Law Council, "An Open Letter to Dean Spies," *VLW,* 9 April 1976, 2; Craig Wagner, letter to the editor, *VLW,* 7 November 1975, 2; "New Professors Encourage Student Contact, Questions," *VLW,* 14 February 1975, 3.

58. Marsico, "New Law School," 11; Scot Butler, "Perspective," *VLW,* 25 April 1975, 2; Pamela Clark, "Physical Isolation Unsolved Problem for North Grounds," *VLW,* 15 October 1976, 4.

59. "Secession?," *VLW,* 30 March 1979, 2; Marsico, "New Law School," 11.

60. Minutes, Special Landscape Committee—Law-GSBA-JAG School Area, 15 March 1973, RFBC, RG 301-78, box 3, folder 7; Teddie Wheeler, "Landscaping Committee Plans Improvements of Duke Tract," *VLW,* 3 October 1975, 2; Blair Gardner, "Plaza and Landscaping Slated as Duke Tract Improvements," *VLW,* 10 March 1975, 1;. Peggy O. Hart, "Meador Discusses Law School Area Landscaping Plans," *VLW,* 22 November 1974, 3.

61. "Clark Hall Replaces Charm with Rocks and Draperies," *VLW,* 30 January 1976, 3. Clark Hall was added to the National Register of Historic Places in 2008; see National Register of Historic Places, Clark Hall, University of Virginia, Charlottesville, Albemarle County, Virginia, National Register #08000871.

4. THE CREATION OF LAW GROUNDS

1. "Mr. Jefferson's Rotunda: A Return to the Original," *University of Virginia Alumni News,* Vol. 64, No. 3 (January–February 1976), 4–17; John G. Waite Associates, *Rotunda,* 136–57.

2. "Phase II's Poor Cousin," 2; Patrick Weschler, "Exploring Phase II Reveals New Facilities, Space Added," *VLW,* 26 January 1979, 1, 3; "Study Space Alternatives Make Phase II Popular," *VLW,* 30 March 1979, 3.

3. "A Look at the Proposed Remodeling of Phase I," *VLW,* 30 November 1979, 3; "Facelift Fails," *VLW,* 5 September 1980, 2; illustration/caption, *VLW,* 2 March 1984, 2; Edmund Kitch, letter to the editor, *VLW,* 18 April 1986, 2; "Around North Grounds," *VLW,* 7 March 1985, 1.

4. "Projected Space Requirements for the Graduate School of Business Administration, 1964–70," 21 April 1964, Papers of the Master Plan Committee, RG-20/26/1.061, box 1, folder "1964, Master Plan Committee," SSCL.

5. Danny Barkin, "Business School to Open," *CD,* 7 August 1975, 1.

6. Mark Reisler, *Darden: A Pictorial History of the University of Virginia's Darden Graduate School of Business Administration* (Charlottesville: Darden Business Pub., 2005), 96, 126–27.

7. "General Discussion Format" section of report attached to letter, Wenger to Jackson and Elaine Hadden, 9 December 1988, Wenger to Jackson, 2 February 1989, Wenger to Jackson and Elaine Hadden, 13 June 1989, and Wenger to Elaine Hadden and Walter Wadlington, 7 July 1988, LSBP, RG 313-05, box 1, folder 1.

8. Robert A. M. Stern, "Notes on Post-Modernism," in *Architecture on the Edge of Postmodernism: Collected Essays 1964–1988,* ed. Cynthia Davidson (New Haven: Yale University Press, 2009), 162.

9. Buildings and Grounds Committee of the Board of Visitors, "A Vision Statement for the Planning and Design of the University of Virginia Buildings and Grounds," provided by Garth Anderson, facilities, University of Virginia.

10. Memorandum by Jackson to Law Faculty, 4 April 1991, LSBP, RG 313-05, box 1, folder 2; Reisler, *Darden,* 154–55, 157; Wilson, Neuman, and Butler, *University of Virginia,* 191–92; Colgate Darden Graduate School of Business Administration, *The Campaign for Darden* (Charlottesville: Colgate Darden Graduate School of Business Administration, n.d.), n.p.

11. University of Virginia School of Law, Capital Outlay Project Request, Draft, 1 February 1993, LSBP, RG 313-05, box 1, folder 4; Reisler, *Darden,* 96. Between 1991 and 2001 the Law School reduced its student-faculty ratio from 24:1 to 14:1; see Robert E. Scott, "Looking Back, Looking Ahead," *UVA Lawyer* 25, no. 1 (Spring 2001), 4.

12. Kent Sinclair to M. Kirk Train, 19 December 1991, LSBP, RG 313-05, box 1, folder 4.

13. Ibid.

14. For Alan Dynerman's architectural drawings commissioned by the Law School, see LSBP, RG 313-05, oversize files. The Dynerman plan resembled the now-demolished Observatory Hill Dining Hall of Robert A. M. Stern, which was a postmodern design with a pergola-like main floor over an arcaded raised basement; this structure likewise masked a more functional 1970s building. See Wilson, Neuman, and Butler, *University of Virginia,* 191–92.

15. Kent Sinclair to Darden Acquisition Committee, 7 April 1992, LSBP, RG 313-05, box 1, folder 4; Reisler, *Darden,* 155.

16. University of Virginia School of Law, *Law Can Lead the Way* (Charlottesville: University of Virginia Development Fund, n.d.); Ribble to Marshall Field Jr., 8 December 1952, RG 107-80, box 15, folder 2, LLSC; David H. Ibbeken, email messages to author, 9 July 2015 and 10 August 2015.

17. "The Law Grounds, University of Virginia School of Law: An Academic Vision," LSBP, RG 313-05, box 1, folder 5.

18. Porter to Scott, 12 September 1992, LSBP, RG 313-05, box 1, folder 5.

19. "Interview Schedule," 15 January 1993, LSBP, RG 313-05, box 1, folder 4; Ayers Saint Gross, "Functional Planning, Space Analysis and Architectural Programming for the Law School, University of Virginia," Technical Capability, LSBP, RG 313-05, box 5, folder 1.

20. Adam Gross to Selection Committee, Facilities Management Department, University of Virginia, 3 November 1992, and "Project Understanding," included in Ayers Saint Gross, "Functional Planning, Space Analysis and Architectural Programming for the Law School, University of Virginia," LSBP, RG 313-05, box 5, folder 1.

21. Ayers Saint Gross, "Project Understanding."

22. Ibid.; Ayers Saint Gross, Process Journal, 22 February 1993, Section 5, LSBP, RG 313-05, box 5, folder 3.

23. Ayers Saint Gross, Process Journal, Section 5.

24. Elise Bryant, "Student Input Needed on Darden Acquisition," *VLW*, 26 March 1993, 1. Scott's first recorded reference to the "front door" concept is in a letter with architect Bethany J. Christenson, 28 January 1992, LSBP, RG 313-05, box 7, folder 13.

25. G. David Gearhart, *The Capital Campaign in Higher Education: A Practical Guide for College and University Advancement* (Washington, D.C.: National Association of College and University Business Officers, 1995), 1–5; Bryant, "Student Input Needed on Darden Acquisition," 1.

26. Ayers Saint Gross, Master Plan Study, University of Virginia Law Grounds Project, 1 September 1993, Section 5, LSBP, RG 313-05, box 5, folder 4.

27. University of Virginia Law School Foundation, *Annual Report 1994–95* (Charlottesville, Va.: University of Virginia Law School Foundation, 1995), 4–5; Scott to Harrison, 20 August 1992, LSBP, RG 313-05, box 7, folder 13; University of Virginia Law School Foundation Building Advisory Committee, Minutes, 11 September 1993, unprocessed papers of Robert E. Scott, folder "Building Advisory Committee," LLSC. Scott specifically credited Harrison with the idea to enlarge the pavilion at the Law Grounds dedication ceremony; see "Harrison Law Grounds Dedication, November 8, 1997," script, unprocessed papers of Robert E. Scott, folder "Building Dedication, Nov. 1997," LLSC; Andy Zappia, "Dean Scott Discusses Law School Expansion," *VLW*, 4 March 1994, 1.

28. Kathleen D. Valenzi, "Building Dreams: Architect Adam Gross on Creating the New Law Grounds," *UVA Lawyer* 18, no. 2 (Summer 1994), 29.

29. David B. Lieb, "Architects Unveil Law School Expansion Plan," *VLW*, 1 October 1993, 1; Zappia, "Dean Scott Discusses Law School Expansion," 1.

30. Carol Wood, "On Mr. Jefferson's Shoulders: Architect Robert A. M. Stern Preserves Tradition in New Darden Grounds," *Darden* 22, no 3 (Summer 1996), 28.

31. Scott to Nicholas E. Chimicles, 3 September 1993, unprocessed papers of Robert E. Scott, folder "Building Advisory Committee," LLSC; Valenzi, "Building Dreams," 28.

32. "Law Grounds Update," flier, November 1995, Papers of the Associate Dean of Management and Finance, RG 111-06, box 26, folder 1, LLSC; Reynolds Wilson, "Eat Your Heart Out Frank Lloyd Wright," *VLW,* 6 September 1996, 1.

33. Curtis Romig, "Harrison Law Grounds Project Passes Halfway Mark; Clay Hall, Caplin Pavilion, and Holcombe Green Lawn to Be Dedicated in May," *VLW,* 24 January 1997, 1; Christopher Bowen, "Jackson Portrait Joins Library Collection," *VLW*, 20 November 1992, 3.

34. Nina McAdoo, letter to the editor, *VLW,* 31 January 1997, 2; Helen Wan, "'Dead White Males' Adorn Hall," *VLW*, 31 January 1997, 6; Mona Harrington, *Women Lawyers: Rewriting the Rules* (New York: Alfred A. Knopf, 1994), 45. For the unabridged version of Wan's article, see LSBP, RG 313-05, box 8, folder 9.

35. David Lieb, "The Deans' Portraits (In Context)," *VLW,* 7 February 1997, 4.

36. Ian Zack, "Hall Called Unfinished Portrait of Law School," *Daily Progress,* 8 February 1997, A8; Earl C. Dudley Jr., letter to the editor, *VLW*, 7 February 1997, 2; Ian Zack, "Deans' Pictures Open Debate in Virginia," *New York Times*, 12 February 1997, B9 (an abridged version of the *Daily Progress* article); "A Hallway of their Own," *Chronicle of Higher Education*, 21 February 1997, A6; Associated Press, "U.Va. Law School Portraits Draw Criticism; Students Point Out Lack of Minorities and Women," *Richmond Times-Dispatch*, 9 February 1997, C3.

37. Petition to Scott, n.d., LSBP, RG 313-05, box 8, folder 9; Scott to Ellertson, 4 February 1997, LSBP, RG 313-05, box 8, folder 9; Curtis J. Romig, "Dean's [*sic*] Portraits Spark Student Debate," *VLW,* 7 February 1997, 1.

38. "School of Law Landscape, Summary of Installation," 7 November 1997, and "Media Fact Sheet," 8 November 1997, unprocessed papers of Robert E. Scott, folder "North Grounds Planning," LLSC.

39. Scott, "Looking Back, Looking Ahead," 4; "Media Advisory," 30 October 1997, unprocessed papers of Robert E. Scott, folder "Building Dedication, Nov. 1997," LLSC; Lindsay Wise, "Rehnquist Uses Address to Criticize Specialization," *Cavalier Daily,* 10 November 1997, 6; "Harrison Law Grounds Dedication, November 8, 1997," script, unprocessed papers of Robert E. Scott, folder "Building Dedication, Nov. 1997," LLSC.

CONCLUSION

1. "Student-Faculty Center Construction Begins," *UVA Lawyer* 24, no. 2 (Fall 2000), 6.

Illustration Credits

Albemarle Charlottesville Historical Society Collection: *page 124*

Albert and Shirley Small Special Collections Library, University of Virginia: *pages ii, vi, 14, 19 (photograph by Eugene A. Perry), 20, 22, 25, 31, 33, 38, 52, 55, 71, 72, 73, 80, 82, 107, 110, first color plate*

Allyn Cox papers, Archives of American Art, Smithsonian Institution, photograph by Blackstone Studios: *page 85*

Ayers Saint Gross: *pages 182–83, 185, color plate 6*

© RMN-Grand Palais/Art Resource, NY: *second and third color plates*

Cornell University Library, A.D. White Photographs, Rare and Manuscript Collections: *page 35*

Darden School of Business: *pages 167, 190 (photograph by Jack Mellot)*

Drawing by Christopher Young: *pages 5, 12, 49, 78, 133, 148, 188*

Harvard University Archives, UAV 605 Box 70, HC 1043: *page 131*

House & Garden 42, no. 2 (August 1922), p. 41: *page 86*

Museum of the City of New York: *page 62*

Photograph by Bill Maris © Esto: *page 138*

Photograph by Ed Roseberry: *pages 128, 135, 145*

Photograph by Gordon Schenck: *page 142*
Photograph by Matthew Riley: *pages 92, 94, 98–99, fourth and fifth color plates*
Photograph by Melba Levick: *page 65*
Sheridan Libraries, Johns Hopkins Libraries: *page 76*
Special Collections, Leyburn Library, Washington and Lee University: *page 59*
University Archives and Records Center, University of Pennsylvania: *page 45*
University Archives Photograph Collection, Special Collections Research Center, Earl Gregg
    Swem Library, College of William and Mary: *page 15*
University of North Carolina at Chapel Hill Image Collection #P0004, North Carolina
    Collection Photographic Archives, Wilson Library: *page 70*
University of Virginia Law Library: *pages 27, 30, 56, 57, 81, 89, 90, 102 (photograph by Steve West),
    105, 130, 132 (Records of the Faculty Building Committee), 158, 161, 163, 164, 174–75 (Alan
    Dynerman), 187, sixth and eighth color plates*
University of Virginia Law School: *page 202*
University of Virginia Magazine Archives: *page 47*
Virginia Law Weekly/University of Virginia Law Library: *pages 113, 114, 126, 146, 147, 149, 151,
    152, 166, 181, 192–93, 194*

Index

Page numbers in italics indicate illustrations.

83, 87, 93, 217n17, *second and third color plates;* unfinished state of Clark Hall murals at dedication ceremony, *82. See also* Mural Hall

Cox, Kenyon (father), 64, 84–85, 86, 93

Cox, Louise King (mother), 85

cryptoporticus, 173

Daniels, John W., 215n32

Darden School. *See* Graduate School of Business Administration

David A. Harrison III Law Grounds. *See* Law Grounds

Davis, John Anthony Gardner, 21–24

Davis, Martha (later Minor), 23

Davis, Rosemary, 107

Dawson's Row, 66, 77

deans, controversy over portraits of, 193–98, *194*

dean's toilet, 144, 228n53

Deglane, Henri, 62

Dillard, Hardy Cross: Clark Hall, obsolescence of, 115, 116, 118, 124; North Grounds, relocation of Law School to, 120–21, 123, 124–25; proposal to name North Grounds law building after, 228n55

Dober, Richard, *Campus Planning* (1963), 118, 119

Dobie, Armistead, 81–82, 100–101, 114

Downing, Andrew Jackson, 123

Dryden, John, *All for Love* (1677), 87

Dudley, Earl C., Jr., 196

Duke, Mary White, 123

Duke, Richard Thomas Walker, Sr., 123

Dulaney, Polly, *164*

Dunnington, Francis Perry, 28

Dunnington, Margaret Bell, 28

du Pont, Philip, 60

Dynerman, Alan, 173–74, *174, 175,* 178, 180, 230n14

Ellerton, Christine, 197

Emmet, John Patton, 21

Engineering, School of: damage to property, in fire of 1895, 29, 214n31; new building for, after fire of 1895, 32–33 (*see also* Cocke Hall); in Rotunda Annex, 25, 29, 213–14nn22–23

English Baroque style, 45

Farmer, Frances, 113–14, 115, 150

Farquhar, Robert D., 63–64, 85

Fayerweather Gymnasium (1893), 32, 43–44, 67

federal funding for college buildings: HEFA and Higher Education Act, 122; Public Works Administration, 53–54

fire of 1895 and aftermath, 8, 13, 26, 28–37, *31,* 160

Flagler Academic Court (Darden School), *190*

Flemish bond, 16, 109, 143

Florida State University College of Law: B. K. Roberts Hall, 198; D'Alemberte Rotunda, 198

Founder's Day (April 13, Jefferson's birthday), 66

Franklin National Bank (Philadelphia), 71

freestanding law school buildings, late nineteenth century trend toward, 33–34, *35*

Frick, Henry Clay, 60

Fuller, Williamson, 87

John Hancock Center (Chicago), 131
Johns Hopkins University, *76,* 178
Johnson, Lyndon B., 122
Judge Advocate General's (JAG) School: in
    Clark Hall, 113, 117, 145, 224n14; in Kerchof
    Hall, 118, 224n14; on North Grounds, 104,
    123, 131, 159

Kahn, Louis, 112
Kelly, Edward J., Jr., 224–25n17
Kelso, Charles D., 139
Kent State University shootings, 127
Kerchof Hall, 118, 224n14
Kimball, Fiske, 67, 68
Kitch, Edmund, 165
Kneedler, H. Lane, 150
Kneedler, Lynn S., *126*

Lafayette, Marquis de, 63
Langdell, Christopher C., 35
"Law Can Lead the Way" campaign, 176
law education in U.S.: ABA-AALS accredita-
    tion standards and postwar competitive-
    ness, 115–16; admission standards, 36,
    57–58, 115; Clark Hall and, 79–80, 82, 100;
    expansion of curriculum, early 1900s, 57–
    58; liberal arts curriculum, law conceived
    of as part of, 3, 17–18; North Grounds and,
    104, 137, 141, *149;* practical legal education,
    early efforts to provide, 23–24; private for-
    profit schools and legal apprenticeships, 18;
    Progressive-Era emphasis on specialization
    of disciplines, 4–6
Law Grounds, 9, 159–201; Ayers Saint Gross
    plans for, 178–83, *182, 183, 185,* 185–89, *187,*
    193, 200; Business School's move away from

North Grounds and purchase of buildings
    by Law School, 160–61, 171–72; Caplin
    Pavilion, *158, 161,* 180, *185,* 185–89, *188, 192,*
    193, 199; Caplin Reading Room, *164,* 198,
    eighth color plate; Clark Hall, nostalgia
    for, 161, 165, 172, 177, 179–80, 184, 185–86,
    203–4; Clay Hall, *161,* 192–98; construction
    of, 191–93, *192, 193;* Darden Building (later
    Slaughter Hall), 171–73, 178, 182, 184, 186–
    89, *187,* 191, 192, 199, 200, 203; dedication
    ceremonies, 199–200; Dynerman plan for,
    172–76, *174, 175,* 178, 180, 230n14; floor
    plan for connecting pavilion, *188;* funding,
    160, 168, 172, 174–77, 184, 186, 199; Hunton
    & Williams Hall and Scott Commons, *202,*
    203–4, 206; Jeffersonian architectural style
    and, 177–79, 180, 191, 200–201; land-
    scaping, 199; "Last Party in Red Square"
    (autumn 1995), 191–92; North Grounds,
    later building and remodeling (1974–90)
    of, 162–71, *163, 164, 166, 167;* portraits of
    former deans, controversy over, 193–98,
    194; Rotunda referenced by, 185–86;
    Rotunda restoration program and, 159–60,
    161; site plan (1993), *seventh color plate;*
    Slaughter Hall, 192; Spies Garden, 180, *181,*
    191, 199; student input into design of, 183–
    84; transformation of North Grounds into
    (1990s), 160–62; Withers/Withers-Brown
    Hall, 172–73, 177, 178, 180, 182, 184, 186–89,
    187, 191, 192, 198–99, 200, 203
Law Library: Caplin Reading Room, Law
    Grounds, *164,* 198, *eighth color plate;* in
    Clark Memorial Hall, *vi,* 67, *80,* 100, *113,*
    113–14, 115, 121, 156; fire of 1895, survival
    of, 29; in Minor Hall, 50, 58, 59; in North